# I'VE ALWAYS LOVED YOU

## ANN SEYMOUR

*To dear Joseph, Jeff's papa, from your girlfriend, Ann with LOVE*

*firefall* ™

First Edition: November 2009

Cover Design: Barbara Joyce Robinson
Printed in the United States of America
by RR Donnelly

ISBN: 9780915090822

FIREFALL EDITIONS
Canyon California 94516-0189


firefallmedia@att.net
www.firefallmedia.com

In memory of my father, Maj. Frank E. Ribbel

# Acknowledgments

My HUSBAND is an expert on the war in the Pacific and I on my family.

I have the letters my family exchanged during the war as well as my parents' diaries, but without my husband as my collaborator, this book could not have happened. I'd have placed Nimitz in the Mediterranean, MacArthur in Copenhagen, or at least would have pointed them in those directions. Thanks, my love, and thanks to the children and grandchildren you gave me who inspired me to tell this story of the family hero.

In my journalism years, many gifted editors guided me, and I thank you all, especially Gardner Mein, Merla Zellerbach, and Stefanie Lingle.

Many talented friends advised me as the manuscript evolved: Patricia Burke, Mona Skager, Patsy Pope, Sharon Owsley, Kirk Kirkham, Connie Bertrand, and Nicole Bestard. Elizabeth Pomada improved my mind – a lot. Jerry Hume took the cover photograph.

Friends like Genie Callan, Dede Wilsey, Lili Monell, and Ann Getty make anything seem possible.

Sen. Dianne Feinstein's office obtained my father's war records as well as those of the Fortieth Division for me. Stanley Dollar, Dick Bradshaw, and Ollie Meek, and the Fortieth's commanding general, Harcourt Hervey, who was my brother's godfather, shared their stories also.

My husband and I were brought to Manila by Lexie McMicking Ellsworth, and her cousins, Connie McHugh and Rod Hall, offered their stories then. We lived through the war without knowing one another, but its experience still binds us together.

Every writer should work with a publisher who has incredible talent and sensitivity. Thank you, Elihu.

And finally, a special salute goes to Brigadier General Charles Viale.

Ann Ribbel Seymour

# CHAPTER ONE

*December 7, 1941, Cayucos, Central California*

I DIDN'T UNDERSTAND. I was only four.

Unaware that my life was reversing, like the tide before me, I played on the beach. The sun brightened the cloudless sky, turning it a silvered winter blue, perfect for Sunday, Daddy's day off. As he and Mom raced to the sea, the foam slapped against the shore. One strap of her bathing suit slipped. In the water, she wrapped her arms around him, her neck pliant, her back limber. Despite the water's chill, they rode the waves together.

Dripping and sleek, Daddy waded out of the water. His black hair shone with a blue iridescence. He dropped a few steps behind Mom, and watched her hips sway as she walked. Slowly they crossed across the sand, their white stucco house perched on the succulent-covered bluff ahead of them.

Relaxing on our picnic blanket, Mom examined her red fingernails for chips in the polish, and then turned over, the seawater glistening on her shoulders. With combs and hairpins, she tried in vain to tame her wild auburn hair. Untamed, her hair excited Daddy; it reminded him of women dancing in Old West cafes while patrons drank their whiskey. Her eyes were gray, pure gray - no little leopard spots of brown or hazel.

I sat next to the blanket and began digging. Deliberate as a fern unfurling, Daddy smoothed oil on Mom's slim back and khaki-freckled shoulders.

"More on the right," she said in her indolent voice. "That's it . . . Up a little. To the left . . . Yes. I've got you pretty well trained."

"That's because you reward me." The tones of warm youth flowed through his voice, and, moving his hand to the small of her back, he began to sing, "Mary-Helen, Mary-Helen, my own Mary-Helen," to the tune of the UC Berkeley fight song.

Daddy kneaded Mom's shoulders, and then rolled over on his back. He winked at me. I knew what that wink meant: he loved me best.

"Nap time," Mom said, so I ran away from her, heading toward the sea.

"Ann, come here this minute." She caught up with me and grabbed my wrist. I had almost made it to the water. As we turned, an army officer appeared on the bluff. To me then that bluff rose immensely high,

7

and the uniformed man seemed to tower up to the sky, looking down like a god in the corner of an old map, one who determined destinies at his pleasure. Actually, the bluff was quite small, but I had the perspective of the very young.

"Captain Ribbel, the Japanese have attacked Pearl Harbor. Report for duty immediately!"

Daddy quickly got to his feet, stood at attention in his bathing suit, and saluted the officer.

"Darling – " Mom touched her cheek with her fingers.

"I have to get going, Sweetheart."

Her eyes welled up, but she said nothing more.

He gave her a quick hug, patted me, and, in five or six strides, dashed up the bluff and disappeared into the house. She gathered up the picnic things and followed, shock slowing her walk. I trailed along after her, as the Pacific boomed and hissed.

Oh, Daddy, Mom. I still can see their faces before he went overseas – innocent, brave, unknowing – see the way they leaned toward each other as they walked along in step – naive and graceful.

\* \* \*

Hours earlier, Imperial Air Captain Mitsuo Fuchida had boasted that he'd pull the eagle's tail feathers. He and 350 other pilots donned white hachimaki headbands to signify preparation for death and launched from the carrier Akagi in a long, vivid stream.

At Pearl Harbor, he called out the "Tiger" radio signal, "Tora-Tora-Tora," and his men dropped their payloads. For two hours, they pelted our ships and aircraft, destroying most of our Fleet.

Later, aboard the flagship Nagato, Admiral Chuichi Nagumo, commander of the Pearl Harbor carriers, slashed the air with his father's samurai sword to celebrate the destruction of America's Pacific Fleet. With it gone and unable to help its allies, the Dutch would have to leave the East Indies and go home to plant tulips; the English would scuttle out of Asia and nestle on their foggy island among their little knick-knacks. Sake arrived, and the celebration began. "Dai Nippon, Great Japan."

It ended with Admiral Isoroku Yamamoto. The unfortunate man did not want war with America, but when commanded to plan and lead the strike, he obeyed. What choice did he have? He regarded refusing an imperial request as dishonorable treason. Pearl Harbor's success felt ominous to him, and sorrow brushed his soul like the wing of a crane. A Harvard-educated economist and brilliant war strategist, he knew our country well, when he said, "People think Americans love luxury, their culture is shallow and meaningless, but they are full of adventure and the spirit of justice. I fear we have awakened a sleeping tiger that will consume us."

Tokyo shook with victory celebrations, throbbed with music, with revelers who laughed and sang, with crowing roosters, and dogs barking enthusiastically under bobbing red paper lanterns. Firecrackers popped. Gold banners fluttered. Women prepared white rice and red lobster symbolizing health and good fortune, and they flew victory kites with their children.

Beyond a moat, beyond towers and high walls, Emperor Hirohito Yamato stood in the imperial palace and raised his hand in triumph. His narrow, chinless face broke into a smile. Most of his subjects believed that if they looked into that face, they would go blind, and viewed him as a divine being who lived above the clouds.

A Darwinist, he saw himself more as the apogee of evolution. However, he realized that if others believed in his descent from Amaterasu, the Sun Goddess, they would obey him unquestioningly, which simplified his life. When a conflict arose, he changed the subject to botany. "Lichen is an entanglement of fungus and photosynthetic symbion," he would say, "usually green algae or cynobacteria." Twenty minutes later, he would still be lecturing. No need to address the issues. His underlings were only shadows calling attention to themselves if they disagreed with their emperor.

For years, he had festered over the "sinister" Roosevelt's "evil plots against Japan," regarding our Two Ocean Diplomacy as a duplicitous euphemism for a spying operation and our Lend Lease program as the blatant arming of Japan's enemies. When FDR embargoed Japan's oil and steel, a furious Hirohito decided to take action.

Preaching surprise and secrecy, he selected a Sunday for the Pearl Harbor strike because he knew that Americans like to relax on weekends. Had anyone in history made a better assessment? He doubted it.

He celebrated his triumph with his wife, Nagako. Sure of her beauty, she walked with fluid movements, and her straight little toes charmed him. When they first met, she let him see the bones of her life, hear her voice with its haunting, wistful quality, as if she were ownerless, ready to devote herself to him. Soon she became his only confidante, and talking to her helped him find clear lines in a confusing world. After they married, everyone marveled that he did not also take a mistress, wanting only her.

Now, while husband and wife toasted victory, Hirohito received a respectful cable from his ally, Adolph Hitler. The German chancellor congratulated the emperor and complimented his Mitsubishi A6M Zero fighters, which he said would terrorize the Pacific. He considered Americans too degenerate to win anything since the Civil War, when the "timid shopkeepers" of the North defeated the "once-proud plantation owners" of the South. Japan had nothing to fear from the Americans, most of whom were pacifists.

The emperor seated himself at his desk, pulled a sheet of paper toward him, and picked up his pen. With pleasure, he wrote an official pronouncement:

We, by the grace of heaven, Emperor of Japan, seated on the throne of a line unbroken for ages eternal, enjoin upon you, our loyal and brave subjects: We hereby declare war on the United States and the British Empire.

# CHAPTER TWO

OVER CAYUCOS, a lone cloud masked danger as the fog will mask the sun. It hung weightless, its edges bright, as Mom called Alice, the wife of General Rapp Brush. They lived next door, and Mom considered Alice the ultimate source of information, given her husband's rank.

I remember Alice's hair and eyes that gleamed like topaz, her round face with tiny features, and her mouth whose corners turned up no matter how she felt. She often made sentences sound like questions. Her husband had big bones, not big like a giant's, but big.

Now, Mom poured coffee in a slow, silent stream. Nearby, I played with my doll, Tinesey Gretchen, speaking to and for her. A blonde, fat-cheeked baby, she always smiled when she played with me, as her blue glass eyes opened and closed.

Mom and Alice lit up. As usual, Alice clamped her cigarette between her first two fingers, which she extended, and she bent her wrist back when she exhaled. Mom's cheeks sucked in, becoming concave with the ferocity of her smoking. She turned on the radio, and we heard the newscaster begin, his voice tinny, as he spoke of fighter planes called Zeros, of how they flew so low people could see pilots hunched, faceless under their oxygen masks, shaking their fists in triumph. Then he described our dazed survivors searching for family members as oily fire on the water illuminated the bodies that floated like kelp. The emperor's fire.

"Werz Purl?" I asked Mom.

She pointed at the horizon line where the sky touched the sea. "Over there."

I went to the window, screwing up my face for better vision, but for the life of me could not see the empor fire. Not even any smoke.

"Isn't it horrible?" Alice moaned. "Tragic? Tragic, so tragic. Those poor men. I'm in shock." She took another drag on her cigarette. "Now we'll fire the Hawaii commanders, wait and see. Do you call that fair?"

"I guess not. Who are they?"

"General Walter Short and Admiral Husband Kimmel. Yamamoto? The famous Japanese admiral? Well, he went to Harvard, and studied economics. Did you realize that? Everyone liked him. He wrote haikus to his friends – you know, those little Japanese poems? And he loved poker. Played it all the time."

Scowling, Mom stubbed out her cigarette. "Then why'd he bomb our Pacific Fleet out of existence?"

"A Japanese sees himself as the sword of the emperor, period? Rapp says so."

"For that matter, why did the emperor have to drag us into his war?" Mom's voice trembled with rage.

Alice exhaled without moving her lips, just opened her mouth and let the smoke drift out. "He apparently blames the 'sinister' Roosevelt. That's how I hear it?"

I climbed on Mom's lap. Tomorrow I would plan a tea party – just Tinesey, Henrietta, my glass hen, and me. Not Mom and Alice. They acted too nervous over this strange radio talk.

I did not know Japanees and did not care about them. No, I did care, because they upset Mom. I went to the kitchen, scooped a bite of butter, and ate it in my little rocking chair.

A stressful hour later, Alice said, "Time for me to go? Don't expect Frank home for dinner."

Mom shook her head sadly and fluttered her fingers good-bye. When she felt nervous, she'd dart her fingers through her cloud of auburn hair or chew her lip. Now she did both.

"Nap time," she said.

Though I usually liked to nap, I couldn't sleep that day. I sucked my thumb, held my yellow blanket with the satin trim and my doll, Tinesey. No use. I got up and looked at my scrapbook, especially the pictures of my last birthday party in Berkeley.

We used to live there, up north in Berkeley, but six months before Pearl Harbor, FDR called up Daddy's National Guard unit and assigned it to Ft. San Louis Obispo. Mom rented the beach house in nearby Cayucos, a house almost entirely surrounded with yellow daisies and perched on the bluff overlooking the sea. When we left our Berkeley home and my sand box, I cried, but Cayucos had sand everywhere. Clearly, we moved there to enjoy the beach.

Now the change scared me, and I wanted to go home to Berkeley.

The scrapbook burst with birthday pictures from there - many with nut cups made of accordion pleated paper filled with jellybeans, gumdrops, and peanuts. Mom's sister, Aunt Lenore, gave me hers, so I had two in the picture.

The only glitch came when a playmate won pin the tail on the donkey. I expected to. Never mind. A birthday cake – white frosting with pink roses – arrived, and I blew out both candles. To this day a white cake with pink roses like that one absolutely thrills me.

Before my birthday, I hold only random images: Daddy's face, Mom's, the feel of their skin – Bluebirds and robins warbled outside my bedroom – From the Victrola came the sounds of "Once in a Blue Moon." In the corners of our house: footballs. Daddy would pick one up, toss it in the air making it spin or pass it fast from hand to hand. He could, he believed, live life like a football game, where he, as quarterback, controlled the plays.

Now, in Cayucos, I closed my scrapbook, tried once more for a "snappy nappie," as Mom liked to say, but gave up. Aware that it would annoy her, I returned to the living room, where she sat fixated as the newscaster spoke rapidly and with alarm.

In the background, I could hear the telegraph clicking. It made more sense to me than the announcer's words. But these shattered our happy day. I knew that much. Mom wrote his confusing words down, then switched off the radio and staggered to the kitchen, her expression somber, unapproachable. She took a chicken out of the refrigerator, smoothed butter over it. Quiet, remote, she didn't meet my eyes. In silence, I embraced her above her knees.

"Would you like some nice chickie?" she asked. "Maybe with some peas?"

"Ice cree," I said.

"You know ice cream's for dessert," Mom said, "First you have to eat dinner."

"Why?"

A siren howled, lights blinked out, and she made me dive under the table with her. I began to shiver.

"Don't worry, baby. It's just an air raid drill."

"What?"

"An air raid drill. A little practice."

"I don't like it. Let's go see Daddy."

"I know the darkness scares you, but – "

"I want my Daddy."

"Shhh," she whispered, "we're not supposed to make a single sound during air raid drills."

When the lights came back on, she served dinner, but neither one of us felt like eating. She changed me into my pink bunny pajamas, popped me in bed, and took Daddy's place reading my favorite story "Ping," the tale of a Chinese duck with too many relatives. Her cheeks began to quiver.

Daddy could read much better, and he liked to make up his own tales about Greenie the Hop Toad. Bedtime stories filled him, intertwined, waiting to be told. He would begin in funny sentences, end with morals of the story, then sing my lullaby, "The Sturdy Golden Bear." Everyone knows that's Cal's fight song. And everyone knows the University of California Berkeley students sang it to him, the quarterback, when he and his teammates surged onto the field at the start of a game.

But tonight, no Daddy. When would he come home?

Mom lay down on the bed beside me. As I tried to fall asleep, she stayed with me and listened to my breathing.

# CHAPTER THREE

ON DECEMBER 8, President Roosevelt, calling Pearl Harbor the "day that will live in infamy," declared war against Japan and its allies, Germany and Italy. Mom leaned toward the radio, not in tears, but frozen with terror. She and I listened, speechless, united.

FDR's declaration became a call to arms, and nothing could keep men away. Gladly they left their families, schools, jobs and lovers to enlist in the armed forces.

Before Pearl Harbor, we loved Cayucos. Daddy and I skimmed the waves, and he would pretend to be a whale by rolling over on his back and spitting water out of his mouth, straight up. Sometimes we found pink seashells the size of thumbnails along the shore and an occasional sand dollar or starfish.

I went to a play school run by a girl with butterfly hands and large green eyes who taught us to wrap bright tin foil on foxtails for bouquets, paste shells on boxes, and try to dig holes in the sand all the way to China.

When she held a sand castle-making contest, I created one fit for an enchanted princess: square w1th a round tower and bits of shells decorating the sides. I smiled modestly when prize moment came, only to learn that someone else's castle won. Maybe because it had a moat. Daddy always spoke of sportsmanship, so I didn't kick the victorious castle down or start crying.

But now, war. Daddy would have to fight. I sensed a horrible threat, as a cat does, as any beast. It beat in my heart. Outside, the Pacific splashed, unconcerned, its great beds of foam breaking against the white sand.

# CHAPTER FOUR

IN MANILA, CHURCH bells pealed good morning from cupolas, the sounds cresting, suspended, and six-inch long monkeys went swinging among the tall lilies as if they were trees. Janitors polished floors with banana leaves, chefs prepared sweets called bibingka, and women filled vases with purple frangipani.

MacArthur heard about Pearl Harbor and immediately convened his advisors. General Richard Sutherland said they had to get the planes off the ground in Clark Field, and Joseph McMicking agreed. However, MacArthur said there was no hurry; the Japanese wouldn't attack until January.

Nine hours later, a bright flock of Japanese planes streaked across the Philippine sky and attacked Clark Field, where the US Pacific force of three dozen B-17 bombers conveniently nestled wingtip to wingtip. Molten metal smoked on the airstrip as the lords of the rising sun flew back to their carriers, and terrified Filipinos ran for cover.

After the attack, a collective anarchy grew as people shouted, "Los Japanese, they bomb, they bomb!"

On December 22, the emperor's finest invaded the main Philippine island of Luzon, and in no time, MacArthur's men beat a retreat to Bataan and Corregidor. Without adequate provisions, they soon began dying from starvation and malaria, as well as enemy firepower. General Jonathan Wainwright gave his utmost, fighting in the front lines.

MacArthur established headquarters in Corregidor Malinta Tunnel and busied himself issuing 109 press releases that described himself as "The Lion of Luzon" and "going in everywhere."

* * *

Emperor Hirohito had more to celebrate. His forces sunk two vital British heavy cruisers off of Singapore, HMS Repulse and HMS Prince of Wales. He had named his reign, "Showa, Peace and Prosperity," which reminded him of the numinous sound of whistling reeds, and then began Japan's sacred mission to acquire all the rich western colonies of the

Pacific. "Hakko Ichiu," Bring the Eight Corners of the World Under One Roof. He enjoyed impressing Japanese culture upon conquered people and believed they benefited from it.

His wife, Nagako, agreed. The managerial type, she saw her word as the law, a good quality in a person faced with overseeing a staff of ten thousand and surrounded by scores of in-laws. Yamatos popped out at her wherever she turned, forever fond of telling oft-repeated family stories.

Raised a Christian, she worshipped in private, participating in public Shinto ceremonies for her husband's sake. Though a hawk at heart, she developed a talent for asking philosophical questions like "Does war come unbidden, or does it have to be induced?" The queries gave her a reputation for wisdom rather than blood lust, which pleased her.

She and the emperor often strolled in the palace garden. Maple trees shaded green grasses where small green birds sought worms; cypress and pine trees cast shadows over twisting streams of water connected by subtly varied bridges, a progression into the floating world. Willow tree branches swayed, and granite rocks turned blind white at noon. In the carp pond swam a lively crop of young fish, cross bred between the beautiful shishigashira, whose brain weighed but one percent of his body, and the much plainer-looking fish, the murmured, whose relative brain weight was higher.

A team of gardeners shaped bonsai trees every day as if there were no war.

The emperor liked to brag that he positioned his conquests just so, the right distance apart, as stones in a garden. Hong Kong, Saigon, Batavia, Rangoon – all part of Dai Nippon now. The Empire of Japan had become history's largest. Conquering Australia and New Guinea would follow, just as sunrise followed sunset. Soon Dai Nippon's military elite would race horses in Melbourne and linger there over fine meals in wood-paneled dining rooms, he believed.

# CHAPTER FIVE

AT 5'10" AND 180 POUNDS, Daddy had to outwit much beefier quarter-backs when he led his high school team to the state championships. His parents called him the "bright star of the family," given his fame as both quarterback and captain of the "Wonder Team." A sportswriter described him as, "a slender and lithe man whom nobody can contain. He's the sorcerer of the single wing, the enchanted quarterback."

He'd grown up in San Diego, then a little village of stucco houses that dotted the slopes above the sea, houses with red tile-roofs, splashing fountains, and wrought iron balconies. Spills of sunlight heightened the pinks and yellows of blooming vines and made galloping horses in the distance look like specks of flying dust. His adolescence consisted of one glorious football victory after another, and he'd married his college sweetheart, a beauty whose family fortune went back to California's land grant days. Such people don't expect catastrophe, so, as history caught my parents in its maws, they patiently waited for their inevitable happy ending.

When he married Mom, they filled their house with art deco furniture and me. The days floated by as they shared their love of animals and nature, their belief in the basic kindness of humanity, their time together filled with music and making love. At night, they burned can-dles in the center of our kitchen table and talked for hours, especially about history, their favorite subject. They only faintly heard the back-beat of Germany and Japan. The history they liked to discuss was written on a page, but a newspaper page rather than a history textbook. Once Daddy did say, "I hear lunatic Hitler's, 'Mein Kampf,' started out as, 'My Twenty Year Struggle With Lies, Stupidity, Blunders, and Treason.' His publisher suggested he shorten it."

However, the Battle of Britain brought it home. When the air raids began, the Chronicle's headline quoted Shakespeare, "This Island, this England." Mom began to cry, and Daddy said, "We have to join the fight."

As Mom and Daddy slowly faced reality, their country geared up for war. Factories rose that soon would produce more weapons than all the other countries of the world put together.

Daddy had such arresting blue eyes that if he didn't laugh and joke so much, he'd have made an ideal poster boy for the armed forces. In those blue eyes, a light of hope always shone, and just looking at them filled a person with optimism. He wanted to help his country, and understood a fair fight, and believed he knew what war could mean.

But "naive" best describes him, and naivety is its own failing in the end.

Now the days became cold; the birds huddled deep in the pine trees. War or no war, Daddy embraced the Christmas season, singing carols, kissing Mom under the mistletoe, and cuddling me by the fire. Mom made me be really good, because Santa might come, and I dictated a letter saying how hard I tried and what kind things I did for people. Daddy actually wrote it, but he made me delete some toys off my list. "It's too long," he explained. "You'll overwhelm Santa if you ask for so much. He needs room in his sleigh for everyone's toys, don't forget."

I couldn't decide which items to skip, and made several revisions before allowing him to mail the letter to the North Pole.

Mom said for the hundredth time that she couldn't understand the Japanese stupidity at bombing Pearl Harbor.

And for the hundredth time, or so it seemed to me, Daddy again explained, "With the US fleet gone and unable to help its allies, the Nip Emp figures the Dutch will leave the East Indies and the English will quit the rest of Asia."

As always, Daddy brought home every joke he heard, laughing before the punch line but trying to stop. I asked what Mickey Mouse and Donald Duck wanted Santa to bring, and he replied, "Mickey wants a chunk of cheddar cheese, and Donald wants a fingerling fish." His basso voice made words sound like music.

He took me in his arms and danced me around the room singing, "She's the sweetheart of Sigma Chi." Then he counted the freckles on my nose, "One, two, three, four, and one to grow on."

When he put me down, I began playing with Henrietta, placing gumdrops in her nest and stroking her.

"Peep, peep, peep," Daddy said. "Will Henrietta lay me an omelet?"

Mom joined us and started stringing popcorn and cranberry garlands for our Christmas tree. "I'm going to serve turkey with corn bread stuffing on Christmas Eve," she said, "and set out a plate of chocolate-chip cookies with a glass of milk for Santa."

On December 17, Daddy's orders arrived: report for active duty in Los Angeles. Since Japanese submarines had appeared off the coast there several times, the brass considered it a prime attack target.

We would drive south immediately. Mom stood in front of her mirror holding up dresses and trying to decide which ones to pack and which ones to give away. All her life, she tended to head for her closet by way of solving problems. When she finished sorting, she smoothed down her hair, applied a new coral-toned lipstick, and smiled at Daddy. "Does this color make my two crooked teeth more noticeable?"

"I never get beyond the eyes," he replied.

After stroking her hair, which she criticized as looking "much like a chrysanthemum," he began fitting his life into his suitcase. Then he herded us into our de Soto, and we rattled off.

Gauzy sky spread a veil of light on the Pacific beyond the sand dunes where the cattails grew, on orchards of blossoming walnut trees, and on redwoods towering in dark majesty.

Impatiently, he wove through the dragon tail of cars and moving vans that crowded the two-lane highway. The huge war migration had begun, so we "crawled," as he kept saying with a scowl. Then he'd talk about "our enemies," calling Hitler a dangerous lunatic and Mussolini a bon vivant who spent too much time with his lady friends.

Mom tucked a strand of hair behind her ear. "I'm glad I don't live in Europe."

"Or Nanking," Daddy replied. "Ask those who tried it when the Emperor of Japan paid a visit. At least the Europeans think they're sons of men. This bird believes he's the Son of God."

I whined about stopping for ice cree, so Mom pointed out the sights. "Look at that old hotel with the white curtains drawn tight across its windows. See, Pooksie, see the neon signs flashing? The colorful lightning."

I am Ann, but Pooksie was my nickname.

20

I was at an impressionable age, and my life was being disrupted. The details seared into my memory and maintain their force in retelling now. My mother confirms them still.

In Los Angeles, my parents rented a pink bungalow near stables, which gave the air a rich scent of well-groomed horses that savored the occasional apple or sugar cube. Mom looked out the window. Tall sentinel palm trees stretched toward the sapphire blue sky that domed the city, miles of orange groves surrounded it, and, in the distance, snow-capped mountains rose. "This place is gorgeous," she said, "really quite sensational. We're going to have some fun under those palm trees."

Daddy gave her his warm blue stare and started singing "The White Cliffs of Dover." A horse clopped by, and Daddy interrupted his singing to wiggle his nose. "The horses can smell an enemy a mile away and warn us with their snorts."

Mom laughed. "I'll get some potted lemon trees for the porch and fill the rooms with roses. I'm mad about them, mad about L.A."

They listened to the radio, and Daddy said, "The Nips have bombed Pearl Harbor, invaded the Philippines, Guam, Wake, Malaya, Shanghai, and Midway. The emperor's about the size of Thumbelina, I hear, but he dreams of his rising sun flag waving over all of Asia."

"Yes, and enslaving the defeated citizens?"

"He's a master of the euphemism, I hear. Calls his empire The Greater East Asia Co-Prosperity Sphere."

"Does his Co-Prosperity sphere include Washington DC?"

Daddy put a pan on his head to look like a helmet-crown. "No chance, Nip baby."

Walt Disney invited some of the Army men and their children to the studio for a Christmas party. All of Walt's friends also attended: Mickey Mouse, Donald Duck, Pluto. Big, the size of Mom and Daddy, their quacks, barks, and squeaks mingled with the Christmas music. I couldn't contain my excitement. If a child could burst from so much, I would have then. Inspired, I tried to invite Minnie Mouse over to play, but she didn't understand. Walt sat me on his lap, sang, "I Wish You a Merry Christmas," and gave me a drawing of Santa on celluloid that I still have. Small and twinkling, Walt reminded me of an adult elf, one who could see into my heart.

Daddy seemed so happy at that party. I remember him throwing back his head and laughing at Walt's jokes, most of which I didn't understand. Did I ever hear Daddy laugh in such a carefree all-out way again? I don't think so.

Mom wasn't there, and the next morning, he described the party to her over scrambled eggs and toast. She smiled. "What a marvelous man to do that. Los Angeles is a paradise. I wouldn't mind spending the rest of the war here," she said.

Daddy shook his head silently. His worries worried her. Her face became still and white. "Will you fight the Japanese? In the Pacific?"

# CHAPTER SIX

ON FEBRUARY 22, 1942, ROOSEVELT ordered MacArthur to leave for Australia, plan a counteroffensive, and give Wainwright command of the Philippines. MacArthur, his wife, son, and staff members bravely departed in a PT Boat that somehow managed to elude the Japanese blockade. When it landed in Australia, he raised his fist and shouted at the waiting press, "I give the people of the Philippines my sacred pledge: I shall return!"

Singapore, the so-called "Gibraltar of the Pacific," remained in British hands and became headquarters of the first Pacific Allied Command: British, American, Dutch, and Australian, called ABDACOM.

However, soon, during the first week of February 1942, General Yamashita attacked Lt. General Arthur Percival's eighty-five thousand man garrison there. Mitsubishi G3M Niels and G4M Bettys took off from Japanese-occupied Indonesia and bombed Singapore, while Yamashita, the "Tiger of Malay," attacked with ground forces. By far Japan's most gifted tactician, he devised new ways to maneuver that surprised the British.

On February 14, a man emerged from Alexandra Hospital with a white flag, but the Japanese ignored it and massacred patients and staff. Five miraculously survived to tell the tale.

Percival decided to surrender in order to prevent further civilian casualties and drew up a list of "terms of surrender." Yamashita agreed to them. Percival surrendered, saluting and presenting his holstered revolver with a flourish. Yamashita accepted it with a bow.

Then The Tiger of Malay went back on his word, unfortunately for the Singapore civilians. And, 80,000 British, Indian, and Australian POWs joined 50,000 others from Yamashita's Malayan campaign. The conquered troops were herded into holding pens, where their captors forced them to bow to the general, touching their foreheads to the dirt. He told them they'd committed grievous crimes because their slimy government cockroaches lied to them. But they could atone by laboring on railroads and landing strips throughout the Greater East Asia Co-Prosperity Sphere."

In Los Angeles, Daddy took me on a horseback ride to see orange poppies blanketing green spring hills. Brilliant flash of inspiration: I wanted a horsie of my own. A girl horsie. We'd get her a straw hat with holes in the brim for her ears, tie a bow in it.

I spoke to him about it, and he said I'd have to wait a little while. No matter. It wouldn't be long. After the ride, I drew a picture of him with the sun shining above. He studied it as if it drove all other thoughts from his mind, then picked me up, waved me over his head, and settled me on his shoulders. I put my arms around his neck and talked to him, my mouth moving right next to his ear.

Next, he interrupted Mom's crossword puzzle efforts with a kiss and filled glasses with ice cubes. Sullen over his shift in attention, I went upstairs and played with Tinesey and Henrietta. Instead of a real egg, I placed gumdrops in Henrietta's nest, then stroked her saying, "Peep, peep, peep, peep" like Daddy did. Soon Henrietta shared her gumdrops with Tinesey and me. Friendly and silent, my hen and my doll kept me company.

Later, when Daddy left for the base, I ran to Mom with my horsie proposition, but she ignored me.

"Pea tenson me," I said, as best I could.

"I pay attention to you morning, noon, and night, Pooksie, but right now I have other things to worry about besides horses."

She turned on the radio and started chain smoking as she listened with those terrified eyes. "The omnivorous Japanese have attacked all Allied possessions in the Far East," the announcer said, calling the Pacific "their private pond."

# CHAPTER SEVEN

THE SPEED OF JAPAN'S conquests stunned Americans at home. Adults tried to cope with the disaster, while children chased each other around trees shouting, "Tora! Tora! Tora! The Nips will come and cut off your head!"

FDR told the Joint Chiefs to plan a dazzling attack that would thrill us and teach Hirohito that distance did not protect his home islands. If B-25 bombers launched from the carrier USS Hornet, they could hit Tokyo itself, and then land in China. No one had tried to launch these ungainly planes from a carrier before, but the daredevil Flyboy, Colonel James Doolittle, agreed to command the attack, which his eighty pilots called "the suicide mission."

They relied solely on Capt. James Cook's charts from the 1700s, as updated versions didn't exist. With huge courage, Doolittle selected a launching site, which FDR named "Shangri-La," and on April 18, 1942, his planes took off, making a silver waterfall in the air.

Near the Home Islands, a Japanese skipper spotted our carriers and went below to shoot himself.

Even closer to Dai Nippon, a Japanese on a fishing boat spotted the Hornet and radioed in.

Result: Doolittle launched two hundred miles farther from Tokyo than planned - not good when you're short on gas in the first place. However, his men managed to hit a few targets in Tokyo, and seventy-one of the eighty pilots survived. In their hearts burned the hero's joy.

\* \* \*

At home, Daddy tossed a football spinning into the air, then caught it. "The Nips call Doolittle's strike the 'Do Nothing Raid,'" he laughed, "but it scared the imperial commanders' pants off." He balanced his football on his forefinger. "And I'll tell you what: the aircraft carrier's king of the sea now. Battleships will have to accept prince charming roles."

I considered asking him for a boat to use in my bathtub but decided my rubber duckie might not like that. Instead I reviewed what he'd said about the "do nothing" raid and concluded the Japnees were not good sports. "Be a good sport," Daddy always said, and he meant it.

Tonight Nancy Dollar would throw a party to celebrate Doolittle. This delicate girl-woman had a radiance even the war could not dim, and no one could make her guests feel happier. Plus tonight they'd celebrate the original "mission impossible." All the girls loved Flyboys, those sexy things, and Doolittle had already won every popular award.

Mom held up her two favorite dresses: a white organza embroidered in lilacs, and a white silk with red and gold ribbons woven into the fabric. Selection made, she "beautified" herself for the event. Nancy and her husband, Stanley, were old family friends, like many couples in the Fortieth. In those days, a boy dated a pretty girl and soon found the chocolates passed around the sorority house. "Yes, we're engaged!"

The newlywed men joined the same National Guard unit, so at least my parents faced the war surrounded by many best friends.

The morning after the party, Aunt Lenore called to say, "Doolittle certainly put the Emperor of Japan in his place."

I told my doll, Tinesey, a quick learner. Clearly Do Little made my parents happy, which allowed me some latitude. I held Tinesey in my arms and sang to her, then surprised her with a new outfit — an old dress that I updated with a bright spot of Mom's lipstick. Not that Mom realized, as she laughed and talked to Aunt Lenore on the phone. Prudently, I wrapped Tinesey in her blanket, which covered the dress.

* * *

On May 3, 1942, Daddy's National Guard unit became the 40th Infantry Division, XIV Corps, of the new Sixth Army. Division commander: General Rapp Brush, our friend.

The Sixth Army's chief, Walter Kruger, called it "Born of War," and declared it had but one mission: defeat Japan. It would march toward the Philippines island-by-island, and then on to Dai Nippon. At the same time, General Joseph "Vinegar Joe" Stilwell, became Commander of the CBI Theater (China, Burma, and India). Here the British presence was vital, especially in India.

Daddy joined the 143rd Field Artillery Battalion, the Red Devils; their small red flag sported crossed cannons. He let me wave it, while he sang:

"Over hill, over dale

As we hit that dusty trail...."

Lieutenant Colonel Wallace Nickell, the battalion commander, assigned Daddy to the G-2 unit, Intelligence.

"It's not because I'm smart," he told Mom, "just lazy. We sit around and shuffle papers only we can read. The troops think we're ivory tower fools; it's hard to live down."

"You'll manage."

"I'll tell you all our secrets," he said. "You'll know more than FDR."

"Has your training changed?"

"You bet. Now that we're at war, the CO complains I sing too much. He says I can't be warbling on combat patrols or in foxholes."

"What's the news?"

"Yamashita grabbed Singapore, you know that. Rapp heard from someone that the POWs are forced to work as slaves."

"In the boiling sun...Those poor men."

"They'll outwit their captors sooner or later. I'll place my money on a Brit any day."

On May 4, his orders came: Report to Fort Lewis, Washington, alone. His face burst with eagerness, and Mom pictured him greeting his buddies there with his big smile and warm handshake, and his, "Hey, you're looking good, kiddo." She held him and rolled his hair between her fingers. "I'll miss you, Frank."

He took her small hand, warming it in his. For a long time that night, they stood at the window and watched the black Pacific swallow the tiny lights along its edge, and then they turned and walked toward their bed, blind in the dark.

The next day she began to pack. The Los Angeles apartment took on a different aspect, unfamiliar: she always found a place strange and indifferent when she was about to leave it. "I want to take Pooksie

27

and return to the East Bay where I grew up," she said.

Daddy nodded. "Right. Be near your family."

"The aunties will help. They always do. Besides, Alice, Nancy, Phyllis – everyone, really - will go home, too."

Like Mom, I call Marie and Nini "the aunties," but you must mentally add the "great," as in great-aunts. Uncle George should be designated "great-uncle," but I never said that either. Forever swathed in pearls, their pale silver hair pulled back into French rolls to set off their elongated eyes, the aunties wore silk, boas, hats with little veils, and, always, gloves. Uncle George, ever the gentleman, opened doors when he visited and pulled out chairs, exuding la politesse du coeur – a sincere courtesy.

As Mom and her sister, Lenore's, parents died of galloping consumption, the aunties and Uncle George raised "the girls" in their huge belle epoch house. Marie and Nini had two other sisters, Catherine and Theresa, but they married and left the East Bay. Mom loved the aunties, and she loved her mother and father, now angels in heaven who sent her Daddy as a gesture of atonement for leaving her.

On her last Sunday in Los Angeles, Mom went to church while Daddy stayed home with me. As she entered the sanctuary, she felt like a child again, transported by the strong scent of incense, adobe, and old wood. The candles flickered in their tall brass holders. Blending with the candlelight, colorful rays of sun streamed through the stained glass windows, falling on the nave.

She knelt in a pew, and a priest in white robes performed the daily ritual of communion, witnessed by various carved martyrs of the faith and Mary, Mother of Jesus, in her turquoise robes. Mom felt the pull of the ritual cord and raised her eyes upward toward the crucifix as her tears fell. "Please," she prayed, "help me become strong; cure the fear inside me for the sake of my family, and transform me into someone brave, as you transform the bread and wine into the body and blood of Christ."

After church, Mom picked up a picture of the aunties and Uncle George, wrapped it in tissue paper, and added it to the box she'd packed. Later she wrote in her diary:

"Raised by such retiring people, I married a dazzling quarterback

28

who would never sit out a game on the sidelines. To my Frank, even war's a game. "

Now she shook her head with hopeful resignation, pushing aside thoughts of the size and might of Japan's empire.

# CHAPTER EIGHT

WHILE I TRIED to touch my nose with my tongue, spending long hours before the mirror, Col. Wendel Fertig seized a Philippine Island, Mindanao. A noisy, devoted soldier with a round, red face, he simply refused to surrender and inspired 30,000 American and Filipino troops to follow him.

However, on Corregidor, bullets flew around like shooting stars, until, on May 6, General Jonathan Wainwright surrendered and the victorious Japanese herded 65,000 Allied POWs to prison camps 60 miles away. The horrific journey became known as the Bataan Death March. Nearly 11,000 Allied and American POWs died from starvation, thirst, untreated disease, or the samurai sword. Those who made it to prison received an ounce of rice a day in return for good behavior, and often the guards amused themselves at the POWs expense.

Later, as an adult, I met Joe Martin, a former POW. One afternoon about ten years ago, he and I chatted on a veranda in Woodside, just south of San Francisco. In the distance, I saw gnarled trees, dry grass, and the soft mountains, their slopes gathering the light. In his prison camp, he worked so long under the sun that his face became a mass of scar tissue, and some of the skin around his mouth burned off altogether.

He said, "The enemy isolated Wainwright in Manchuria so he couldn't create problems in the Philippine prison system. But just knowing he was alive gave us the illusion that we served under him, not the Japanese, and we felt like fighters rather than slaves."

The idea kept them alive, according to Joe, though Wainwright himself spent tortured days asking himself if he should have fought to the last.

That same afternoon, Joe told me that major Japanese corporations, thriving unpunished today, rented slaves from the POW pool to work in their factories. Every morning, POWs assembled in large courtyards and kowtowed to their Japanese masters. Joe remembered bowing but clinging to his courage, though he could taste death in his mouth.

As he spoke, he peered up at the sky as if it bore down on him, closing in, stifling him, especially when he told me more, about the less fortunate POWs who went to Manchuria to become fodder for Dr. Shiro Ishi's biological research laboratory. There, POWs lived shackled and handcuffed until a researcher needed a brain or another organ. Some had five hundred cubic centimeters of blood drawn every few days for experiments involving anthrax, glanders, and plague. Within a month, they died naturally or by injection.

Joe felt grateful to have escaped that fate. Despite the scares on his face and his soul, he took his place in the greatest generation, eventually serving our country as an ambassador and a presidential advisor.

He devoted considerable time to studying the labs in Manchuria and recommended some books on the subject to me. Reading about the labs made me sick, and I will only share a little of what I learned here.

In 1932, Prince Kuni, the emperor's father-in-law, suggested that POWs who became too weak to work should go to Manchuria to participate in medical experiments for the benefit of mankind. Hirohito, as the self-styled scientist, loved the idea and began with the Chinese.

In Zhong Ma, Manchuria, the "Ishi Corps," unit 731 within the Imperial Army, conducted human experiments from 1932-1945. The hoped for happy ending: develop devastating biological and chemical warfare weapons. Off-limits, the "experimental lab" stood surrounded by moats, brick walls, barbed wire, high-voltage wire, and powerful searchlights. Soon he began gleefully killing hoards of people in the spirit of a mad scientist, and every day he impressed his men with the importance of their work.

When in time our POWs heading for Manchuria chugged along in unmarked boats, the US often sank them, unknowing. Some POWs did reach Manchuria, where, in their tiny cells, they lost their manhood, becoming little more than mollusks washed up on the shore. The staff exposed them to poison gas or jolted them with electricity to see how they reacted. With eyes filled with despair, beyond speech, the POWs submitted, their gazes shifting downward as their medical tormentors approached. The Japanese defended their behavior this way: honorable men fight to the death, and those submitting to capture warrant total contempt. Joe Martin summed it up, "I've heard many excuses for unseemly conduct in my day, but none to equal this one."

# CHAPTER NINE

I MET MY HUSBAND before my fifth birthday, though he didn't propose at that time. After Daddy received the Ft. Lewis orders, we drove to San Diego to spend a little time with his family. We rented a beach house in adjacent La Jolla, and once again I could dig in the sand while several gregarious porpoises turned somersaults beyond the breakers. Daddy made up stories about forgetful porpoises. He called himself "the beach tour director." He took me out to inspect the tide pools. "See?" he said. "That's a purple sea anemone, and that's a hermit crab walking sideways. Look at that pink starfish." Magic.

A seven-year-old boy stood on the rocks next to us with his grand-mother. His name was Bob Seymour, and he was scanning the waters for Japanese submarines. "I see one, I see a sub!" he cried, jumping up and down and pointing at the horizon.

Years later, he and I met again at Stanford. I saw something unique in him, something large in his stillness and in the way he moved, not hurrying but purposeful and intent. However, as children on the beach, we only thought about tide pools and submarines.

Soon Daddy's orders to leave La Jolla arrived. His mother, my Grandma, organized a farewell dinner. Her once silky hair had coarsened to the texture of a lion's mane, and her right eye was half closed, but with determined energy, she hurried from room to room, her heels clattering like bamboo sticks against the floor. "I need to keep things running smoothly," she liked to say.

Since his heart attack, Grandpa's world shrank down to the size of his chest cavity. Grandma urged him to eat more and rubbed his chest with cocoa butter. "So enormously helpful to the heart. Don't let your bed claim you," she'd say.

The night of the dinner, skirts and awnings swayed in the wind, a flat wind that blew in from the Pacific; whitecaps tossed dinghies, and anchored boats reeled. Daddy, Mom, and I pulled up at the curb, she in a silvery silk dress and the usual family pearls. I wore a blue and white striped dress with a white pinafore and a big white bow in my hair. Through the windows of the house, we could see Grandma's silhouette moving in welcome. She came out the door, waving, and we got out to embrace her. She kept wearing her smile, but somehow the energy had gone out of it.

Grandpa staggered forth from his injured misery to grasp his son's hands.

Daddy hugged them both, with his boyish smile. "I'm hungry as a wolf in a rainstorm," he said. "What's in the oven?"

"Roast venison."

Daddy's wide blue eyes opened wider. "I want my portion to be bigger than my head."

"See?" I waved my ID tag stamped with a number corresponding to one on a list held by Civil Defense; children wore the tags in case of evacuation.

"Yes, it's very grown-up," Grandma said.

Daddy went upstairs to check his old bedroom, with me scuttling behind. In his diary, he wrote that it remained the same, jammed with books, pennants, and trophies from floor to ceiling, two unmatched shoes, and an unstrung tennis racket twisting in its press. His mother never moved a thing, and glancing around, he remembered good times, but in a distant way.

The room looked familiar and at the same time unfamiliar. Once time seemed infinite to him, as it does to most youth, and the days moved by so slowly he hardly noticed. Now, since Pearl Harbor, they moved fast, piling one on top of the other.

He picked up his high school football and tossed it from one hand to the other, back and forth, faster and faster, and then returned it to its accustomed corner. I opened my arms so he could throw it to me, and with the gentleness of a feather, it landed in them. Briefly. I did drop it.

After a last look at his room, he returned downstairs.

The family moved to the living room with its array of heirloom colonial American furniture and a radio playing "Till We Meet Again." Over the lit fireplace hung a painting titled "Drakes at Sunset," and embroidered antimacassars rested on the arms of velvet chairs.

Grandpa flopped in a chair, rested one hand on his lap and picked at its skin with the other. "Remember, Frank," he said. "There's one thing more important than winning, and that is coming home."

Mom raised her glass and smiled approvingly. "Right!"

Uncle Arthur arrived with his wife, Virginia, pale dress and blonde hair swinging, her ivory skin reflecting light. She blew her hello kisses here and there, and Daddy took her for a quick spin around the room singing, "Carry me back to old Virginny."

My uncle had hair like Daddy's, dark and wavy, and a quick wit. Though he had wanted to enlist in the armed forces, his bad eyesight had disqualified him. He and Mom clasped each other's hands, until, pulling away, she lit a cigarette.

The doorbell chimed, and Aunt Ruth wafted into the room, trailing her scent of tobacco, face powder, and Chanel No. 5. An evanescent, instinctual creature, she had a delicate face surrounded by a cloud of black hair. I ran over to her, and she picked me up in a big hug.

Aunt Ruth. I adored her. During our brief stay in La Jolla, she spent an afternoon with me. She smiled with her perfect mouth lipsticked in the color of an American Beauty rose and produced a blue taffeta-covered box. Filled with pressed flowers, paper lace, ribbons, and cutouts, it enchanted me. She taught me to make collages and Valentines. Later she let me sit in her lap while she brushed my hair. The next day, she taught me to dance. Or so I thought, but at least she tried, whereas Daddy's idea of dancing was to pick me up and whirl around the room singing, while I just hugged him.

Tonight she traced his jaw line with her forefinger. "I can't believe this is your last night here, sweet brother. I guess you've heard about Gil. I mean that he, um . . . "

Her husband, Gil, enlisted in the navy and asked for a divorce one quiet afternoon, just as her roses began to bloom.

"None of us gave your marriage five minutes," Daddy said, fixing her a scotch and soda. "Mary-Helen didn't monogram the silver tray we sent, you notice."

Mom interrupted. "Frank – "

"Gil's the toughest kind of man to make into a good husband," Daddy continued. "He slicks down his hair with goose grease, which I think seeps into his brain."

34

Aunt Ruth looked down. "Well, you're sweet, but I blame my neighbor, Maud. She always has that recently bedded look, if you'll excuse my saying, and she's buried four husbands. She marries old moneybags who die shortly."

"Let's call her 'the Embalmer,' " Mom suggested, and crossed and recrossed her legs, exposing her delicate knees and long, slim ankles.

Daddy started pacing. "I'm frightened if he's joining the navy. The Japanese command every ocean in the world except the Atlantic, so we need good sailors, and Gil certainly won't be one of them. He's a weasel, a bloody cad, a bloated – "

Grandma rustled. "That's enough."

Aunt Ruth kept chocolates in her handbag and paused to pet stray dogs. Why would a man pick on someone so beautiful? I didn't understand it. Life became latticed with riddles; facts my mind could hold, but at that age I didn't know that facts build uneasy lessons, half-truths.

She lowered her head in a gesture of profound grief, so I put my arms around her. "Come live with us, Aunt Ruth."

She smiled at me, shook her head. "I need to be independent."

"In a dent? Why?"

She laughed, extended her arm so she could inspect her wedding band at a distance, then shrugged. "But all I really care about is my family. You, especially, my dear, brave Frank."

With a series of hand movements resembling a dancer's, she lit one Old Gold cigarette after another, chain-smoking. Daddy said they needed to invent a cigarette she could eat.

Grandma headed for the dining room now, where dark red roses decorated the center of the long mahogany table, and portraits of her ancestors, the Austins, scowled down from oval gilt frames. One wall bristled with antlers, Grandpa's hunting trophies, and a huge painting titled "Women of Thebes" covered most of another.

As usual, dinner began with a toast to the President of the United States and to King George of England, my grandparents being the California colonials that they were.

Then Grandma passed around a platter of asparagus, and Daddy raised his glass. "Whichever way the wind blows, the asparagus tips," he said. He took his food to his mouth, and chewed firmly with pleasure.

Beeswax candles flickered in silver holders, turning Grandpa's skin the color of Swiss cheese. He smiled at his family and raised his glass, "Here's to Frank. No man is honored for what he receives; he is honored for what he gives." His gold fillings gleamed, and his tongue moved slowly.

"Thanks," Daddy said. "You gave me everything." He dug into his venison. "Great! Pink and juicy. The army has an insane hatred of wasting food, so at the base we get limp lettuce, two-day-old coffee – but never mind. I want to know what's going on here. How's the old gang?"

"You remember Bill Nevin," Uncle Arthur said. "Well, he's over in England. Flying, I think."

"It's the place to be. The government's sending 85 percent of our forces there. Plus equipment."

"Leaving just 15 percent to fight Japan? Its empire's triple the size of Germany's. I call this ludicrous."

"Go figure. But I'm not worried; we have the spirit. Our guys burn to score all the touchdowns. This war will end in no time."

My uncle frowned in concentration. "So, have the Joint Chiefs defined the Pacific playing field?"

Daddy nodded. "Admiral Chester Nimitz will command the Central Pacific, CINCPAC, and he delegated Vice Admiral Robert Ghormley to handle the South Pacific and Guadalcanal.

"That leaves the Southwest Pacific, SWOPE, where you have larger land masses. I hear that when FDR suggested MacArthur as SWOPE chief, some of the Joint Chiefs objected. So did 'Ike,' who complained about the nine years he'd spent 'studying dramatics" under him.'"

"But MacArthur has brilliance and charisma, along with a genius for using the press as a propaganda tool," my uncle said.

Daddy nodded. "Besides, he knows the geography of the Pacific, including the 1,000-island Philippine archipelago."

Grandpa chimed in, unusual for him: "Most Americans haven't even gone to Hawaii, let alone the Pacific beyond."

Aunt Ruth nodded. "People like London and Paris."

"Funny," Daddy said, "when they could just as easily be visiting

Ulith and Tarawa. Anyway, MacArthur got the job. He's the best."

Grandma had a big pepper tree in the back yard, and I decided to try to climb it, but Mom stopped me before I got out the back door and dragged me back to the table. By way of revenge, I sucked my thumb instead of eating.

Smiling, Grandma offered Daddy a second helping of venison. He selected two thick slices, and my uncle said, "They called Louis XV a walking stomach. When he fled the Tuileries, he demanded a three-hour stop for lunch. That's how they caught him at Varennes."

"Should I take this personally?" Daddy asked.

"No insult implied."

The subject shifted to the Japanese. "They never rattle before they strike by declaring war," Daddy said, "but they've totally overextended themselves. You put too much air in a balloon, it pops."

"The sooner I hear that pop the better," Mom replied.

Everyone agreed and put in opinions without paying attention to each other. Mom can still remember snatches of the cantata: "Bob Hope plans to entertain the troops."

"I'm going to cut my hair myself until the war's over."

"We'll squash the enemy like worms."

I went over and climbed on Daddy's lap. He held me and sheepishly pointed out it was past my bedtime. Mom gave both of us a stony look.

Grandma brought in her homemade pie with the apple slices laid one on top of the other in a spiral, set it on the table, and handed the first piece to Daddy. "You'll be safe, don't worry."

He gave me the first bite. Mom steepled her fingers, and everyone began laughing and crying, and telling stories.

After dinner, Daddy hugged Aunt Ruth. "Goodbye, Stardust," he said, and her wide brown eyes filled with tears.

He shook Uncle Arthur's hand, "So long, pal."

"Happy landings." Arthur's voice caught.

"That's my favorite expression," Daddy said with a big smile.

He patted Grandpa's back and he rested his hands on his mother's shoulders as he kissed her good-bye.

"I love you, little boy," she whispered.

# CHAPTER TEN

AN AUSTRALIAN FRIEND remembers his mother keeping two bullets in her gun during the war years - one for herself and one for him, in case the Japanese invaded. Rumors about what happened to those captured terrified her. At age six, my friend collected silkworms in shoeboxes and made thread with a tool fashioned from his erector set. He believed his silk could make parachutes and help win the war.

On spacious beaches, waves broke with slow, majestic sounds, while fearful Australians watched for battleships bearing the sign of the rising sun. They scanned the sky for bombers, and, in the bush, waited for a sudden glint of samurai steel, the flash of sun on a helmet.

When MacArthur arrived, he rallied them with his fighting spirit and genius for words, giving them the greatest gift: hope. He assembled his team and eagerly put pins on his maps, each movement fueling his bounding will to win. Strategy and panache – that's what was needed.

The Imperial troops heavily outnumbered his own, so he devised a brilliant leapfrog strategy – an adaptation of the classic strategy of envelopment based on the method of the wolf.

With speed and surprise, Allied amphibious forces would capture the small garrisons in between the large, heavily defended ones, thus isolating them. The Joint Chiefs ratified his plan for the Allies' southern advance, and this moment marks the beginning of Daddy's walk on a road of terror, his link in the chain of war. However, even knowing the future, he would not have flinched. He did not have to define duty; his quarterback's temperament did that for him.

\* \* \*

In 1995, fifty years after Japan surrendered, I sat in a good friend's garden in the Makati section of Manila eating cueta, a fattening but delicious pork dish. Wind chimes rattled on eaves, frangipani filled the air with scent, and in one corner, afternoon shadows began to play on the raked patterns of a sand garden. A Japanese sand garden, in itself an emblem of forgiveness, I thought. I chatted with a group of Filipinos, some of whom idolized MacArthur's memory. Others did not.

One man in our group fought on some of the Pacific islands at age eighteen, and he described the combat, "Enemy soldiers hid up trees like monkeys. Sometimes when they attacked, they screamed like terrified lambs in a slaughterhouse, or they'd wave white surrender flags to suck us into traps."

After awhile he asked how I remembered the war years at home, and I replied, "More than anything I remember the longing. Always longing for Daddy."

Ambassador Johnnie Rocchia told me that during the Battle of Manila, American crossfire killed his mother as she walked to her sister's house. Later he introduced me to a local professor who taught the full history of the Pacific War. He said, "The Philippine story in the war is probably not what you think. We all know the truth from word of mouth, but this year the Freedom of Information Act goes into effect, and the previously classified records will corroborate the rumors. Read books published in the next few years. You'll learn a lot."

I did, especially about the blunders of the American commanders, but I found the quotations from Hirohito's private diaries that Count Makimo published the most fascinating of all.

The Imperial Yamato family kept diaries, and in 1946, the emperor gave recorded interviews for several months, all from memory. They showed him to have been aware of every aspect of the war effort and to have participated in all decisions. Then, forty-six years later, Hirohito's testimony and the diaries became available to everyone.

He believed that when scholars read all the war's diaries, his own would stand as courageous and inspirational, and historians, he often wrote, would name the twentieth century the "Age of Hirohito."

# CHAPTER ELEVEN

WAVES OF LUPINES and poppies blanketed the California hills as Daddy drove us north, whistling and singing, while I bounced around in the back seat or looked at my favorite book, "Sunbonnet Sue." Mom rested her head on Daddy's shoulder, kissed his neck, and whispered private words to him.

In Berkeley, we rented a brown shingle house with window boxes where scraggly tendrils of potato vine drooped wearily. Immediately Mom added daffodils. The house stood on a hill behind the university, and here's what I remember: fireflies. Yes. They came out at night, bursting into the dark from nowhere, and danced round and round. I could never catch one, so concluded they possessed magic powers.

Aunt Lenore wanted to visit us. Her husband was risibly named William-Joseph, but we called him Billy Boy. He developed an ulcer after Pearl Harbor, and spent the war years resting in bed while she brought him silver trays with bowls of milk toast, presenting them in a manner a pampered princeling would envy. Uncle Arthur had wanted to fight but was turned down. On the other hand Billy Boy painstaking filled out his medical incapacity forms.

Mom complained, "One day my sister will die of exhaustion from waiting on that man. She runs up and down stairs with milk toast while he sits in bed, or she crawls on her stomach to untie his shoelaces with her teeth. When she's dead, he'll run off with a younger woman." (She was right.)

"He's the barnacle clinging to the rock," Daddy replied, "but give the man credit; his sick act is worthy of Olivier."

"He obviously believes himself underrated," Mom grunted.

"Right. The rarified creature unsuited to the routines of daily life."

"She only married him because he's good looking."

"That's why you married me."

"But you have charm, but if that creature has any, I certainly can't see what it is."

Daddy stroked his chin. "Whenever a woman approaches a dining table, he leaps to his feet fast, way before the rest of us. In college, he'd

40

go into a bar, sit next to someone's girl, and ten minutes later she'd be charmed. He's one of those sophisticates with a line of hot air women love. But never mind. Your sister's swell."

True. Long-legged and turquoise eyed, Aunt Lenore had a sporty glamour, which, like all true elegance, seemed completely unstudied. Today she arrived in a long, dark skirt and a white silk blouse with a wide collar. In common with the other women in the family, she always wore her "good pearls." Pearls and silver tea services – the emblems of Mom's family.

Lenore called herself "delighted" to see us, but it soon was apparent she was not in a particularly jovial mood. She wanted a baby, and the stork kept bypassing her, though considering how much attention Billy Boy required, the bird probably bestowed a favor on her. I didn't think the baby issue made much sense, considering her perfectly good niece – me.

She started in on the war. "MacArthur's supposed to be a genius."

Daddy nodded. "I've heard a lot of men say that they'd follow him anywhere."

After glancing around our apartment, my aunt said, "Mary-Helen, you should get slip covers, decent-looking blue and white checks."

Mom nodded, feeling vague and formless around her strong and definite older sister.

Daddy smiled at my aunt. "Catch me up on our Cal friends," he said. "Remember Rae Okomoto on the team? What happened to him?"

"He's joined the 143rd Regiment. The rest of his family's in the Utah internment camp."

Daddy got mad. "So they draft the Nisei or lock 'em up. The Nisei were born here, but we slap them in camps. That's executive order 9066. Not the way to treat citizens."

"But this is war," Aunt Lenore replied, as if he didn't know.

Next, the aunties and Uncle George arrived, accompanied by their priest, a man with a tiptoe walk and salmon-colored lips. Today he told Daddy, "We will pray for your safety at every Sunday service."

"That's a relief," Daddy replied. "Now I know I'll be fine."

The aunties, as usual, talked in unison, either saying the same words or else snapping at each other. Now everyone joined them. "Hitler like a mad crow with a Charlie Chaplin moustache." "The emperor of Japan's no bigger than a groundhog, and he's blown his gaskets." "The French call Churchill a courageous drunkard." "Where did you hear that?" "Who cares? Monsters are on the loose in Europe and Asia."

The family sounded much like the Ribbels did at Grandma's.

"Now, now," the priest said, "remember that even with the war, we are all God's children. We must pray for peace, but as good Christians we don't want to condemn other individuals."

"Conversation would completely dry up if we stopped," Aunt Lenore replied. "By the way, have I ever mentioned I met Nimitz once? Blonde, blue-eyed, your basic Apollo Belvedere. And down to earth."

"Swell guy. He started the navy ROTC at Cal," Daddy said. "The boys practiced maneuvers on a cow-studded hill; Nimitz called them the Battles of Cow Flop Hill."

On Daddy's last night at home, he took me for a walk under the stars, holding my hand. The infinite sky dwarfed us, the more so the longer we looked. We stopped under a bowl of stars he called the Milky Way, and it poured into my senses until I felt filled with stars, up to the brim.

Later I woke up and crawled into bed next to him. "I'm scared of the dark."

He held me in his strong arms. "As long as I'm alive, you need never to be."

The next morning, a light breeze rocked the treetops gently. Mom pulled the white sheet up over her ears and sank further into the pillows, breathing in the astringent smell of cologne and fresh linen. Then she rose and pulled open the blackout curtains to invite the sun to come in and stay. She put on her favorite dress, sleek and pink, and went downstairs to cook breakfast.

Daddy shaved and showered, singing "The Sturdy Golden Bear." Mom usually complained that he used up all the hot water in order to finish every verse, but not today.

He went downstairs, and, after finishing his Aunt Jemima pancakes, began talking about the Pacific War, striding back and forth, hands in his pockets, shoulders hunched a little.

He sat down again, and Mom began massaging his shoulders. Around her neck, along with her pearls, hung the St. Christopher's medal and gold cross that she would wear for his safety until he came home. "I'm worried," she said.

"Don't be silly. I'm just going up north a little way." He gave her his happy smile. "Besides, wherever I go in this war, I'll be back. I've always been lucky."

We drove to Oakland's Spanish-Colonial style train depot, and Daddy picked me up, saying, "Sweetheart, you're a brave little girl."

His tone of voice sent a wave of fear through me; I felt the warmth of his skin through his clothes. "Don't go, Daddy."

Mom began to cry.

"All aboard," the conductor shouted.

Daddy kissed Mom good-bye. "I love you, my precious," he said, and he climbed aboard the train, almost fell out the window blowing kisses to us. Mom took my hand, and I could feel the moisture on hers, the planks of the platform under my feet. The air seemed to tremble.

I blew kisses toward the train and called, "'Bye, Daddy. Come home soon," but I thought, don't go. Stop, train. Let my daddy get out, return with us to the beach, and pretend he's a whale while we ride the waves.

Puffing and rattling, the train chugged along the track, on and on, moving away. Mom let go of my hand and wrapped her arms around herself as she watched her husband disappear.

# CHAPTER TWELVE

JAPAN'S RUGGED, floating Home Islands teemed with women in meager houses who waited and sacrificed. Their faces lacked animation, as if they could endure only through lethargy. Their men had gone to fight, and their places stood empty. Though their homeland bloomed with tea bushes, quince, and cherry trees, they fought depression, tried to bolster one another. "Dai Nippon's brave warriors will prevail," they said, but they dreaded that bloody General MacArthur, whom they called, "Makkasa."

They warned their children that he could harm them, and only good behavior would keep him away. If the children became too frightened, their mothers told stories of the Yamato family or ancient myths about monkeys who worshiped a frog god who saved them from starvation. If these tales didn't work, the ladies could always fall back on a female Horse-Headed Buto-Kwanon, whose bio sheet rivaled Joan of Arc's. Most days, mothers and children went to temples and bowed before portraits of the medieval holy man, Seshin, touching the floor with their foreheads.

Though the nearsighted emperor stood only five feet, six inches, he tended to stoop, and, though timid at times, he found within himself invincible yearnings and hungers. He believed that had he not been born an emperor, his genius might have flourished in a field other than leadership, probably literature or science. In any venue, he could transform the world, of that he felt certain.

Along with Hirohito and the powerful, secretive businessmen called kuramakus, Premier Hideki Tojo ran the war. As a general, he'd conquered large portions of China, and reportedly he combined the soul of a warrior with the body of a slimmed-down sumo wrestler. He reeked of old cologne and sweat, and his face almost appeared jovial until he cocked his head to watch a person warily, like a gecko looking for food to devour.

Today he crossed the Sukurada bridges, the "gates of heaven," that traversed the wide moat around the palace compound. Its curving roofs and eaves rose, one above the other, designed to produce the effect of a shimmering mirage. The kongorikishi, tall guardian figures, discouraged evildoers from entering. Surrounded by fire, their snarling faces threatened, while they brandished chains and swords.

A guard dressed in black led Tojo to the emperor, who, after accepting the premier's deferential bows, motioned him to a carved gold French chair that once belonged to Louis X1V, a man with whom Hirohito compared himself. Most people meeting with the emperor knelt on a pillow at his feet throughout the conversation, but Tojo deserved the privilege of a chair. The emperor sat on the Chrysanthemum Throne.

No Yamato ever visited Europe before Hirohito, but, priding himself on his "modern" eclecticism, he added numerous foreign furnishings, like the chair, to his palace.

After the preliminary obsequies, Tojo said he wanted to invade Hawaii, now that it stood unprotected by the fleet. Hirohito agreed, but an amphibious assault couldn't succeed unless Dai Nippon's navy first attacked Midway, the Allies' Central Pacific bastion — a sentry for Hawaii.

Tojo sat in silence. He wanted to cut back the navy's radar and let submarines patrol only. No more Long Lance torpedoes. Though he resented the navy, he truly hated his old army rival, General Yamashita, the Tiger of Malay, who once called him more a bureaucrat than a general. Tojo now intended to assign Yamashita to the training command in Mutankiang, Manchuria. The ultimate backwater.

\* \* \*

Lieutenant Commander Robert Dixon, the historic USS Lexington's Second SBD leader, went about his chores, dashing like a racehorse from one sortie to another. He sank the imperial carrier Shoho in the Coral Sea on May 7, 1942. "Scratch one flattop," he gleefully reported.

However the following day, he and his men wept unashamedly when the Japanese hit the Lexington, and, forced to abandon ship, they watched their beloved carrier sink.

He moved to another ship and hit back with a passion that forced the Japanese to abandon their drive toward Australia and head for the Aleutian Islands.

Meanwhile, a nearly intact Zero had crash-landed on Akutan. Allied aircraft engineers crawled all over it, analyzing what made it fly so fast. Next, off to their drawing boards, where they developed a plane that climbed faster, higher, and maneuvered more easily than the Zero. Our newborn FSF Hellcat Fighter soon wiped it out of the skies.

# CHAPTER THIRTEEN

SINCE DADDY WENT away, Mom became high-strung, uncertain; sometimes she chattered like a bird in a forest so not to be aware of lurking danger. At night I lay in bed, trying to fall asleep, hearing her footsteps elsewhere in the house. They seemed aimless, and she kept opening and closing doors.

In early June, 1942, I made Daddy a card showing a little girl (me) in a sunbonnet holding a watering can. Added flowers and grass. Using a brand new box of crayons, I drew the card over and over until it looked perfect. In the sky, blue jays appeared. They visited my windowsill, pretended to befriend me, hoping for a breadcrumb, and once one of them brought me a morsel of something squishy. I appreciated the wormy thought. On the grass near the little girl I drew a pile of crumbs, yellow dots – my food for the blue jays.

Also, I learned to play hopscotch, to jump from square to square on the sidewalk without touching a line. In order to complete the jump, I'd bend down and surge forward with great precision. When I showed Aunt Lenore, she smiled with love and invited me to Fenton's for a chocolate ice cream soda. With sugar rationing, Fenton's could only open one day a week, so reservations took forever to get.

A Chinese man named Ching presided over big cans of ice cream, syrups, and, from his fountain spigots, bubbly colas and waters. In old China, Mandarins like Ching's family let their nails grow long to prove they didn't work. Now employed, he grew only the nail on his pinky finger until it curled. A display of rank.

He had an unlikely sign on the wall of a soda fountain that said, "Soft water erodes hard rocks, as a kind word erodes anger. All of life consists of complimentary opposites from which derives its energy."

Aunt Lenore and I sat on wire-legged stools at the counter while he scooped chocolate ice cream and syrup and mashed them together in tall glasses, then squirted in the soda water. Delicious. Chocolate sodas ranked as my favorite food.

They cost five cents apiece, so Aunt Lenore said, "At these prices you must finish every drop."

Ching nodded in agreement, looking apologetic over the high prices. He'd lived in Manchuria before the brutal Japanese "Rape of Nanking" occurred in 1937 and felt unbelievably lucky, as he'd immigrated here in the late 20s.

He often said that myriad rituals of politeness governed Japanese lives at home, but in conquered countries, it was a different matter.

After our soda, Aunt Lenore told me, "You must be strong like Ching."

"Ching! What about my daddy?"

After she dropped me home, the phone rang – Alice Brush calling, excited beyond belief. She wanted to come over and tell Mom a thrilling story. Mom picked some sweet peas from the garden and arranged them in a frosted glass vase, then put on water for tea, fished around for some snacks, and decided to open a bottle of Four Roses whiskey as well.

The ladies decided on tea, but laced with a little of the Four Roses. "You just won't believe?" Alice gushed. She truly sounded breathless. "It's a long story? But we broke the Japanese code."

"Glorious!" Mom added a little more bourbon to the tea.

"It gets better. Nimitz learned from it that Yamamoto planned to attack Midway Island. So? He had a chance to head it off."

"Perfect," Mom replied gleefully.

"Twenty-five of our submarines moved silently underwater, while carriers circled Midway on the sea's surface."

Mom smiled with relish. "Meanwhile, the Japanese steamed toward the island, unaware they headed into a trap?"

Alice nodded. "Because of the imperial commanders' general hubris? That's what I say, anyway."

"So what happened?"

"Well, my dear, on June 4, our Dauntless Dive Bombers turned four of Dai Nippon's carriers into flaming pyres. It took five minutes? Yes. That's all. Can you believe?"

Mom raised her teacup in salute. "Wonderful!"

"An armada of Japanese bombers pounded the island, but we whipped them. What's his name, Nagumo? He lost 3,500 men to our 307, and four times the planes. Rapp told me, but don't say anything.

You know the rule: pass it on if you see it in the paper, but not if you hear it from me."

Mom beamed. "I have a feeling I'll be seeing it in the paper."

She added more bourbon, and the two friends clicked their teacups together happily.

Mom was right. Soon the Chronicle announced that on June 5, Yamamoto ordered a withdrawal in the first Japanese naval defeat in almost three and one-half centuries.

When Mom, Aunt Lenore, Nancy, Alice, and everyone cheered together on successive phone calls, I waved my own little flag.

Mom clung to the idea that our country, beneath its surface, like a huge rock, possessed the will to win this war quickly. Daddy's departure for Ft. Lewis seemed bearable, because, though she missed him achingly, he had honor; he made her proud. However, her existence teetered on the edge; she lived it forward and backward, grasping fragments of the future and the past.

She liked to remember the day she'd met Daddy in a Cal history class. Later he told her he considered her "a beauty," claimed that when she first touched him, she "made him follow her, reveal himself in a way he never did before."

The early days of their marriage floated by like music. Daddy liked to laugh, sing, and make love, and cherished animals and nature. As a journalist, he wrote articles for newspapers and coached football on the side. Mom thought he should spend more time on his half-finished novel about a football player with too many women. "It's funny," she'd say. "You write the way you talk."

But now he had gone away, and soon afterward Mom announced the stork planned a visit. Not to Aunt Lenore; to her, which didn't seem quite fair. Every morning she got sick. She shopped for fuzzy bunnies and yellow checked curtains, read the latest books of infant psychology, and cheerfully predicted she would have a son.

What was so good about a son?

When the aunties heard the news, they fell on their knees in church to give thanks. (I didn't). Aunt Marie began a petit point rug for the nursery; Aunt Lenore bought a bassinet decorated with white tulle and yellow ribbon. It would have been nice for Tinesey, if Mom didn't insist on saving it for the baby. Friends sent silver cups, tiny pajamas, and satin-bordered blankets. It became annoying.

Once a week, Aunt Lenore took me to a restaurant, but she didn't like the way I played with the catsup and salt. She'd grab them so fast. She once won the state doubles championship in tennis and was still lithe and strong of hand. Possessed with understated wit, she had a genuine ability to see the humor in everyday life. She gave no feeling of upset, rather of solidity and peace. In memory, I still revere her, because she gave praise only when I earned it. Also, she took action, rather than asking, "Is there anything I can do?"

Mom neared full term. She sat at the round walnut kitchen table, said she looked like a hippopotamus, and constantly thought about her next piece of rationed fudge with walnuts. She tried to charm me by letting me feel the baby kick, but I made it plain the subject did not fascinate me.

Diana Hickingbotham (now Knowles) gave me a daschund puppy. She lived across the street and had a diamond-studded blonde glamour that still shimmers. All their lives, she and her brother, Stanley, dined on Caneton Nantais au poire vert and mousse de fruite perigeuse. They owned only the finest, and knew glamorous people all over the world. Their father didn't light cigars with hundred dollar bills like Diamond Jim Brady, but he cultivated the tastes of a Sun King.

The puppy licked my face and wagged his tail so hard it made his hips swivel. He hid behind the dining room drapes not knowing his tail showed. I hadn't been so happy since last time Daddy took me for a ride in his jeep, so I named my puppy for the vehicle. Every minute I stroked his ears, kissed his forehead, and called him a good doggie. Aunt Ruth sent him a big box filled with collars and sweaters. "A dog is such a comfort," she wrote.

From then on, I didn't care about one other thing besides Daddy and Jeep. Mom could have all the babies she wanted.

Having procured lightweight V-mail stationery with red and blue along the edges, she wrote Daddy:

"To tell you truth, I felt the need for a dog myself. Please don't joke about him being 'better than a husband' – he isn't, and he's too small to scare off intruders; he'll just be a good friend for us."

Soon she received a reply:

"Give Jeep my kind regards, and tell him to watch it on your rugs.

"The Japanese could surrender by the time our baby's born and I, for one, am glad. The food here is disgusting. You can't imagine how much I miss your rabbit; in fact, next time you fix it I'll call it lapin aux whatever.

"Our CO, a giant of a man, has a wide forehead that gives his face a lightbulb shape, and a forearm so muscular, Popeye looks puny by comparison. He issues his orders as though there's inspirational music playing in the background and his words have to ring above it. But ask him a direct question, he makes a propeller-like noise and saunters off.

"His second-in-command is a deferential lip-synchor. Being a little short on language skills, they constantly say, 'You're in the army now.' No. I'm being unfair. This morning the CO said, 'There's a war going on.' Insightful. I replied. 'Yes, sir,' is all I ever have to say.

"Remember the man who told us about Pearl Harbor? Greer Brown? I think of him as 'OB,' for Officer on the Bluff. He's determined to win but always asking the burning questions about the bleary-eyed multitudes and luring us into heady philosophical discussions about the nature of man.

"No need to memorize the other officers' names, they're all 'sir.' We are, I should say. No hope of my wife calling me 'sir,' of course.

"One of my intel buddies said that the Nip emperor originally intended to bring the royal family closer to citizens of Japan, but in 1923, an assassin's bullet nearly hit him, and the kuromakus rushed in to isolate and control him. These players, like puppeteers, run the home show through conglomerates called diabatsus.

"But who cares? I prefer to think of you. I'm lucky to have my memories of such a beautiful wife, and I see your hair swinging as you walk. You slip off your shoes and sit with your legs drawn up beneath you. I love you."

Mom put the letter aside. She could visualize her husband walking along with that fast stride, combing his wavy black hair with his fingers and rubbing his neck when it felt stiff. She knew her baby would take after him, or at least have his blue eyes.

One day she began brushing my hair, and the phone rang. Daddy could come home on forty-eight hours leave to meet his baby. The doctors would induce labor, a common practice during the war. She sat on her mauve silk chaise lounge, eyes down, as if in the midst of a pleasant recollection.

Soon Daddy walked through the door, stroked her swollen belly, held her and kissed her lips, her cheeks, and her neck. They drove to the hospital, he steering with one hand as usual and stroking her knee with the other, while her arm circled his shoulders.

Baby Frankie arrived in time to meet his father. He looked quite comfortable for a person just expelled from a womb, and, holding him, Daddy said, "He's a nice, fresh boy, but don't spoil him, Mary-Helen."

He gazed at the baby, talked to him, stroked his head, and sang him "The Sturdy Golden Bear." On the nightstand stood a bouquet of roses nasturtiums, peonies, bluebells, and daisies he'd brought, with a card saying, "LOVE." He also pinned a gardenia in Mom's hair.

For her hospital stay, she wore a peach satin bed jacket hand embroidered with fine gold thread. She wore the same one for me, and her granddaughter wore it for the birth of her son. It hangs in her closet, frail from years but rich with memories.

Now she allowed me to inspect the baby closely. "A baby! For me! My baby," I said, feeling thrilled at last. He looked so small – hardly bigger than Tinesey. I counted on having babies someday, and Frankie would be good for practice. Soon I'd teach him to play with my doll.

I offered him a bite of my chocolate fudge, but Mom said he didn't have any teeth for chewing. Sure enough – a fish mouth.

At home that night, I lay down beside Daddy, rolled into his arms, breathed in his male scent. Against the pillow his face shone like an angel's. I wished I could enter the light surrounding him. He told me that when he came home for good, he'd catch moonlight as it fell from the sky and wrap it around me.

He and I compressed the next morning together; the waste of even a second seemed unbearable. I obsessed over pleasing him, would stop the sun in its course for him if possible.

We went to the hospital to see Mom and the baby. She could hardly stand, and she couldn't control her weeping. "Be careful, Sweetheart," she sobbed. "I love you with my whole heart."

They held each other, and the emotion between them filled the air, making it hard to breathe.

We visited Frankie in his quarters. Patting his little back, Daddy said, "Be a good boy, OK, Pal?"

His son burped.

Aunt Lenore dashed in to pick up Daddy and me. We left the hospital, and Mom's eyes filled again, blurring the image of her departing husband.

As we drove along, Daddy promised to buy Aunt Lenore a chauffeur's cap when he returned. A spring rain poured down, and at the depot, it gave the platform water streaks. A poster said, "GIs, defense workers, and families only. No Tourism for the Duration." Another showed a Red Cross lady holding a child with war raging in the background. "Everyone Can Afford a Little," it said. "Give Gladly."

Soldiers hugged and kissed their families and sweethearts as the steam locomotive approached. With signal lights flashing, it pulled up, bellowing out blasts.

Aunt Lenore hugged Daddy. "Take care," she said.

He tweaked her cheek, and a half sad smile lit his face.

"I don't plan to play the lead in any funerals. I'm a simple man with two kids who wants to finish this war and come home."

"Stay home, Daddy," I said, grabbing the cuff of his sleeve.

"I have a commitment, my precious," he replied, stroking my cheek with one finger.

"Com?"

"All aboard," the conductor called.

I began to cry. "I'm scared."

"Don't be, Pooksie. Be brave. Don't cry. I'll be home before you know it. You'll hardly miss me, and I'll bring you a present." Stepping back, he smiled. "Help your mother take care of the baby. I'm counting on you."

He hoisted his duffle bag, walked away from us, climbed on board, and waved from a window as the train chugged off, its iron wheels clattering along the tracks. When he waved good-bye, a feeling of uneasiness swept over me. His presence that filled rooms, filled lives and made them light, that presence had gone away.

As Mom later wrote in her diary:

"Frank has crossed to the war. His mind is traveling to the Pacific now, and nothing can change it. I feel that reality's taken the wrong turn and there's no way back."

# CHAPTER FOURTEEN

MOTHERS-IN-LAW and daughters-in-law sometimes don't get along. Such was the case in the emperor's family, where his hawk wife pitted herself against his dove mother. Though Japan allegedly teems with ten thousand kami spirits who reside in the rocks, fields, and trees, their holy presence could not save the emperor from the struggles of these two strong women.

He feared his mother, adored his wife, Nagako, whose patriotic haikus stiffened his resolve to fight with greater ferocity. However, his mother, Teimei Kogo, Dowager Empress Sadako, took a resolute antiwar stand. She dreaded the Americans and believed they would crush Dai Nippon. When she wasn't lecturing him, her thin, dry lips trembling, she sent him haikus around themes of the traveler who seeks the seed of the green tree of peace or a moment of peace as a bar of gold. Worse, she called everything he did a "stupid mistake."

He would point out that the pride of conquest united the Empire of Japan, and added that Westerners did not learn the customs of others, befriending only each other. Now Shinto priests migrate through the empire teaching Dai Nippon's ancient ways. Asia for Asians.

Instead of agreeing, she'd stare at him with hostile black smudge eyes that unnerved him.

He called her the world's "most ungrateful mother," while she referred to him as "delusional." They scowled at each other, he with his thick eyebrows, she with her delicate arches.

Supposedly no insults existed in the Japanese language, only infinite degrees of apology, but the dowager empress forgot this courtesy when speaking to her son. When he replied, she crossed her arms to signify boredom. What an anomaly she was in a country where a tiny breach of courtesy prompted the apology, "Moshi wake gazaimasen, if you please, my transgression is unforgivable, and I wish I were dead."

After encounters with his mother, the emperor rolled round crimson rubies in his hands like worry beads to calm himself. She thought of herself as Japan's true ruler, and schemed with her snickering sycophants, which created yet another morass of problems.

Today, she paid him a rare visit, and he wanted to palliate her, especially after the Midway news. He presented her with a magnificent Burmese necklace of egg-sized emeralds and rubies. Did she thank him? No, she said she would have one of her advisors sell the necklace for money to spend on her peace efforts, and added she doubted that her son obtained it in an honorable way.

He pictured the advisor selling the necklace, pocketing the proceeds, and telling his hoax of a mother that every penny would go to printing her haikus on fine paper, and offering them to worthy Japanese homes.

In Hirohito's opinion, the sly American president, operating under a "constitutional dictatorship in time of war," actually had far more power than the Emperor of Dai Nippon did.

After she left, dusk arrived. Bats flew in circles around the imperial palace, and new guards arrived, bearing lanterns. Dark, sealed people, they swerved in tandem. The emperor brooded within. The palace seemed somber to him at this time of day. Its post and lintel construction made the interior quite dark, so large screens with burnished gold backgrounds covered the walls.

Even the sumptuous sliding wood panels, carved and lacquered in bright colors, seemed to absorb the scarce light. Still, he liked them, as they illustrated myths and historical triumphs of the Yamato family. Tonight, however, past glories couldn't cheer him. The Americans had avenged Pearl Harbor at Midway. He insisted that his people never hear about Japan's first significant defeat in more than three centuries. He would have to camouflage it for propaganda purposes into a triumph and issue an imperial rescript praising his Midway victors. Then he would crush the barbarians before another summer replaced plum blossoms with leaves.

Beginning with Midway, the imperial commanders tried to explain Japan's deteriorating military position to Hirohito, only to hear lectures on botany by way of reply. As the war progressed – or regressed, from Japan's perspective – they became frantic, but the emperor refused to discuss surrender. When it came to native intelligence, his commanders reminded him of the nearly decerebrate shishigashira in the palace ponds.

# CHAPTER FIFTEEN

THE SUN HUNG IN the center of the sky, touching the East Bay with summer warmth, a warmth that now extended from me toward the baby. In fact he was so cute I loved him even more than Tinesey.

Mom wondered how long she would have to raise the baby and me alone. She could manage, though; after all, hadn't she been captain of the relay team in her all-girl high school? She wanted to become a model of stability and strength now, and she would.

Her vibrant energy surged back, and she bought a house in Crocker Highlands, a white stucco with a thatched green roof, tall arched windows, and a garden with the verdant look of a forest. In the middle grew a grove of fruit trees and tall pines that filled the air with scent. Beyond, eucalyptus trees stood like old bones.

On moving day, she sat in a ladder-back chair on a floor littered with magazines and documents, unhung paintings, pots, pans, and – somewhere – an ashtray. She wanted a cigarette. Tinesey and I sifted through boxes looking for Henrietta while Frankie squawked for attention in his bassinet.

A week later, Mom was bumping into stepladders, hanging swatches of fabric, polishing mahogany beams, scrubbing fireplaces. She loaded tables with lacy ferns, jaunty English ivy, and red geraniums. Aunt Lenore gave her a globe where she struggled to find the battle-fronts on pinprick-sized islands, some of which did not appear on our globe. Not brilliant at communing with maps, she experienced daily frustrations, but kept trying. She wrote Daddy:

"You'll love the house like we do. The street has such a romantic name: Clarendon Crescent. In the garden, fruit ripens on trees; succulents tumble out of turquoise pots. I've just about finished unpacking, even put your football in the corner of your den, as usual. Looking at baby Frankie wrapped in his fuzzy blue blanket cheers me up so much. He smiles at me, blows bubbles, kicks, and grows more precious and chubby every day. I'm so crazy about him. He's so, so adorable. Radio commercials now govern Pooksie's life. Yesterday she said, 'Get some Kilpatrick's bread. It's the freshest thing in town.' She's going to be the dancing cabbage in the school musical, so I bought yards of light green fabric to wind around her. She practices in her costume, and her skinny little knees tremble, as she's so nervous over the big performance.

"I'm trying to do a good job with the children and all, but I'm so lonely for you. Especially your blue eyes. And other things."

She still bathed with new Camay, "the soap of beautiful women," creamed her elbows with Ponds, painted her fingernails and toenails red, and struggled with her wild hair, though it all seemed wasted effort without Daddy.

I made progress in life: got a new tooth, grew a little taller, and learned a French song called "Frere Jacques." Aunt Lenore taught me to color between lines and to sharpen a pencil, smell the wood and lead as the point came into focus. And I held on to my memories. Before he went to Ft. Lewis, Daddy, Mom, and I had walked among the willows and rhododendrons beside Lake Merritt in Oakland. The lake's green water looked as smooth as stone, except when the swans, ducks, and geese rippled it. Frogs croaked and kicked, their souls pulsating under thin green skin, and coveys of round brown birds ran beneath shrubbery or suddenly took flight.

My parents had given me slices of bread to break off and feed the ducks. They flapped and quacked as they fought over each crumb, and I laughed so hard. Then Daddy led us to a large oak tree, and we sat under it. He put his arms around us, "My girls," he said, and then again, "My girls."

His tone of voice sent a wave of anxiety through me. "I love you, Daddy," I whispered.

After he had left, I kept asking when he'd come home, so to divert me, Mom bought a series of Mickey and Minnie Mouse balloons which she inflated, tied, and inserted into cardboard feet so they stood. I still remember making my doll Tinesey laugh by patting them so they swayed on those cardboard feet.

While Mom wrote, I entertained my baby brother, waving cotton balls at him. "Teeny wow-wows," I called them. He chuckled his fat chuckle, his happy face never betraying how difficult he would become, especially years later when we played Batman and Robin. Of course I should always be Batman, as I was the elder, but he stubbornly demanded a 50-50 split then. "It's my turn to be Batman," he'd say. "I'm always Robin. Mom, she's being selfish!"

With the house more comfortable, Mom rode to lunch with Alice in San Francisco. watching the city rise from its shore, with its cable cars and spires, cypress trees, and striped awnings. The Golden Gate Bridge glowed, distant and mysterious, and the flags on the St. Francis Hotel danced in the breeze, as she walked through the carved doors of El Prado.

She followed the maitre de to a table, shining with the richness of handmade accessories, a crisp white cloth, and a single red rose in a silver bud vase. As a violinist played "Auf Wiedersehen," women wearing suits with stone marten furs waved, calling across tables at each other.

A superannuated waiter hovered while Mom ordered tomato aspic salad with bay shrimp; Alice chose artichoke hearts with crab legs and sourdough French bread. The waiter creaked off, and Mom and Alice let the conversation drift to the ruinous nature of newcomers to the Bay Area, the insane rise of house prices, war taxes (complainers should be jailed), and volunteering at the Red Cross, where, in Alice's words, "Some go to really work, others to gossip and social climb."

By the time she and Mom finally faced the war topic, the women at the next table had finished their snails, helplessly drowned in garlic and butter. Attentive, the women lit up, and their narrowed eyes flicked speculatively at Mom and Alice.

Mom weighed Alice's every word, searching for hidden meanings, desperate for reassurance. She moved her head sideways until it almost rested on her shoulder as she listened or lit up and took quick, nervous puffs of cigarettes.

"MacArthur? He's sending troops into New Guinea," Alice said. "Locals call it dehori land? Manana. Wait a while. Plus I hear it absolutely pours for months."

"Yes, I read that they call it the 'wet time.'"

"You know Guadalcanal in the Solomon Islands?"

"I've read about it, of course," Mom replied.

"Well, the Nips decided to build an airstrip there. You know, to fly off and sever the US-Australia lifeline. But? When they began to level and pave, one of our reconnaissance pilots spotted the project, and we flew to Savo Island. Next step? Guadalcanal."

Mom gave her a grim smile. "But what's his name, Nagumo, he wanted revenge on the snake that lay in the waters off Midway, right? And ambushed us, from what I've read."

"Um. We lost four cruisers at Savo Island."

"Covering the ocean floor with the bones of heroes."

Alice clasped her hands in silence for a moment. "But here's good news: our sub, the S-44, sank a key Japanese warship, the heavy cruiser Kako."

They clinked their glasses in salute.

Then, after analyzing the 40th Division, Alice switched the gossip. Amusement flickered in her eyes as she explained that one of the generals stole his first wife from General Pershing, but she soon got bored and wandered off. Next, he found a svelt Eurasian model and kept her in claustrophobic isolation, so his mother wouldn't find out about her. "It all became too much for the model," Alice said, "so one day she asked for money to send to her family overseas. And spent it? On a vacation with another man."

Mom chuckled with appreciation. "The general's remarried now, isn't he?"

Alice nodded, made a coy rosebud mouth, and started furiously fluttering her eyelashes. "Poem of womanhood? He calls her that, you know?"

Mom laughed for the first time since her husband left home. "I take it she has a higher regard for him than her predecessors did."

"Worship? She bows down at the mere mention of his name."

Like Lenore with Billy Boy, Mom thought. "The general's brilliant, isn't he?"

"Oh, absolutely. At West Point? He graduated number one in his class."

The waiter tottered over unsteadily to pour coffee, and, after a dessert of minted oranges, Mom and Alice split the check and said their good-byes.

Once in Oakland, Mom pulled up at I. Magnin, an art deco building fashioned out of turquoise granite, with a polished brass door and smoked-mirror elevators. She needed a birthday present for Aunt Marie and found a little black velvet hat with a demi veil. Pleased, she headed for home.

On Clarendon Crescent, her car barely avoided one of the neighbor's Siamese cats lounging in the middle of the street. When she honked, it glared at her resentfully, then dashed to her flowerbeds and trampled her pansies.

In the house, she poured herself a glass of Jack Daniels, switched on the radio, and listened to the quarrelsome tones of the announcer, "submarines . . . torpedoes . . . bombs." Anxiety rose, so she turned off the radio and lit a cigarette, practicing blowing smoke rings, shaping her mouth in an attractive "0" and sending the rings straight up. Wearing her sling-back patten leather shoes, she crossed her legs, flexing her ankle up and down to the rhythm of the smoke rings.

She wanted to compete with Daddy, and I knew it. Absolutely no one blew smoke rings like his. He would pull on his cigarette, inhale deeply, form the requisite circle with his mouth, and blow one ring after another in an endless, ephemeral parade to the ceiling and beyond, the place where angels played.

I asked if I could blow smoke rings, too, and she replied, "Little pictures should be seen but not heard." She spoke slowly and calmly, as if setting me a good example of how to sound.

Infuriating.

* * *

In Fort Lewis, Daddy received orders to "strengthen the defense of the Hawaiian Islands." The Japanese sent more submarines there, and an invasion seemed imminent.

He wrote in his diary:

"To cheer myself, I picture Mary-Helen at the top of the Mark Hopkins hotel. It's sunset, and she's standing near the windows, the city over her shoulder. Or it's late, when the foghorns sound from the bay, and I imagine drawing her close, across a bed of scented linens. In my dream, we live in another city, country, time, I don't know where, but I know when she's touching me."

After a slow voyage, he debarked in Oahu, the first step in his journey to the dark Pacific war. He walked through ankle-kissing thickets of orchids. The Polynesians sat in trees or stood by the road, watching the soldiers with their guns. Daddy called them "a relaxed, soft-spoken bunch," and wrote, "I still love the sunsets here. Beautiful as ever."

His drills included gunnery training and artillery practice. The blasts fluttered his clothes and knocked his brain against his skull, as he fired howitzers, Long Toms, and antitank guns. When he earned his sharpshooters' badge, he celebrated by taking a swim among the red and yellow, turquoise and violet reef fish.

He collected seashells for me, and, on his first free day, bought gifts: for me, a Polynesian doll named Leilani. A dark-skinned girl with elegant lines, she wore paper leis and a grass skirt. For Frankie, he got a Polynesian rattle, and for Mom, a vermilion sarong printed with small white pineapples.

He wrote Mom:

"My only complaint is the food, which is as bad here as at Fort Lewis. The regular army, being what it is, has language experts peeling potatoes; our vegetable chopper has a Ph.D. in Asian religions. Either the chef goes, or I do. Will step aside and make room for someone more deserving. Just kidding, but I swear to you, his food would make a sword swallower gag. Fortunately, I can sneak away and pick a pineapple every so often.

"A turquoise and yellow parrot lit on my shoulder and fluffed out his feathers to show that this perch was his. I named him Boss. (Maybe he's a she. In that case, Boss makes an even more appropriate name). Love him, and I love the sea; it always reminds me of riding the waves with Pooksie at Cayucos.

"Our radio operator, Charlie Harrington, tells shaggy dog stories until we fall asleep, and they're always about women who drool over him. We figure he has a big imagination. Last week he had KP, and he talked so much, they let him go after three days. When he's not talking, he's searching for hula dancers, army nurses — you name it. Last night at mess we celebrated in spite of the food, because I won enough points to get my regimental combat badge. Let's hope it isn't a flash in the pan. It's entertaining to watch the army thrash around trying to turn easygoing American guys into fighters, but I must admit we've developed real comraderie here. We're a team."

The same days, the same weeks, and the same months repeated themselves until Daddy felt his existence coming to a halt. He counted the endless hours, waiting to see some action.

One night he had a dream. He often thought he saw Mom somewhere for an instant, or experienced such strong feelings and memories they mimicked reality, but this dream moved to a new level: he could reach over and touch her. Just as his fingers made contact, he woke up amazed to find himself alone, and he realized, he said, that only an ephemeral wall separates the past from the present.

# CHAPTER SIXTEEN

ON THE VAST WATERS of the Pacific – one third of the earth's surface – anything can change quickly: the Allies turned the next engagement into a victory of sorts. In Vella Gulf, part of a sea passage called "The Slot," Japanese vessels appeared every night, flowing like a great school of pearly fish. Masthead beacons plus port and starboard lights shot out beams for half a mile, silvering the water with an exhilarating display of light. Australian Coast Watchers warned of their approach, and Allied ships, waiting in ambush, opened fire with earsplitting noise.

Haphazard skirmishes erupted, with half the damage on both sides coming from friendly fire, and several of our ships, overloaded with ammunition, exploded far too easily. The brass decided to replace Ghormley as commander of the South Pacific, the biggest shake-up since poor Kimmel and Short took the fall for Pearl Harbor.

Enter Admiral William "Bull" Halsey. On October 18, 1942, he took over from Ghormley, advising his men to tell the reporters when we declare war and tell them when we've won. But nothing else. Nearly parboiled by the heat, he crafted his plans with bravado. They must be bold; he loved rushing into danger and uncertainty.

On Oahu, Daddy felt a dark shadow, thinking that destiny passed him by. While the real war raged in the distance, he stood in danger of losing a mighty and terrible opportunity. Surely, something different from his present existence would come along, something worthy of a quarterback.

If his friends felt the same frustrations, they didn't say so. Being soldiers, they kept their intimate thoughts to themselves. Enviously, he wrote in his dairy:

"When the First Marine division went ashore on Guadalcanal, the men fought with a killing enemy in front and the Pacific behind, while sea birds, unknowing, circled the large sky. Undermanned and under equipped, our marines called Guadalcanal "Operation Shoestring," but they had the toughness, the unity, and the knowledge that we were fighting for all that is good.

"Meanwhile I sit around warming the bench on Oahu. At least I've organized a couple of teams so we can play a little ball during time off."

* * *

When he heard about Guadalcanal, the emperor skipped his usual monologue on botany, in favor of a baleful demand for victories rather than bad news. He also learned that British and Indian forces in Burma were hitting imperial troops with guerilla warfare.

He went for a stroll among the intricately shaped areas of vegetation and green ponds in the palace garden to try to calm himself. As usual, he fiddled with his glasses, which never seemed quite strong enough. The Doolittle raid raised Yank morale, Midway stopped Dai Nippon's expansion. Did Guadalcanal begin the US offensive toward Tokyo Bay? He observed a small bird searching for a worm and dreamed of his beautiful silver-white bombers lifting off, riding the air, bursting out of clouds, and shattering the Americans and the British.

* * *

At their monthly El Prado lunch, Alice told Mom about the marines' crazy-making jungle skirmishes – hit and miss, come and go. "Unpredictable ambush calls for higher qualities of courage and steadiness? I mean, compared to campaigns full of charges and countercharges where they can keep score?" she said.

Mom agreed. "I read that by the end of October, Halsey sunk twenty-one Japanese escort carriers. So many ships went down, and so much metal covered the ocean floor, that he changed the name 'Slot' to 'Iron Bottom Sound.' "

Alice smiled. "That's true, and I love it. The Nips suffered ten thousand casualties in Guadalcanal? And the few survivors starved until they lost their hair and fingernails. Worse, in their twisted opinion, they'd lost face."

"They're going to lose a lot more than that," Mom said, and she and Alice clicked their glasses.

Home again, Mom repeated the news to Aunt Lenore on the

phone, and I decided I should go to El Prado, too, hear for myself. Mom gave me her favorite "We'll see," which meant, "no," and hinted that I try to mind my own business. That, I thought, was exactly what she and Daddy should do. He should come home now and mind his own business. I started to tell Mom that, but she gave me, "He belongs to his country . . . he loves his country . . ." I'd already heard all that but, in my childish way, believed we should take our lives into our own hands rather than sit around waiting.

Though I really wanted to join the army, I settled for homemaker, like Mom and Aunt Lenore, and so studied under our maid, Juanita. She had a wide-mouthed face, long, thick eyelashes, and a melodious voice that filled the air with friendliness. I always smelled chile on her breath. Clanking with silver jewelry, she hummed as she walked along, swinging her ruffled skirts. She let me crank the washing machine wringer to squeeze water out of the clothes, mix blue starch with water, or press the pedal on the steam iron. You could lay a shirtsleeve on it, clamp down the top, and voila: the French-hand-laundry look. Together we displayed a little American flag with a stand I made on my bedroom windowsill.

One day I asked Juanita if I could ride her broom and play witch, but she didn't let me. All my fears and frustrations burst forth, and I sobbed with rage. Mom announced I was "acting spoiled" and put me to bed, her remedy for everything. I sucked my thumb and considered running away to join the army. There, I could roll bandages like Mom did at the Red Cross.

Just as I began to refine my plan, she invited me to help arrange flowers from our garden and make tollhouse cookies to mail to Daddy. With sugar rationing, we couldn't save many for ourselves, but the ones we did became my favorite food. That was before jalapena poppers.

One evening, when the sky turned the color of tea, Mom mixed Manhattans and told Aunt Lenore about her dream the night before. In it, she groped through a midnight forest until she found a house that glowed with the phosphorescence of a night sea. Someone crouched inside, someone unknown but important, and she wanted to walk over to it but couldn't move. She had to move, and kept trying. In the distance, she heard a faint melody, perhaps from a bagpipe, playing in the unusual key of D flat minor, and it grew louder, pressing in on her eardrums. Dancers wrapped in white gossamer swirled in and began to rhythmically dismantle the house, first the doors, then the shutters, finally a wall. Then they began on the next wall. They seemed to understand something, a secret, perhaps. As she watched, she tried to see their faces, but they eluded her, and she still couldn't move, so she called out to them, her voice emerging in a strange language she did not recognize.

"Sounds balmy to me," Aunt Lenore said. "Dreams? Hocus-pocus, if you see what I mean."

Mom began to sulk, ran her long painted fingernails over her arms beneath her sleeves.

When Aunt Lenore left, we ate dinner and went to bed.

Early in the morning, the phone on Mom's nightstand shrieked. Jolted awake, she answered and learned that an old friend of Daddy's had half his face blown off on Guadalcanal. The gyration of fate had moved too close. I heard her talking and pieced together what happened. I decided that if my Daddy lost half his face, I would kiss the other half.

Mom couldn't get back to sleep, so, as night moved into day, she thought, "As long as I live, I don't want to ever see another war. When I look at little Frankie, I can imagine how Frank's mother felt saying goodbye to him."

She wrote in a letter to Daddy:

"Frankie has fat little cheeks and wrists and ankles, a dimple in one cheek, and your blue eyes. I love to cuddle him and kiss his little toes. Pooksie complains that he isn't a good playmate for Tinesey, so thank you for Leilani. The dolls will have each other.

"My Hawaiian sarong works wonders. Even on days like today when my hair looks like a bird's nest, it gives me an exotic glamour. Wait till you see me in it.

"Family news: Aunt Nini, after years of loyalty to Gary Cooper, has fallen in love with Gregory Peck. She saw him in a movie last week and said he looks exactly like you, plus the story had a happy ending. Every day, Aunt Marie works on needlepoint slippers for you – a nice change from army boots, and Uncle George continues to complain about his sisters.

"Lenore keeps me company every day. Billy Boy swishes around acting cute until someone says 'war' or 'work,' which sends him straight to his ulcer bed.

"Your mother fears rationing might affect the cocoa butter supply, and your brother's a reporter at the San Diego Union now. Your father hung a flag in his bedroom, in your honor.

"Enclosed is a picture of your new nephew, Arthur, junior.

"Ruth briefly took an interest in a Spaniard, here escaping one side or the other in the civil war, I forget which. Full of old world charm, she thought, but now she's decided he has 'a calculating mind.' She could write a book. Or maybe help you with yours. Just kidding.

"Blue-eyed man, your letters take my mind away from the news and all my worries. When I read your words, the world becomes absolutely quiet.

"PS – I've dabbed eucalyptus oil around the garden to repel the neighbor's Siamese cats, so they'll have to sleep on their own trees."

When church bells chimed noon, Aunt Lenore came over, her eyes looking wide and childlike, aided by her array of pencils, shadows, and mascara. Gold bracelets jangled on her thin arms, and her auburn hair looked sleek in its pompadour with curled bangs. She always tried to curl her hair, while Mom tried to straighten hers.

"Let's have a tuna sandwich on the porch," Mom said. She'd trained honeysuckle and baby roses around the railing, and their scents blended with the jasmine perfume she wore. After lunch, Aunt Lenore would watch Frankie and me if Mom went to Magnin's for a new handbag, shoes and gloves, or maybe a belt.

"Nice hairdo, Sisterkins," Mom said, settling into a white wicker chair.

Aunt Lenore smiled and nodded.

"I did my last haircut myself," Mom continued. "Do you like it?"

Aunt Lenore's bright eyes honed in piteously, making Mom wonder if she had greasy roots.

"No."

"What's wrong with it?"

"Everything."

What did my aunt know? Her hair obeyed, rather than running its own life.

"In a minute you'll be telling me to stop frowning and pull back my shoulders," Mom sulked.

"You should."

"Peter Posture Perfect Lenore."

"You've never taken criticism well."

Mom's chest swelled defensively. "And I suppose you do?"

"I only try to keep you steady."

"You? You who have always chain smoked, quit, gained and lost weight, developed crushes on every priest, every choirmaster, every – "

"Look – I'm sorry. Wear your hair any way you want, though I think it's too short, and furthermore you're too thin. Frank will think you've turned into a little boy when he sees you."

"I whacked my hair thinking it would be easier to keep smooth, but it's just as wild. Worse."

"It looks fine. I'm already getting used to it." Aunt Lenore smiled. "Um, okay, guess what? We're on solid foods now."

"You mean Billy Boy?"

"Bill, yes, of course that's who I mean. He's feeling much better now."

"How very wonderful," Mom lied.

Aunt Lenore turned an angry pink. "Thanks for sounding so enthusiastic. Look, I know you feel abandoned, and you miss Frank every minute and hate being alone, but I wish you'd try to – "

"I'm not good at being alone. I don't really understand how things work in the world." Mom twisted a tendril of hair tight around her forefinger. "I think about how things work, think about it a lot, but I'm not getting anywhere."

"It's better not to think. Do it as little as possible, except about practical matters."

"I heard something good from Alice. One of the big Nip commanders drowned trying to cross a river in New Guinea. MacArthur called it a fitting death." Mom's lips formed a small smile.

"I agree with MacArthur." Aunt Lenore slapped the wrought iron table for emphasis. Then she shook her head. "But it's a shame we lost the Hornet off Guadalcanal."

Mom nodded sadly. "I know. Losing anyone or anything hurts, but the Hornet was so special since it launched Doolittle."

Time to climb a pine tree, I decided.

"Pooksie, stop that," Mom said. "Come down this minute; that tree's too tall."

"Tinesey, Leilani, and I sat in it yesterday. The tree's our friend."

Aunt Lenore raised her eyebrows. "You have to give my niece rules and regulations. Lay down the law."

"I know. Frank used to do that. It's so hard without him. I even miss his corny jokes."

"As a matter of fact, I do too." Aunt Lenore took a couple of drags on her cigarette. "Here's to pulling through."

"I got a call from Ruth this morning," Mom said. "I've found the man for her – Paul Henries. In the movie 'Two on a Match,' he lit two cigarettes at once and handed his woman one of them. Wouldn't that drive her wild?"

Aunt Lenore crossed her elegant legs. "She's had two husbands. That's enough, as far as I'm concerned."

"She has an instinct for finding and repairing."

"Um."

Mom rose, and, with Aunt Lenore following, carried Frankie into the kitchen while he tried to chew her cross and gold chain. She kissed each of his hands, and put him in his playpen, then fed the turtle in its Pyrex dish. A tropical paradise of rocks and shoots of greens, it looked like a turtle's Hawaii. She said, "I always feel so tired. It's because I miss Frank's energy."

Aunt Lenore nodded; then her lips tightened. "I got my period again."

Mom got a look on her face that read and Billy Boy remains the prospective father – the coincidence is no less than astonishing. But she said, "Keep trying. You'll get pregnant someday." Mom pasted on her fake smile. "Meanwhile, you've your hands full with your husband."

"What do you mean?"

Gosh. So obscure. "Well, you know – "

Aunt Lenore scowled and lit up a Pall Mall.

"Um, do you mind if I run downtown?" Mom asked.

"Go ahead. I'll watch the kids. Would you mind picking up a pair of white kid gloves for me?"

"I'll get you two pairs."

I went back into the garden with its grove of fruit trees, sunlight seeping through – my favorite place, next to beaches. Robins, bluebirds, and wrens sang ceaselessly in the morning, a sound wave on the tide of time that never fades away. White butterflies and iridescent humming-birds would chase away the blue of an afternoon sky. I liked to smell the roses, watch them open, or pull the stamen out of the honeysuckle and taste the nectar with the tip of my tongue. Most of all, I liked to climb the plum tree that became my friend, partly because it stood apart from the pear, apple, and cherry trees. I would sit on a strong branch with Tinesey or Leilani and talk to the birds.

The birds talked to each other, tree to tree. "I know a bird who knows a bird who knows . . . "

Mom walked through the brass and glass doors of Magnin's and did her shopping, saving the shoes for last. She wanted another pair of pumps, preferably open-toed with bows.

After she finished, she became absorbed in walking around testing perfumes and looking at hats until she decided to go to the powder room and refresh her appearance. When she emerged, she no doubt looked marvelous, but it was past closing time. She got into the elevator, and the operator said, "You're lucky. I was about to go off duty."

The elevator started down and stopped with a groan and a shud-der. Tepid and tentative, the operator pressed bells and buttons, but nothing happened; the elevator remained as still and silent as an animal that has stopped breathing. Mom glanced at her watch and decided to wait five minutes before asking what they should do. Six minutes later, for good measure, she said, "What do you do when an elevator stops this way?"

"You ring the alarm, but it's not working," the operator replied in an uncertain, reedy voice. His hands trembled, and she heard his hard panting, smelled his fear. His lips twisted, and he said, "This is my first day on the job. I don't know much about these damned things."

Mom winced.

With a strangled yelp, he pressed the emergency button again, which did nothing but set light to his panic, and he gasped about "having to work in these conditions." He moaned and kicked the doors, screamed for help, and pounded the walls that sealed them off from the world.

Mom's stomach lurched; she gagged, having a flash of how a breakdown felt, a sense of going out of control. To steady herself, she thought of Frank's voice, low-pitched and resonant with a certain amount of sexy gravel mixed in.

She tried to call out for help, but could only manage a petrified croak.

Two hours later, the night guard found them and called Otis, the elevator company.

On Monday the store manager called Mom and apologized. "We have a terrible time with repairs," he said. "All the mechanics have gone overseas or work in the munitions factories."

"So much the better," Mom replied. She hung up and thought, no more elevators for the duration. She called Aunt Lenore, "I don't really like going downtown these days anyway. If I set foot out the front door, I trip over a newcomer eyeing the neighborhood."

Aunt Lenore emphatically replied, "Call the dentist, wait weeks for an appointment – newcomers. The aunties complain about the 'insufferable crowds' and claim that if it weren't for the war, they'd sell the house and move to Cannes. I can see their point."

Mom nodded as she spoke. "You're right. It's turning into a mess around here, and I'm sick of it. I write letters and more letters to the Tribune editor, but he's too busy selling papers to the newcomers to reply."

The next time Mom introduced me to someone, I said, "You nu cum?"

Later she told me I "shouldn't repeat family secrets." So. The newcomers were a family secret, along with all the war talk with Alice. This war wasn't worth it. Every time I asked, in my fashion, why we bothered, someone repeated the story about the Japnees and the purl. I got sick of it.

However, even the young can master logic, as I did when I realized we had nothing to fear from the Japanese with all the newcomers around. Too many for the Japnees to hurt everybody.

But I couldn't convince anyone.

# CHAPTER SEVENTEEN

EMPEROR HIROHITO REALIZED that his financial problems stemmed from his too-generous nature, just as his leadership problems stemmed from his international sophistication. Before the war, he'd enjoyed outfitting himself in western-style suits, but now he usually wore military uniforms, as a gesture of respect to his commanders. But did they deserve it? He spoiled them, provided them with sake made from rice milled until only 70 percent of the kernel remained; it fermented into smooth perfection. They expected jummai shou or dry karakuchi before dinner, and sweet amakuchi after. They dined on delicacies such as ebi shinjo, shrimp wrapped in soybean paper. Meanwhile, the foreign Yank devils ate nothing but K-rations.

More and more, the emperor felt that his reverence for his prodigal warriors corroded their strength. Japan now employed over 100,000 comfort women in brothels in occupied territories, attractive women skilled in dancing, singing, and playing instruments, and in other arts. No doubt visiting these establishments took energy and could be the main interest of some of his commanders, considering the war news.

Hirohito knew one thing for a fact: Roosevelt didn't pamper his troops with women of the pleasure quarters. The loathsome American president, though an evil monster, did know how to define ascetic living for warriors. Hirohito considered Dr. Ishi's Unit 731 in Manchuria. The emperor, still loyal to his samurais, felt that if the camp saved one officer's life, it was well worth the expense.

Today he decided he would eat only rice in the morning, instead of his English breakfasts, and give up his morning visits to his botany lab as well as his horseback rides. He would also act on the latest advice from the kuromakus. Unlike the commanders, they understood finance, and suggested adopting a series of measures regarding Jews on Japanese soil: ban their immigration into occupied territories, systematize surveillance of their homes and offices, and impound large portions of their assets.

Japan's allies, the Nazis, seized Jewish assets to help the war effort, so why shouldn't Japan do the same thing? Hitler would appreciate the responsiveness. Besides, the emperor described Marxism as a "Jewish disease," once and in response, the American general Vinegar Joe Stilwell called him a "Yellow Aryan."

Hirohito went inside, sat at his official desk, and issued a directive: courtesy to Japan's allies and financial expediency necessitate an assessment of official conduct toward Jews.

* * *

Mom tried to avoid the far end of her mind where dread lay. One day she decided to go to Chinatown in San Francisco to buy gifts for Aunt Lenore, Aunt Ruth, Alice, and possibly Grandma and the aunties. Christmas was a long way off, but she could save the presents on her closet shelf. She carved her way through the crowd inside the great tile gates. A group of men placed bets on a cricket race, while on a balcony, laundry flapped in the breeze. Shop windows burst with silk embroideries, rose quartz and jade animals; inside, abacuses rattled as sales progressed.

She bought lacquer trays of togetherness, henian quanhe, filled with the fruits that invoked good fortune – the perfect gifts for everyone. Then she found a white jade carved with a bat for happiness.

Once home, she took off her pheasant-feather hat and placed it in its round pink box, placed her gifts on the closet shelf as planned, and found an old sepia photo in a carved gilt French frame. It showed her parents on their wedding day. Her mother in filmy white looked evanescent next to her husband under a bower of limes. Mom took it to her nightstand and placed it next to a picture of Daddy smiling at her. It stood in a leather frame that his college football team gave him. She placed the white jade in front of his photo, to bring him good fortune, figuring that an Asian amulet, along with the saints' medals from the aunties would cover all the bases.

Sometimes I dreamed Daddy came home, bounced me on his knee, lifted me, and danced round and round. Or pushed me in a swing, higher and higher, his hand firm and trustworthy on my back. Awake, I consoled myself with the idea that he served America and did the right thing. I, too, tried to do the right things: pray, help Mom, entertain

Frankie, so that my good behavior would assure Daddy's safe return.

\* \* \*

In Hawaii, Daddy wrote in his diary:

"Despite bench warming on the sidelines, I feel my life has become larger, brushed by so many other lives here. Good men. But sometimes I think if the regular army does something that makes sense, it's unintentional.

"Today a letter from Ruth arrived; she's taken a job. Good. Maybe she'll finally stop marrying these well-dressed, fragrant Adonises."

In the next day's mail, he received a letter from Mom:

"Every time I turn around, there's more lonesome boys waiting to be shipped out. A lot of them look pitifully young – eighteen, nineteen, with muscular arms in rolled up T-shirt sleeves and a determination to defend their country. They stand straight but with scared eyes."

He wrote her back:

"Hold a good thought for those scared boys. But I'm fine. Believe me, you work a lot harder at home than I do. Here we just relax and hold 'one potato, two potato' contests.

"Still the same old K-rations. You don't acquire a taste for them. Mess hands them out nervously, fearing an insurrection just might be brewing.

"I close my eyes and see you lounging on the sofa, one arm cocked behind your head, the other arm stretched out by your side. Letters help. Thank you for saying my last one made you smile. I'm glad I can still bring a smile to your face at this distance. Makes a guy feel better."

# CHAPTER EIGHTEEN

ON CLARENDON CRESCENT, Jeep barked to announce my rising, and I banged around upstairs after saying an extra morning prayer for Daddy. Outside, geese flew over our house in a long watchful V for victory, like the raised two fingers. I considered that a good omen.

Again today, we would celebrate Daddy's birthday, even though he was overseas. The actual date: April 8, but Mom celebrated the event four times a year, once every season. Now, in autumn, the morning air exuded scents of fallen leaves piling up in gutters, red berries ripening on bushes along the sidewalk, and apples simmering in the kitchen. I came downstairs, and stared out the window, squinting at the distant stripe at the edge of the world. "Can my birthday kisses for Daddy travel that far?"

"Yes, easily." Mom knew that at my age, I found it difficult to relate a narrow blue line to Daddy's whereabouts.

Then we sent him gifts. I love gifts, with the atonement, love, and hope conveyed in their bright wrappings. For Daddy I drew pictures of dogs on the wrap and made curls in the paper ribbon with scissors. While we worked, we listened to Vera Lynn singing "Harbor Lights" on the radio.

Japanese children heard stories of Shigisan Engi, the miraculous golden bowl that lifted bales of rice from the storehouses of the greedy rich and delivered them to priests who lived in solitude and poverty. We had Walt Disney's stories, the very man who gave the Christmas party. Mom put on a record of Donald and Daisy Duck, and they quacked their way through our burned toast breakfast.

Once we'd "cleaned our plates," mindful of "the hungry children in England" (I only pretended to see the connection), Mom produced my favorite thing: an envelope with Daddy's handwriting, which slanted forward as if in a hurry. She read it aloud:

"Pooksie, thank you for your happy birthday letter. I hope you're having fun on my big day. Here I'll sunbathe and drink coconut milk, as usual, plus swim.

"I can imagine the party at home: the Siamese cats next door watching, eyes narrowed, as they plan a strike on the food. Your mother writes that she doesn't like the cats because they follow her with their eyes when she's trying to garden. I gather last week while she picked a bouquet of roses one of them snuck up behind her. When she turned to shoo it away, the other one pounced on her bouquet and started shredding it. She says they usually sit in their own garden, and when Jeep scampers over to play, they peer at each other conspiratorially and thump their tails. They probably think of your dog as a self-warming tree stump, and do cats pay attention to tree stumps? Only if birds perch on them.

"But we have to admire the cats, because I hear they often scan the sky for enemy aircraft.

"I'm told that Jeep, though consistently snubbed, has decided he, too, is a cat. Is it true that he licks his paws, tries to climb trees, and stalks birds? A dachshund doing these things must look silly, but he will teach you valuable lessons about self-concept and the power of your imagination."

After hearing Daddy's letter, I popped a birthday present into his secret box. I hid treasures to give him after the war – a mussel shell from Carmel, a "V for Victory"-shaped twig from Tilden Park, a wishbone from the aunties' Easter chicken. Today I added a smooth green pebble from Lake Merrit to his homecoming collection.

Juanita bounced in with a corn tortilla decorated with a cross of chili peppers, "to will make Senor Ribbel safe," and said that in his honor, she lit a candle to Santo Antonio Isobel, patron saint of travelers. She'd stayed up late sewing bright suns and moons on a handkerchief for Daddy, showed it to me and then told me about day and night: to form the sun, Tezcatliupoca, God of Night, transformed himself into a ball of fire to light the earth. For rest, the sun hides in a subterranean passage, and darkness falls. Her matter of factness convinced me she knew the straight story. Pointing the moral, she said when Daddy came home, days seemed sunny; now that he's gone, they seemed dark. But sun would follow as day follows night, and soon all my days would be bright.

When she finished, I stretched out on my tummy and wrote:

"Dear Daddy, I mis you. So dus Jeep. We pla but we want you. Be karful. Pleas. Be karful. I luv you. Ann."

Then Aunt Lenore sashayed through the door wearing gray slacks and a white blouse with wide shoulder pads and seams that followed the line of her slim torso. For the first time, women wore pants in public. Embodying the spirit of Rosie the Riveter, they worked at aircraft factories like Lockheed and Douglas or joined the military auxiliary branches: Waves, Wacs, and SPARs. They wore slacks every day, regarding their skirted sisters as fossils.

Aunt Lenore put one hand behind her head, the other on her hip, and slowly turned around. "Aren't my slacks snazzy?"

"Yes, you look so modern. Really smart."

"A woman should be able to put on her clothes and then forget about them."

Trust Lenore to accompany a pair of slacks with a lecture, Mom thought. "Exactly."

"I'll get you a pair. By the way, your hem's crooked. I'll have my dressmaker work on it for you." She always spoke right up. No need to pussyfoot around on Mom's account.

"That's not necessary." Mom's lips tightened, as she changed the subject.

"How did you like 'Casablanca?' Didn't you see it last night?"

"Marvelous, I loved it, even though someone with a huge head sat in front of me, bobbing in agreement every time the actors spoke. Ingrid Bergman and Humphrey Bogart – simply wonderful, but in the end, she gives him up. Sad."

"Now that I know how it ends, I guess I don't have to go."

Aunt Lenore's back stiffened. "You should. Bill loved it, though going exhausted him. I don't know why he progresses so slowly."

"I'm sure he'll pick up."

Aunt Lenore lit a Pall Mall. "Just as well you skip 'Casablanca.' You always cry in movies, and this one's a tearjerker. Want the rumor du jour? I hear FDR's gone back to Lucy Mercer, his old girlfriend."

Mom smiled. "How do you suppose Eleanor likes that?"

"Not much, I guess, but she's a good woman. Wants to be sure workers have enough ration coupons to survive. Plus she visits the troops."

"You've got to hand it to her," Mom said, tugging at her hair, which felt like straw to her. "She sticks up for the everyday people. And she's no queen bee. She just goes ahead and scrambles eggs for dinner on Sundays when the help's off, serves them herself to him and all those friends of theirs who live in the White House."

"What are their names? Hopkins, Hitchcock, Lash – "

"I guess so.

Aunt Lenore's eyes softened. "Well, I can understand all the White House campers. I mean, FDR's polio makes it hard to get around, so I guess he likes to bring the world in."

"Makes sense. You know."

Aunt Lenore crushed her stub in a silver ashtray. "Speaking of crowded households," she said, "I hear that pair, the Duke and Duchess of Windsor, invite Nazi buddies over to their house in the Bois de Boulogne for wiener schnitzel or whatever. The Nazis call them the 'D and D'."

"Possibly the Duke wants a crown with a swastika on it."

"Or she might." Aunt Lenore rolled her eyes. "What does he see in her?"

"I'm stumped. Not for the first time in my life."

"Whatever. He's peculiar, in my opinion. Not in the same way as Henry the Eighth. The D doesn't go around chopping off people's heads the minute they annoy him, but he's nuts just the same."

"That's for sure. He resembles those dogs he likes – the pugs."

"I hear she fills the house with pillows embroidered with pugs, porcelain pugs, paintings of pugs, jeweled pugs, plates and cups decorated with – well, you get the idea."

"Too cute for words," Mom smirked. "How do the French like the D and D's Nazi soirees? The Resistance grows stronger every day, I'm told."

"Yes, they have courage, and some of our best people help them, but what about the others?"

"Taking serious measures like hiding the Margaux and selling the wrong length skirts to the Fraus." Mom smiled. "The resistance people are tough. Don't forget that when we saved France in World War I, the girls found lovers who didn't call them Fraulein."

"True. Plenty of American blood over there. But not enough. By time we rescue them in this war, they'll all be singing Horst Wessel."

Mom laughed. "What would I do without you?"

"It's been really difficult for you, raising two kids with Frank gone."

Mom nodded, her hand fluttering hopelessly. "He was so cheerful."

"And he really observed life closely. That's what made him so funny. I mean, what makes . . . "

"I still keep reaching for the phone to tell him something or roll over in bed expecting to touch him."

As a surprise, I came in wearing a black beaded cocktail dress of Mom's, a string of her crystal beads, and lipstick smeared around my mouth like fried egg.

"Pooksie, take my dress off," she said, with no result. "Right now. I mean it."

Finally, in response to her outraged glare, I climbed out of the dress and stood on my head. "Look at me," I said.

"That's good, dear," Aunt Lenore replied, and I tumbled down, landing on top of Frankie.

Mom gathered her squalling son into her arms. "I wish you'd be more careful, Pooksie," she growled. In a pointed tone, she told Aunt Lenore, "Yesterday her teacher made her stand in the coat room again for talking during lessons."

I stuck up for myself. "Donnie asked me a question, and I just answered. The teacher made a mistake. It wasn't fair."

Aunt Lenore nodded sympathetically.

Mom went into the pantry to mix Manhattans, and I asked Aunt Lenore to jump rope with me.

"No thanks," Aunt Lenore said.

"Why?"

"Because I don't want to."

"Why?"

"I simply do not."

"Why?"

81

Jeep followed the words, his gaze moving from one face to another, ears shifting to gauge tone.

"You're giving me a pain," my aunt said.

"Where?"

"In the neck, that's where."

Puzzled, I began rubbing my own neck.

She produced a kaleidoscope, and we rotated it, watching the infinite glittering shapes form against the afternoon light.

The phone jangled from the hall and Mom went to answer it. I tiptoed over to eavesdrop. A friend, Major Patterson, was coming home, but with both legs shot off.

I climbed on Mom's lap. "Dear Lord," I prayed, "please keep my Daddy's legs safe, especially today, on his birthday."

At midnight, Mom wrote Daddy:

"Pooksie asked me if you were safe, and I said yes, so she asked, 'How do you know?' I replied you're safe because you're enchanted, they used to call you the Enchanted Quarterback; now you're our Enchanted Warrior."

# CHAPTER NINETEEN

DAI NIPPON'S rising sun slowly changed course and began to sink toward the horizon. The imperial commanders no longer considered world domination a given, nor did they believe that Australia, New Zealand, Hawaii, and the United States would fly the rising sun flag over their respective seats of government. Around Japan, bamboo groves rustled and golden pagodas reflected on lake waters, bells rang from red toris, and blue morning glories closed their petals for the winter – a chilly new winter for commander morale.

The emperor tried to calm himself when he thought of his mother, who now wanted to purchase doves of peace to fly over Tokyo. Before meeting his military leaders, he also tried to calm himself. First he would made his disappointing "warriors" bow not only to him, but also before a Nara painting of languid Amaterasu with her plump cheeks, pencil-thin eyebrows, and pea pod-shaped mouth. Feathers in iridescent hues covered her gown. Behind her, an indigo inscription read:

"The emperor cannot be removed from the throne for any reason, and he is not to be held responsible for overstepping the law in the exercise of his sovereignty. Sonno foi: revere the emperor."

A subtle reminder of who was boss. Hirohito doubted his generosity created the loyalty it should among his commanders. On their faces hung forced smiles, and they hid their true thoughts behind ceremonial ritual. He needed constant vigilance to assure himself that they didn't steal his money rather than spend it rightly.

Worse, their incompetence cost him more every day. Lately he'd been sending fewer and more restrained congratulatory messages to them when an American ship or plane went down. When he held meetings, he tracked enemy progress with little red flags on maps and demanded explanations "to learn how to avoid future disasters."

The commanders confessed their latest dishonorable defeats, followed by a melee of cross accusations about each other's blunders. Then the fools described new plans and hinted at future triumphs, without saying a word about economizing.

As tempers escalated, they described one another as stupid and irrational, stopping just short of drawing swords. He accused them of developing a dishonorable air of defeat, as victory receded ever farther away, like Mt. Fuji glimpsed through a snowstorm.

# CHAPTER TWENTY

THE LONGER THE WAR went on, the more often we heard about dead or captured friends. With time, fear mounted; Mom's girlfriends in the Division and the Red Cross became more and more upset. Many developed symptoms of chronic stress, like crying jags, insomnia, crippling headaches, backaches, and stomach aches. Her friends made her jumpier than ever.

I redoubled my efforts to be a good girl so she would be happy, and Daddy would come home. For instance, I saved all my pennies and nickels to help her buy War Bonds. The effort filled me with a sense of accomplishment and peace. And I had my memories: quiet days of barelegged beach walks and sunlit meals, of sidewalks veined in moss, and old stone houses.

One day I heard Mom talk about the emperor and concluded he was a slant-eyed version of the giant in Jack and the Beanstalk. "Fee fi fo fum, I smell the blood of . . ."

The thought made me uneasy. Though friends turned happy faces my way, I sensed anxiety, as all children do. Of all the happy faces, the aunties did it best. Everything was "lovely," we possessed "good taste," that mattered more than anything. "Well bred" people lived "quietly." The war didn't sound very quiet, but unscrambling the secret codes of adults remained beyond my reach.

Still, Alice brought good news, at least it sounded good to me. The intel people said the Nip foreign minister realized Japan's hegemony in Greater East Asia had crumbled, and if the emperor now negotiated a surrender, before the situation worsened, he could demand honorable terms.

"Probably the emperor told that minister that he sounded like a calculating old woman," Alice said. "In the Nip emperor's opinion, laying down arms would be sacrilege. Cowardly? Hirohito's grandfather, the Meiji Emperor, never listened to cowards. His commanders, if they erred, sat outside the Gate of Heaven, you know, the palace gate? They chanted apologies for their mistakes, and then committed seppuku."

"I'll drink to that," Mom said.

\* \* \*

In Hawaii, Daddy received his orders: Report to the Guadalcanal garrison for combat patrol. Oahu receded behind the ship's lacy, curling wake, as he sailed toward the dread island. Would the enemy sink his ship as it cut a path across the sea, plumes of gray rising from its smokestack?

He responded to the pull of distant action like a man making his way through a dark tunnel. Nervous, eager to help at last, he walked around the deck with his hand hooked by the thumb to his cartridge belt. Now. The game. Soon the ref would blow the whistle and toss the kickoff coin. Up and down over the lulling swells his troopship moved, the hum of the engine, the heat, and the endless days never changing. Time passed too slowly; everything in this blue world of water and sky became unreal.

On December 20, 1942, the slopes of swamp-infested Guadalcanal ridged the pearl pink horizon, and as Daddy's ship drew nearer, the afternoon sun slanted against the eerie mists above the steamy jungles. The El Dorado of mosquitoes, the island had fetid air, soggy heat, rodents and slithering reptiles. The ambiance here did not resemble Paris or London's.

Hoards of battle-seasoned Japanese fighters remained in Guadalcanal, hidden in jungle foliage and bamboo groves. Also, Admiral Raiso Tanaka's Second Destroyer Flotilla landed fresh troops, artillery, tanks, and supplies. We nicknamed the flotilla the "Tokyo Express."

Soon after Daddy debarked, a shot rang out, exploding a friend's head. Daddy felt as if blood poured from his own arteries. Something opened within him, full and frightening, and his heart galloped against his chest, as terror drew him into the reality of war. It became part of him, burned in.

When he and his men won a skirmish, he liked to say, "Didn't expect us, apparently. Shows how important it is to RSVP. Not enough people do out here."

One day he called to a nearby captain who didn't reply. A samurai had slit his throat in silence and disappeared, so the captain just lay there looking unperturbed in death. Daddy checked his own throat to be sure he felt no blood, and then, to steady himself, he wrote Mom:

"We pleasure seekers are getting well acquainted with Guadalcanal. We've got the Nips scrambling up the trees trying to hide from us. They're a joke, and this is just easy-breezy practice for when we retake the Philippines. That's when the fun will really begin. No decent cigarettes here. We have to smoke tasteless Fleetwoods and use special black lighters. The government should not be involved with a man's stomach or his cigarettes. I miss my Lucky Strikes.

"I'm having fun but hate being separated from my family. After we win, all I'm going to fight is the weeds in the back yard.

"I can picture our CO here in the privacy of his home, sitting at attention by the fireplace, lying at attention in bed. He calls everyone by his rank, first and last names – 'Good morning, Captain Frank Ribbel.' It gets on my nerves. Another thing, he asks a question and then answers it with oracle-like wisdom before anyone else can. 'Captain Ribbel, how is the weather today? Hot and humid.'

"You'll like my buddy in the foxhole, our air officer, Jim Williams. He's a typical Flyboy - brown hair shot with red and relaxed, funny bravado. He managed to squeak through college with a major in parties and came to the Sixth Army like me, via ROTC. He learns the island songs, wishes he could stroll along under balconies, singing and playing. It would suit him better than foxholes do.

"He took me up in a reconnaissance plane, and I want to tell you: he's the quarterback of pilots. I watched the ground sink away; installations became empty shadows, the rivers, unmoving lines, the colors of the earth, soft and muted.

"My neck tingled when we took off, but he enjoys flying more than a seagull does, and the three dimensional experience of the air! There's nothing like it. The airplane's tamed when he flies it, as if it understands the game. I'd trust Jim with my life. Like a good quarterback, he makes a plan, and if things go wrong, he improvises. And he knows how to analyze plays. I mean flight patterns.

"I love your beauty, I love to talk to you, be in your presence. These letters help, at least."

87

A plane! I thought when Mom read the letter, I'll have Daddy take me for a ride the minute he comes home. Or after we buy my horse.

She wrote back:

"Stay on the ground where you belong, I don't trust those stupid little planes. They're sitting ducks. OK, flying ducks. I miss the many loving things you did for me every day. I know you want to win and get home, and I know you're excited about the Philippine invasion, but please don't try to pull Excalibur out of the stone. Be careful, my love. Pooksie told me to say she agrees with me."

Then she helped me write Santa:

"Dear Santa, I hav ben a gud gurl 4 one hole year, so send my Daddy home. Now down to prasunts. May I pleas have if posibal sum rollerskats and sirprise me too. Luv, Ann Ribbel."

I made a Christmas card for Daddy, using all my favorite bell and angel stickers, and bought him a chocolate bar with money I earned selling homemade lemonade.

On Christmas Eve, Aunt Lenore created a feast for us so we would not feel sad. Her house perched on a hill where staggered, slanted roofs caught the sun, and geranium-filled terra cotta pots lined the patios. Its leaded glass windows and mansard roof exuded rarefied ease. She'd filled it with masses of pine boughs and red berries, and the scents combined with the delicious aromas from the kitchen.

Tonight she swept up her hair into three large buns, which set off her aquiline profile, and wore a blue halter dress to enhance her turquoise eyes and display her fine-boned back. She hovered, making sure everyone felt welcome, and Billy Boy, who usually rested with an unmatched thoroughness, greeted people as Santa in an outfit she'd bought for him. He gave Mom a thin smile and nervous squeeze of the hand, after which she followed Aunt Lenore into the kitchen to help put the finishing touches on the dinner.

In the living room, Billy bent over me and honked, "Ho, ho, ho."

I pulled down his beard. "You're not Santa."

"How can you behave like this after all I've done for you?"

"What have you done?"

His ears twitched. "Extended endless hospitality, that's what."

"What's that?"

He wagged his forefinger. "I've been gracious about having you with us morning, noon, and night. This is our house, you know. You're a guest, Pooksie, and you need to behave like one. Besides, you scurry around excessively. It's not feminine."

"What's fe-man?"

He began clicking his tongue against the roof of his mouth as if to aid his thought process. "You need to act more like a girl. Be quiet, ladylike, less razzmatazz. Well bred."

I ignored him.

He continued, flicking his tongue, "Your mother took Child Psychology 1-A at the University of California, and she worries about 'complexes.' Less spoiling and psychology, more rod, that's my recommendation."

Concluding that his Santa outfit had flopped, he stomped upstairs to change, and I, rather than scuttling after him, began playing with a glass globe, turning it upside down to stir up its snow.

He reappeared and lounged on the sofa with aristocratic nonchalance, his burgundy cashmere scarf resting next to him. He gave me one more bit of advice, "I live carefully, take a step only when the ground feels firm beneath my feet. You should learn from my example."

I began galloping around the room, whinnying and calling myself a horsie, while Aunt Lenore and Mom returned with drinks, soda crackers, and cheddar cheese. "It's a shame the priest couldn't join us," she said.

"That priest calls on the Holy Mother for everything, even directions to the men's room," Billy Boy retorted, "but he knows a thing or two about women in black underwear. He just wears that crown of thorns in church."

Frankie, dressed in a red outfit with white pom-pom buttons, practiced his vocabulary: "Mama, baba, numnum, da, An, me, Nor." I began playing "This little piggy went to market" with him, and he made funny little sounds like nascent jokes, laughing at himself.

The aunties waltzed in, all pearls and silk, followed by Uncle George, who seemed like a bit of a maiden aunt himself. He wore his usual dark pinstripe suit, the starchiest white shirt, and his trademark linen handkerchief. Aunt Nini often said that except for his slight over-bite, he looked like Gary Cooper.

Aunt Marie's delicately penciled eyebrows rose in lofty arcs, as, steepling her fingertips, she asked me, "Have you been good in the eyes of the Heavenly Father?"

"Yes, Aunt Marie," I replied.

"Fine, then, heaven be praised." As always, she followed this Q and A period with a saying for me to remember. Tonight's: "Resentment is a poison you swallow thinking the other person will die." With a regal air, she stretched her pink bow lips into a smile and displayed the petit point bookmarks she made for "our boys overseas."

Aunt Nini announced that she now helped the Coast Guard scan the skies for enemy aircraft. "I hope I spot something," she said. "I want to help people, help someone sometime, the Good Lord willing."

Yesterday was a bad day at the races, so Uncle George gloomily replenished his sherry, while glancing at his sisters and saying, "Of course I drink. Alcohol keeps me sane, the saints be praised."

A maid with a raddled face announced dinner, her lips flapping when she spoke, and the family moved to the dining room table with its red tablecloth and holly centerpiece. At every place sat gifts wrapped in green velvet and tied with red satin ribbon.

Venison had escaped rationing, so a roast, warm from the oven, glowed in the candlelight, surrounded by victory garden vegetables. From the kitchen came the scent of winter apples baking in Brer Rabbit molasses and cinnamon. They didn't smell as good as toll house cookies, in my opinion. The war again, no doubt. Sugar rationing.

Billy Boy investigated the buffet, where his nose scoured the plat-ters of food like a truffle pig's, and he commented on the "marvelous aromas . . . magnificent scents." Once seated, he arranged his eating utensils in a precise, straight line. For his delicate stomach, he had a fried egg rather than venison. He ate it one bite at a time, then plopped the whole yolk in his mouth. Next, he took a bite of his sourdough French bread. As he chewed, his avid mouth worked rapid-fire like a chipmunk's.

"You chew too fast," I said.

Aunt Marie gave me a patrician stare. "If you point out someone's fault, he will cure it but never forgive you." She'd never forgiven Nini for accusing her of eating peanut butter out of the jar.

Aunt Lenore raised her glass, "Let's drink to defeating Japan before the new year."

I pulled at the sides of my eyes so they slanted. Mom told me to stop that, and Aunt Marie suggested concentrating on manners – for instance, curling the little finger when using forks and spoons.

Mom and Aunt Lenore ate with slow grace, holding their utensils lightly. I watched them, and, after a thoughtful silence, said, "Aunt Lenore's eyes are blue, and yours aren't, Mom."

"Never compare two sisters, if you know what's good for you," Aunt Lenore replied.

Billy Boy mentioned that the Japanese hit Calcutta with air raids. No one replied.

Mom started talking about Daddy's letters from Guadalcanal. "He claims that if the Japanese stopped shouting for one single instant to concentrate on fighting, they might occasionally score."

Everyone laughed and raised their glasses.

She continued. "He described the exhilaration he felt – almost dizzying. He's a fighting man now, and he's held his own. It's like a baptism. True, he's a sharpshooter, but motivation matters more – that's what he thinks. A man must face the enemy without reservation."

Billy Boy said he'd read that you couldn't turn over a stone in Guadalcanal without Nips swarming out. And that men easily got lost in the jungle.

"That will be enough," Uncle George snapped.

Even Aunt Lenore glared at her husband for once.

Billy Boy shifted gear and began a rant on the absurdities of history, for example all the people senselessly killed in the crusades. "The infidel remains the infidel, even though we battered down his doors," he said, and then he began sharing his radiant complexity and capacity to view world conflicts from all sides. He summarized, "I just want to stand for grace, kindness, and common humanity."

"You're a goody-goody," I said, and Mom tried not to laugh. Billy Boy fell into an aggressive silence.

Mom began nervously shredding her Parker House roll, as silence fell, except for the sound of the maid rinsing china in the kitchen. Once Uncle George finished his venison, he refilled his wine glass with a flourish, and, sounding patriarchal, toasted Aunt Lenore and Billy Boy, the President of the United States, the Holy Family, his sisters, me, Frankie, Mom, and especially Daddy.

We all chimed in, "Hear, hear!" Clink, clink.

Mom shook back a strand of hair that had detached itself from the rest and stared into her glass of wine as if she could see the world through its bottom. She raised it, trying to keep the quaver out of her voice, "I'd like to drink a second toast to Frank – "

The family members raised their glasses, and an image flashed before me. Daddy stood there, trying to tell me something, but I could not hear him. Though it immediately faded, I could barely disguise my unease.

After dinner, Mom went to "powder her nose," and Aunt Lenore stood with her arm draped over the mantle as she swirled cognac in a snifter. In the fireplace flames leapt; I felt their heat, saw their glow against her frame. I could talk with her about Daddy more easily than with Mom, because she didn't get so upset. "Why didn't Daddy just stay home?" I asked.

"He heard the sound of a bugle," she replied, and she pretended to be playing a horn, singing "Ta-rum, ta-rum, ta-rum."

Ah. I knew Daddy loved music. This made more sense than racing off to confront monsters who cut off legs and bombed pearls.

# CHAPTER TWENTY-ONE

HIROHITO STOOD NEAR a golden screen painted with a field of iris and summoned one of his most trusted kuramakus. He preferred kuramakus to ministers and commanders, because they could think. Today's visitor recommended the emperor organize an asset-stripping plan for occupied countries, rather than letting the commanders continue to randomly loot and pocket the spoils. The Japanese had financial needs – didn't all conquerors?

The emperor smiled for the first time in too long. At last now, a superior concept. He would call his glamorous brother, Chichibu. The emperor trusted his Chichibu-san, unlike his other brothers.

This particular Yamato already realized, the vanquished countries teemed with gold and treasure, so he delighted in taking charge of an operation codenamed Golden Lily. He pretended to need medical leave from the army owing to tuberculosis, and claimed he'd gone to a sanitarium near Mt. Fuji. His people prayed for his recovery, bowing before flickering candles and bowls of billowing incense.

Instead, in the dust of ancient roads, he walked through occupied China and Southeast Asia, his piglet hands clutching at goodies. His men took a dozen solid gold Buddhas, each weighing over a ton. He collected fine Asian art, and he appreciated jewelry, though not as much as his brother, the emperor.

Once Chichibu gathered up a country's bounty, he sent it off on fake hospital ships to various locations. With his cultivated taste and love of souvenirs, he did save some pretty jewels for his wife and daughters, not to mention a few objects to freshen up his palace.

His belief in the sacred also motivated him to collect religious artifacts for the emperor. Hirohito responded to esthetics, especially objects fabricated from gold or jade and encrusted with precious gems. He favored Shakyamunis, (Buddha, the lion of the Shakya tribe), Padmapanis, (queens of heaven), Tao-tieh (tiger-god) masks, and dragons.

In time Chichibu seized so much treasure, it became physically difficult to move it all to Japan, so he conscientiously stashed it in the Philippines, hiding it in over two hundred church vaults, bunkers, and underground tunnels. The hills came to life with the sound of coins clinking. In Ipoh, Malaysia, he melted gold and created bars of bullion bearing the stamp of the Golden Lily logo that he helped design.

The bounty still lurks in caves, and every so often, someone discovers a bit of it. And, a recently unearthed solid gold Philippine Buddha weighing close to a ton reportedly now resides in a Zurich vault.

# CHAPTER TWENTY-TWO

As THE WAR progressed, secrecy deepened at home, and the government censors inked out ever more from overseas letters, as 1943 blustered into the Pacific. Amid pounding rain and twisting wind, guns rattled, bullets whistled, and explosions shook the earth still.

As scarce as truth was, Admiral Bull Halsey believed the supply exceeded the demand. He and the Secretary of War seemed bent on obscuring it, according to Mom. Distorted rumors began gathering around facts like plaque to a tooth, rumors that escalated fear and uncertainty at home.

Military history lists battles, but in the Pacific War, we fought endless encounters on uncountable tiny atolls, jungle islands, and many sea passages.

The Tokyo Express still controlled the Hawaii-Guadalcanal route, but the Allies began to interfere. The Japanese retaliated, and both sides found delivering supplies nearly impossible. Daddy and his buddies nicknamed Guadalcanal "Starvation Island."

Hungry or no, we tried to prevail over the tough imperial rear guard. Daddy, who always said, "I'm starving. Let's eat," learned a terrible new definition of the phrase. He wrote in his diary:

"The hunger! To distract myself, I think of afternoons at home when the thick fog cools the air, and the foghorns sound, see Pooksie and Frankie cuddling in my lap, their little bodies fitting it easily."

He got letters from both Grandma and Aunt Ruth. Grandma's said:

"Arthur's articles are the talk of San Diego. Yesterday at my DAR meeting, the recording secretary said his punctuation's flawless.

"I read that our V-17 air squadron is winning engagements in the Pacific. Good. That helps you. You're the only child who never worries me. You'll take care of yourself and keep safe for Mary-Helen's sake and the children's, I know that."

Aunt Ruth's letter said:

"Last night I had my first date in ages, and halfway through dinner, he started sniggering and calling me 'Melons.' That was the end of him.

"The Embalmer's married again, richest husband yet, on oxygen for his failing heart. Of course, she got rid of stupid Gil, so now he writes me from his naval base. 'I still think about you, made a little mistake, want to see you when I'm home on leave. We can work things through. We should have talked more in the first place.' Oh, Frank, I should throw the letters away, shouldn't I?

"Mother keeps annoying me by saying how grown-up I've become through teaching; she began saying how grown-up I was when I first went to kindergarten and has been optimistically repeating it ever since.

"Last night I dreamed of you. We were young, and you pointed at a shooting star. I stood on tiptoes trying to see it. Finally you turned to me and asked, 'Where's the rest of the family?' I didn't know, but when I woke up, I felt so close to you and so happy. I know, absolutely know, I'll be seeing you soon."

The next day, Daddy and some friends moved through the jungle on combat patrol, dodging snipers who popped up on all sides in the usual horrifying chaos. One man's arm blew off leaving a bloody stump, another man burned to death from a grenade. Charlie Harrington, the man who never stopped talking, disappeared into an area of the jungle teeming with Japanese swordsmen.

"Let's go find him," Daddy said to Jim Williams.

"How?"

"Easy. We'll follow the noise. He's probably still telling a story."

"Or maybe he glimpsed a bare-chested native girl."

General Rapp Brush, Alice's husband, spoke little and stayed inside himself watching and listening. Daddy liked and admired him. Rapp often warned his men not to go off in the jungle except in good-sized groups. Daddy and Jim preferred facing danger to trying to avoid it.

Trying to remain oriented, they moved through the wet, green hell of swamps, past camouflaged steel pillboxes full of firepower, past still-armed tanks. A man's direction sense might falter, and when seven-foot tall grasses rustled, an enemy could lurk.

"What do you suppose the Nip quotient is around here?" Jim asked.

"I don't care, as long as they're sniveling cowards who cringe out of sight and stay out of trouble."

96

Around them, the jungle shimmered, a place with no origin or destination, just infinite moist green.

Jim stopped. "What do you know?"

He spotted Charlie, weakened from several pieces of shrapnel, none of which made a vital hit. Covered with dust and blood, he lay with his back against a banyan tree and stared ahead in silence, his eyes dulled. But a glimmer remained in those eyes, something that had not given up, though insects buzzed around his blood.

Feeling the awful aloneness of dying, Daddy fought to keep his voice steady. "We're here, man," he said. "You're going to be fine."

"May I have a cigarette?" Charlie asked, his tone apathetic.

"Sorry, we don't have any," Jim replied. From the trees, monkeys chattered to alert each other that men had appeared. Parrots squawked as though for treats.

"Somebody shot me," Charlie said.

"Trying to shut you up," Jim replied.

"Talking to yourself?" Daddy asked. "No. We're not giving you credit where it's due. It must have been a jealous husband."

Charlie tried to smile. "Thanks for coming."

"You'd plowed half way through a story when we got separated," Daddy replied. "We wanted to hear the other half."

He lifted Charlie and carried him in his arms. The day stuck to Daddy, hot and thick as fever, and sweat poured down, drenching his back. The slippery ground wracked his muscles, his boots began to hurt as the leather bit into his ankles, and he wondered if he'd misjudged his strength.

"Let me carry him for a while," Jim said. "You're waddling like a pregnant goose."

He picked up Charlie, and Daddy spotted a dead Japanese soldier draped over the branch of a tree. "What happened, Dick Tracy? Did you forget your Crime Stoppers' Manual?"

Jim laughed. "Jesus, I'm sick of these mosquitoes whacking at my helmet," he said.

"Look!" Daddy cheerily pointed to an abandoned Japanese bicycle; Jim draped Charlie over it and pushed it along.

Finally, they spotted the division medics.

"A beautiful sight," Daddy said.

"A little plasma, and you'll feel like new, Charlie," Jim added.

"So, okay, then?" Charlie asked.

"You're lucky these two certified nut cases went in after you," the medic said.

"Heroes," Charlie replied.

"More like dodoes with reckless nerve," Jim said.

* * *

Santa gave me a dollhouse for Christmas, and I adored it as one adores an escape from worry and sadness. I cut remnants of cloth for curtains and made chandeliers from crystal beads, creating a tiny world full of wonder and delight.

At the same time, I began to have nightmares that the Japanese tiptoed into our house and we tried to hide, or they chased me with bayonets, and I tried to run but couldn't. At the movies in 1943, we saw newsreels of the war raging, and I watched terrified as twirling bombs fell, huge battleships sank, and light planes crashed. I did not want Daddy involved in this war anymore. He should come home. Now.

I said so to Mom and quoted what the aunties told me, "Stand on your own two feet." At the time, I thought they meant rather than standing on theirs, but now I understood it meant doing things on your own. On his own, Daddy should say good-bye to the war and come home.

However, Mom said her usual "He'll be home soon," and then answered the doorbell. Alice. "Just think," she said, "it's only February, and already the Allies have invaded New Britain Island, the Admiralties, the Gilberts, Marshalls, and Carolines. That's a lot of islands. Think of the planning?"

Mom smiled. "It's impressive, all right. But what a war. I've read Japan's empire is the largest in history, if you count the miles, but we go from one little rock to another."

"That's how we reach Tokyo? One rock at a time."

Mom nodded and lit up. "I read that the Japanese suffered a particularly unpleasant day at Truk in the Carolines. We downed 201 of their aircraft and sank 21 ships. And only lost 17 planes. That's pretty darn good."

After Alice left, Mom felt so cheery, she decided to take us to a movie. First, as usual, came the newsreel. We didn't know it then, but the Pacific newsreels were highly edited, as the commanders didn't want the public aware of the casualties. They worried over how audiences would react to raw and shocking scenes; brutal images of dead and wounded men might erode public enthusiasm. The newsreels showed little actual carnage, and the only dead were Japanese.

The next day, Mom scanned the morning Chronicle, "Rapid collapse of Lae . . ." Then she read the official casualties article, which toned down the reality. Dead fighters. She wept for the families. The bereaved. Their lives will never be the same, she thought. The man they lost would never vanish from their memory, and memory itself would be forever stimulated by pictures on a living room table, by letters and diaries in a bottom drawer, in odd belongings that from time to time appeared in the back of a closet or hidden in the garage.

She shook off her depression. Aunt Lenore planned to come over for watercress sandwiches around noon. What would Mom do without my aunt? She wanted to try to express her appreciation to her for always being there, but whenever she planned a loving speech, Aunt Lenore sidetracked her with talk of this or that.

Today we would eat on the porch and enjoy the first warm winter day of "fresh air" in ages; besides, Mom wanted to show off our newly potted lime trees.

"Are you sure Daddy will come home?" I asked.

"Yes, I am. I know it in my heart. What you know inside is just as real as what you see outside."

I thought she was kidding.

Aunt Lenore swept in and handed her a box of saltwater taffy. Mom smiled, really smiled. "Candy. What an amazing sister. I love you so much. We have so little since sugar rationing went in."

She unwrapped a piece and ate it with relish. Unbelievably good. "Where did you ever get it?"

"Well, from Hannah Wilson."

Mom looked as if she'd just whiffed rotting codfish. "Hannah? How could you even speak to her? She's the worst person in the world. She probably got it on the black market." She handed Aunt Lenore the candy. "Take it back. I refuse to eat another bite."

I ran over. "Mom, I'll eat mine."

"Calm down," Aunt Lenore said. "Hannah seems to have figured out how money can keep distribution working smoothly, yes, but it would be nice for your children to have some idea of what taffy tastes like, if you want my opinion. You used to live on it."

"Well, I'm not eating another bite. Pooksie and Frankie can have the rest."

"I despise Hannah as much as you do. You should thank me for putting up with her to get the taffy. Not to mention what I had to pay."

"Never again, please. I truly hate her. She's the original purveyor of doom."

"All made up, I'm sure. No one who pours vast amounts of flesh into half the required fabric has much grasp of reality. Not that you can tell a book by its cover, ha, ha."

Condescension saturated Aunt Lenore's voice. "I have more respect for the average codfish than I have for her. Much more. But taffy's a nice treat for the children."

Mom stubbed out a Camel, then lit another. "I call her the Grim Preacher. Of course, you can't listen to a word she says. Unfortunately, you can't believe most of what anyone says. So many unfounded rumors about this war whirl around."

"Probably the more secrecy there is, the more people will make up stories."

"Uh-huh. Creativity flourishes in the dark. Then there's the endless propaganda. Maddening. We should know the truth."

When the mail came, Mom forgot about the Grim Preacher. Her worried spirit soared with elation; she positively fizzed with happiness. The letter from Daddy said he was coming home. Rapp Brush decided that Daddy possessed tactical talent, based on an article he'd written about ladder firing for the Field Artillery Journal. Ladder firing and deployment during island beach assaults. He sent Mom a copy with a note:

"Darling, save this for me; it probably will be my only accomplishment for the year. Rapp's enrolled me in the Command and General Staff School at Fort Leavenworth in Kansas. I get to bring my precious family while I sit and study! Who's the luckiest man alive?

"MacArthur, Krueger, Marshall, and the rest trained there. Rapp told me that when MacArthur first crossed the parade ground there, a man named Sergeant Major Corbett said, 'Boys, there goes a true soldier.'

"Don't worry – I haven't changed my mind about an army career, no matter how often I'm told I have a great start on seniority. When this war ends, I stay home with you, period.

"I'll be home soon. Look for me. I'll be wearing my fashionable khakis."

She read aloud, and a light happiness squeezed my chest. I have a copy of Daddy's Officers' Handbook in my desk drawer now, and it's filled with football play formations. Naturally a quarterback storming a beach to push toward an end zone would devise a better way to do it, so his good article came as no surprise. After all, this war of islands and atolls had no existing blueprints.

Mom and Aunt Lenore danced around the room, wept, and hugged Frankie and me. Then Aunt Lenore took us for a walk so Mom could phone and tell everyone the news. In an instant her energy and spontaneity returned, along with the lilt in her voice. She laughed in a new way, like a child, thinking, I let Frank inside where it hurts, and this past year I've learned just how much. My happiness today makes up for everything, and I burst with love and excitement.

The next morning, Mom said to Juanita, "The cows will tremble, as I'm going to feed him so many. I'm saving every beef rationing coupon for when he comes home."

While she normally spoke of fresh fruits and leafy greens, he considered a meal without meat an insult, and he didn't allow her to hector him about what he ate.

For security and weather reasons, Daddy's arrival date remained classified, so every day Mom excitedly washed her hair and toweled it off, just in case. She chose a dress for me to wear – yellow to compliment my blonde hair, trimmed with blue ribbon to accent my eyes. For herself, a mint green Lily Dasche with padded shoulders, a straight, slim silhouette, and ruffles at the neck and hem.

She planted yellow tree roses and pink rhododendrons in the garden, filled the house with sweet peas, lilac, and made a sign for the front porch: "Welcome Home. We Love You."

One crystal blue day, water swelled through the Golden Gate, the tides carrying the sea into the bay, as Daddy's troopship approached.

We waited at home as usual, Mom making fine adjustments to the seams of her silk stockings and smoothing down her hair.

Frankie rattled around trying to get attention, and I stared out the window. Finally the doorbell rang, and Mom threw open the door. The sun, vast and golden, poured in, and, blazing in the light, stood the blue-eyed man with the dancer's grace and dazzling smile – the beloved father, the husband. His wavy black hair still glistened, he still thrummed with life, and the male smell of his body and his athlete's posture remained unchanged. He still shimmered, though the expression of innocent youth had vanished, and he looked emaciated. Plus he needed a shave.

He drew Mom to him and stared at her as if something inside him had moved and changed position. She lowered her eyes, complacent to his touch, as he turned her around. The moment would radiate in her memory like a phrase of music that stirs an emotion, recaptures it in its brightness.

He stepped inside, and focused, his eyes taking in everything. Lifting me, he danced me around the room, "My angel, you've grown so tall and beautiful," he said.

He held Frankie aloft, pride kindling his eyes like a match touching straw. My brother squirmed with delight, as Daddy jounced him on his shoulder, enjoying his baby powder scent, his chuckles. After kissing the top of his head, he blew on his tummy to make him laugh. "You're a tubby little guy," he said, "and you've got a great sense of fun." He dropped to his hands and knees and gave Frankie a piggy back ride, then headed to the corner, picked up his football, and tossed it from one hand to the other, making it spiral.

Jeep dashed from room to room barking, found his red sponge ball and wiggled over to offer it to the returning hero. Daddy patted his bottom, "So you're the head of the household now. Honored to meet you at last."

Mom played a record of Glenn Miller's "Pennsylvania Six-Five-0-0-0" and went to the fridge, checking her face in the mirror enroute. The fine hair on her upper lip looked too powdery, so she smoothed it. Daddy kicked off his shoes. She brought in champagne and fluted glasses and set them on the rosewood coffee table, then reached down, picked Daddy's shoes up by the heels, and parked them just so in the corner.

She sat on the floral chintz sofa, and Daddy lay down with his head in her lap, relaxing like a puppy that trusts the vet. Her hands moved over his face, his hair, his shoulders, and she touched the top button of his shirt as if it were a jewel. He reached into his pocket and pulled out a string of small white puka shells, which he hung around her neck. His fingers traced her chin, and he gazed at her.

Soon he began his extensive repertoire of Japanese stories, all of which depicted the enemy as harmless buffoons. "I heard about a soldier who hid in the bushes just a few feet from us sharpshooters," he said, "so he could use our showers late at night and raid our K rations. That's what I call desperate."

"I find this hard to believe." Mom smiled indulgently. Then her eyes changed. "When do you think the war will be over?"

"Soon. The score's 100 percent for us so far, zero for the enemy. FDR, Churchill, and the brass met at Casablanca last month, and now we're going to get 30 percent of the forces. Finally. We'll crush the Japanese in a matter of weeks."

I put my arms around his neck and talked to him, my mouth moving right next to his ear. Laughing, he pressed my belly button, "Ding-dong."

Mom went into the kitchen to prepare lunch, and Daddy walked through the house for the first time, humming "Home Sweet Home" and admiring every detail: the daffodil yellow walls and glossy white moldings, the hardwood floor with its golden patina.

"Wood has skin, like a person," he said. "I love these floors. Love this place."

Mom announced lunch, and we went into the dining room. She had papered it with green and white stripes, and hung floor-to-ceiling curtains – white with lipstick red, pink, blue, and green flowers. We took our places and ate the first course, Daddy's favorite, hearts of romaine with Roquefort dressing. Jeep sat gazing at me, hoping for a snack.

"Stay, Jeep," I said, when he tried to jump up on my lap and eat off my plate.

Daddy patted him. "There's a noble creature, treatng my daughter with loyalty and respect, obeying her commands. He'll spoil her for any future husbands."

Frankie stuffed himself with milk and pureed apples, and Daddy said, "That boy really eats. He must have seven stomachs, like a goat."

Then he opened his welcome home gifts: from the aunties, Rosary Beads, St. Christopher medals, crosses, and a petit point vest embroidered with an American eagle. Daddy tried it on, announced it fit perfectly, in no way implying it might be unsuitable for battlefields. Undeterred by not knowing how to do it, Aunt Nini had baked a loaf of molasses bread for him, but it proved to be as hard as cement.

Aunt Lenore and Billy Boy dropped by, she hugging Daddy as tears poured down her cheeks.

After shaking Daddy's hand, Billy Boy sneezed. "I'm not sure if I'm coming down with a cold or allergic to the dog."

Mom turned and just looked at him. In beauty she stood apart from him, silent, willing him to leave. They all finally did.

Daddy looked thrilled most of the time, but occasionally he would remember something, and his face closed, become devoid of expression. He went somewhere else. In these moments, we could see his pain and vulnerability, despite all his strength and spirit. His face looked the same, and it didn't. There were things he knew that we would never know.

After "tucking in the kids" and alone at last, he spoke to Mom of homesickness, the humidity, the long distances you traversed to a battlefield, the sense of being lonely and deserted. Logistics in the South

Pacific? A nightmare, he said.

She put on a record, extended her hand to him, and he followed, pinned securely by her smile, his hand in hers. In the fireplace, flames crackled; on the mantle, a lemon verbena candle flickered. He turned on the Philco radio, found a music station playing "I'll Be Seeing You," and danced with Mom, breathing in the scent of smoke and wood from the fireplace. As he held her, he envisioned a future shining beyond. Dancing was essential to him; he adored it. Swirling, turning, back and forth over the living room floor he and Mom went, the rhythm of the music filling their souls, making them light, inoculated against war.

# CHAPTER TWENTY-THREE

USUALLY EMPEROR HIROHITO considered early spring his favorite time of year, though now even the seasonal weather failed to cheer him. He morosely sat near a breezy door surrounded with a carved ebony panel depicting ancient myths: cranes worshiped a frog god who saved them from starvation, a goat-headed female brandished a sword. Inspiring Japanese stories, all, reflecting a national soul he tried to preserve.

After his first birthday, he'd left his family, so tutors could raise and train him. Mhinomiya, the future emperor, loved his laughing moments with his younger brothers, those moments when he felt like a little boy. But even then, everyone, including his family, had to treat him respectfully at all times.

Now his life changed. Princes Hiagashikuni, Asaka, Fushimi, and Kaya continued meeting with his mother every week and sent him messages labeled "important" in which they shared their "wise counsel." Cowardly surrender counsel. Prince Takamatsu claimed he would opt out of the imperial family and become a commoner if Hirohito did not surrender, and compared him to a monkey falling out of a tree as he reached for a banana.

His mother sent messages saying he should stop trying to be a warrior and devote himself to his botany and marine biology. Then she'd say his head caught fire and burned up his brain or else recited one of her irritating haikus about Japan, a leaf in bitter winds, ending with a phrase similar in sense to the red flowers of Japanese blood.

Hirohito fumed about the collapse of tradition, reverence, patriotism, and family loyalty. He became more isolated and distrustful, stiffly meeting with relatives and associates only to discuss issues at hand, never to relax and enjoy their company.

The Allied flood rose higher and faster than the dikes his people built. In history's fastest-moving offensive, the infected fly foreigners pushed his forces back more than three thousand miles across the Pacific. His commanders functioned as feathers in a gale.

Too few of them committed seppuku, despite their failure to guard the sacred empire: a deep, permanent duty, larger than the sum of rules, strategy, and slogans. Even Admiral Yamamoto faltered lately. A national hero should only report victories to his emperor, but he described recent naval battles as a contest between "unequally matched sumo wrestlers."

Hirohito could not allow these excuses to continue, so he changed the subject to new varieties of mosses and fungi. With escalating losses and rising pressure to surrender, the emperor ran out of material for his lectures and began repeating himself.

He still expected his shrinking troops to press on. A warrior knew his life, a life where death seeks him. It was a fine thing for such a man to give his life for his emperor, and warriors needed to remember that they survived at the pleasure of their emperor, and their lives belonged to him. Surrender to the vicious Allies would result in the massacre of innocent Japanese women and children, the plunder of sacred shrines, and execution the Yamato family.

# CHAPTER TWENTY-FOUR

FROM MARCH UNTIL November 1943, Mom and Daddy's lives became their own again, as they shared the intimacy of dressing and undressing together, hanging their clothes in the same closet, brushing their hair, or putting on their bathrobes. Daddy watched Mom awaken in the morning, stir, stretch, and breathe in the air of a fresh day. Her tumble of auburn hair would cling to the pillow, her face and neck, and she would gather it, pulling it out of the way, to kiss him. In these moments, he felt the peace of the man who is loved. Safe.

Next, his morning shave. Wetting a little brush, he dipped it in a bowl of shaving cream, spread it on his face, and cut it away with a straightedge razor. When he finished, his face looked shiny and new. He brushed his teeth without replacing the toothpaste cap or returning the brush to its holder.

No matter. Mom would soon come in and clean up; she liked everything to be in "apple-pie order." He would drape his tie on the back of a chair, remove his jacket and stick it on the dining room table, kick off his shoes, and sit on the sofa, putting his feet on the coffee table. Or he tossed everything in one drawer, unsorted, and she arranged it. Sometimes he stacked empty Coke bottles and football programs on his desk or the side tables, knowing she wanted everything "put away" and would see that it was.

"Vacation is to get away from hectic living," he said, "not just switch the backdrop and keep running around in circles."

"He wants me to pick up after him," Mom winked at me, then sat in his lap, her hands floating over his shoulders.

Occasionally she rebelled, and to restore peace, he roamed through the house and systematically organized all his possessions: hung up clothes, tossed cigarette butts from ashtrays, and placed his lead pencils in neat rows beside his Parker pen and inkwell. But that didn't happen very often.

Every day he wore his uniform.

"The khaki sets off the blue of your eyes," Mom said.

"That's exactly why I'm in the army," he replied.

He bought his son a teddy, "a baby's version of the Sturdy Golden Bear, the UC Berkeley mascot," he said, and Frankie held it, chewed its ear, clutched it close when he fell asleep.

Mom wanted to show off his brilliance and spent a lot of time holding up objects and saying, "Spoon, spoon, see? Spoon."

"Uh."

"See? He comprehends so many words," Mom gushed.

"No, he doesn't," I said.

Daddy probably agreed with me, but he disappointed me by not taking sides. How could a brave soldier behave that way?

The next day, we packed up the blue De Soto and got in. We were moving, leaving for Leavenworth. Our country manufactured no new cars these days, but luckily ours still performed with brio. Daddy turned on the ignition. Silence. Again. A cough. Again, and the car started. He made an arm signal and we headed off to our first stop. We took Jeep to the aunties', rather than Aunt Lenore's, as Billy Boy suspected he could be allergic to dogs, since the neighbor's poodle often made him sneeze.

I bent down and patted Jeep's head. Suspicious, he stared at me with his questioning eyes. His tail drooped.

"That's one annoyed dog," Daddy said.

Next we drove to Aunt Lenore's to drop off Juanita, and Daddy's eyes turned cobalt. "Did you see the shrug of contempt your sister's maid gave Juanita? The sneer?"

"Lenore will keep them separated – don't worry. Juanita can always comb Billy Boy's hair and brush his teeth."

The car cranked grudgingly along. The delight of being together lit our every word, every small gesture, even Frankie's drooling and bubble blowing. From his car seat, he threw his teddy on the floor, and then motioned me to pick it up.

"See how well-coordinated he is? Imagine," Mom simpered.

"He's acting like a brat," I replied, and started complaining about him to my dolls. By the way, he had turned into a big disappointment. Playing with him in no way resembled playing with Tinesey and Leilani, since he wiggled and ran around too much, talked back, and disobeyed me. I got sick of it. However, Jeep liked him and acted more like a dog and less catlike around him. He would chase the red sponge ball when I threw it and run over and drop it in front of Frankie.

My brother tried to learn to bounce the ball; impossible, only I could do that. He wriggled free when I sat him on my lap and read stories that would improve his mind, but sometimes he would surprise me with a hug, and in these hugs lay his redemption.

As we cruised along in the car, I pretended to be a princess riding an elephant. I could no longer suck my thumb, as Mom painted it with brown medicine to cure my habit. "I have to go pee-pee," I kept saying, to punish her. She coped with her "unruly mass of hair," powdered her nose, or replenished her lipstick, turning the rearview mirror so she could see herself. Sometimes she scratched Daddy's back as he drove, making small circles with her oval nails, or stroked his fingers on the steering wheel, one by one.

Cars didn't have radios then, so we sang songs, and Daddy made up stories about a sneaky tiger, a giraffe that thought he was Moses, and a bear that hiccoughed all the time.

The government prioritized gas rationing coupons "A, B, or C," according to war demands, but Daddy didn't have to use his, as station attendants refused to charge a man in uniform. Mom began complaining about his speeding, and he winked at me in the rear view window. "The Japanese commanders make their wives stay home and not talk back," he said, "and they have to stay out of sight when company comes."

After days of searching, I finally asked, "Where are the fruited planes?"

Under a metallic gray sky, a smudgy brick city appeared, our destination: Ft. Leavenworth. It had tar streets lined with telephone poles linked by sagging wire; sporadic evergreens sprouted and little flags stood on windowsills. Daddy pulled to the curb, and our tired car wound down with a sputter. He patted the dashboard, "You did a good job," he said.

Mom swung her legs out of the car with Daddy mentioning "sleek kneecaps," and I climbed out of the back seat. Mom stretched her long, perfectly tailored arms and suggested we take a stroll.

The fort looked so colorful, with all the international regalia. Officers from all the Allied countries, even Russia, went there for strategic planning and leadership training, so we saw endless bright uniforms, medals, and plumed hats. The soldiers marched at the parade grounds, "Hup, two, three, four!"

Our apartment was on the rear of the building, so we couldn't see anything beyond, except brick and rear windows. The front door creaked as if it wanted to fall off its hinges, but Daddy cheerfully lifted Mom and carried her over the threshold, as he did at all our homes.

The inside smelled dank, and though the narrow, dark rooms were crowded with furniture, we saw no signs of a family – no plants, no photographs, no petit point pillows. Nothing suggested that in these rooms people laughed or children played.

Then, when she stood in the hall, he held her tightly, her arms against her sides, and began rocking her a little, one way and the other, in slow movements.

Mom looked around. "There are some real possibilities here," she said. "I love the old-fashioned atmosphere. All I need to do is buy some colorful quilts and – well, you know."

She soon filled the apartment with bowls of fruit, candy, candles, and bouquets of flowers, gathering life for the rooms.

Drum rolls sounded, bugles sang out, and, at sunrise and sunset, cannons boomed.

One day a soft white powder of snow made the streets and parked cars glisten like wet seals; Daddy blew on the windowpane, creating a circle of condensation and then drew a heart in the middle. Mom looked out another window, and he walked up behind her. Raising his arms, he placed his palms against the windowpanes. I could see his body along hers, see the small muscles on the backs of his hands. It annoyed me. She always considered herself the queen, as far as Daddy was concerned.

Once again, the news from the Pacific sounded distant, more like history than life. One morning at breakfast, Daddy shook his fork of scrambled eggs at the newspaper and said, "There couldn't be an enemy pilot remaining in the air at this point. They lost a slew of A-Team boys in March during the Battle of the Bismark Sea and in Yamamoto's 'Operation I.' He tried to bomb us in Guadalcanal and Tulgari, but turned tail fast. Poor 'Y,' no luck with 'I.'"

He put down the paper, made a halo over his head with his hands, and scowled, "I'm the god-emperor, and I'm fed up with 'Y,' 'I,' and everything else."

Bugles sounding reveille awakened me every morning, and I rushed off to the post school with children from around the world. We sat at our wooden desks with holes for inkwells, and sometimes we earned "V for Victory" stickers, which shone like my old tin foil foxtails.

Daddy marched in the parades, stood at attention for the hoisting and lowering of the flag, his face expressionless, his posture military. Every time he heard of another victory for his country, he clasped his hands together, waved them over his head, and cheered.

Mom asked him about his training sessions with the commanders, and he replied, "I hold the match while they light their cigars. So far all of them just discuss 'complex strategies.' I'm waiting for the guy who says, 'keep it simple and be flexible.' Nimitz has stepped up his Pacific assaults, which is great, but the army brass sulk like kids when they think he's getting more money and men than MacArthur is. They complain about the JCS more than the Nips sometimes."

Occasionally he mentioned the battles of Vella Gulf in the Solomons, the Allies' occupation of New Georgia and progress in New Guinea. If he had heard the Japanese executed 100 POWs on Wake, he didn't say so.

One day Mom said, "You must have learned a lot of strategy by now."

He shrugged. "The fact is, fighting in a battalion's like playing football. You need concentration, have to know how to play your position. And avoid penalties. These tackles who go for the neck instead of the ankles can cost you a game in penalties." He smiled in a strange way. "But on Nip-infested islands, we don't have to cope with the whole hankie on the play routine. That's for sure. The Nips would get a hell of a lot of them if we did. Take my word for it." He shook his head as a fierce look crept into his eyes.

Mom looked worried but forced a quick smile. "You're a very good quarterback, we know that much."

Daddy reverted to the subject of his command training. "I'll do something right, and a CO notes it in a report – says his recommendations will be good for my career. What career? I want the war over and me out of the army."

"Me, too," I said.

# CHAPTER TWENTY-FIVE

ADMIRAL YAMAMOTO knew the world had shuddered over Japan's attack on Pearl Harbor, but considered himself the sword of his emperor who death alone could unsheathe. Though haunted by premonitions of death, he toured South Pacific naval bases to build morale, amid top-secret arrangements. He even wore khaki drill to make his presence less conspicuous. On April 18, 1943, code signals went out informing Bougainville base commanders of his upcoming visit, as he took off from Rabaul, New Guinea, in a Mitsubishi Betty bomber, escorted by six Zeros.

Our code breakers intercepted the signals, and as his plane came into land at Kahili Airstrip, a P-38 fired. Yamamoto's plane burst into flames, sending fragments in all directions as it careened toward the earth and crashed.

Smoke billowed up and finally down, leaving embers to melt on leaves and earth. An army lieutenant on patrol found the bodies, including Yamamoto's, and loaded them onto bamboo stretchers. A guard of sailors took the bodies in a sad ceremonial parade to the top of a nearby mountain, covered them with palm fronds, and ignited a fire. It circled upward, its sparks dancing on the wind, smoke rising like a departed ghost. Soon Yamamoto's ashes flew to Tokyo.

When he heard of the brutal murder of the great admiral, Emperor Hirohito wept, then became enraged, and his rage condensed into loneliness, hard and black as coal. He told his wife this barbaric murder reflected Roosevelt's viciousness, and to retaliate, the emperor would order the assassinations of all American Pacific commanders, beginning with Nimitz and MacArthur. But how? He needed a satori, an illumination, to show the way.

For a month, he kept the national hero's death secret, and then announced a state funeral, only the twelfth in history for a non-emperor. I'm told no one in memory had been so deeply mourned in Japan.

Hirohito's people considered him above life and death, so he sent his mother to the funeral. Perhaps honoring a hero who died for his country would inspire a little patriotism in her - for a change.

On the day of the funeral, the wind came up, the spring leaves sighing in it. Torches blazed and samurai stood at attention as the cortege slowly moved through the streets of Tokyo. White silk and linen banners fluttered from square bamboo staffs forming gates for his soul's passage to heaven. Shinto priests in white robes and Buddhists in saffron yellow beat metal drums and shouted incantations while karate masters dropped to one knee in prayer.

# CHAPTER TWENTY-SIX

A<small>T</small> F<small>ORT</small> L<small>EAVENWORTH</small> Frankie celebrated his second birthday with a parade review. Summer came with thick, hot air and a tangerine sun that hung huge, its edges turning red. Mom bought a fan to "keep us all from spoiling."

One day Daddy took us for a walk around the base. Men along the road stuck their chests out, saluting him.

"At ease," he'd say.

I began to feel shy around him, but my confidence bloomed when he explained, "They're saluting me because of my pretty daughter."

I didn't know whether to believe him, but I did know we stood in the center of all that mattered.

From then on, Frankie saluted Daddy every time he walked in the door, and he toddled around after the football that accompanied us to the fort.

On a starless night, I dreamed Daddy stood nearby. I wanted to join him, but first I had to climb a steep bluff, taller than the one at Cayucos. The ground began to loosen and give way as I walked, feet sliding clumsily until I woke up to the humid embrace of morning. Later I fainted at school and came home with my forehead hot to Mom's touch.

The pediatrician arrived. "Rheumatic fever," he said.

Aunt Lenore sent her recipe for Billy Boy's milk toast. The aunties sent a gold cross on a chain for me to wear around my neck. Just like Mom's cross, only smaller. Daddy sang to me, told me stories, and held me until my fever broke. Remorse touched his soul, and he wrote in his diary:

"My poor Pooksie. Maybe I should stay home to protect her. Go into essential industry instead of fighting overseas. But I can't. A gate has closed behind me."

On November 11, 1943, soon after the Battle of Empress Augusta Bay in the Pacific, Daddy graduated from the Command and General Staff School as a Major. We drove back to the Bay Area. I gave myself over to the traveling process, seeing the nation encapsulated in the car window. White wooden houses with green roofs stood surrounded by fields of precious crops; farmers kicked mud off their shoes or pulled up weeds. Frankie pointed at other cars and practiced new words, wiggled around hogging the back seat, or pulled my hair when I ignored him.

I planned to have a talk with Daddy when we got home, a "sensible," one, as Mom would say. We should return to our first house with the sand box and let the war take care of itself. Since everyone called the Japanese dumb, wouldn't they all fall into the sea very soon and drown? Or something like that? In any case, they weren't really any business of Daddy's. A couple of times I floated the "our old house" idea, but Mom changed the subject without actually admitting she and Daddy had already sold it.

Sometimes she fell into a gloomy silence, while Daddy patted her knee and told his corny jokes. When he felt irritable, he complained about "the brass." Occasionally he became remote, preoccupied, and I wondered what he thought.

At other times he did talk about the Pacific War. "It's prosecuted from Washington, or, as some say, 'by parasitic bureaucrats in Washington.'" He sounded cheerier when he said things like, "Our pilots have bombed the Aleutians, Wake, and New Georgia Islands, to name a few."

Along the road, red and white Burma Shave signs bloomed in clusters of five. Each of the first four signs, placed one hundred feet apart, contained one line of a four-line couplet. The fifth advertised the shaving cream. For instance:

Don't lose your head
to gain a minute
You need your head
Your brains are in it
– Burma Shave


When we arrived home, we went to pick up Jeep. At the aunties,' he ran around in circles yelping with pure joy. Homesick and bored, he'd chewed part of Aunt Marie's petit point rug.

At Aunt Lenore's, Juanita spoke in sentences that took a long uncomfortably time to finish, but soon she brightened and told Frankie and me a story about Uxmal. The bad ant takes bites out of the moon making it smaller and smaller until Tou, the Sun God, replaces it and the moon becomes round again.

These few days at home were the final furlough before Daddy shipped out. In the morning, he would go walking with me, enjoying the day's first breath, the birds' wake-up calls. He pointed out grass growing along crevices, the geometry of a shadow that changed, or silvery clouds as they formed and re-formed.

He and Mom acted uneasy, as if fear contaminated the air they breathed, the water they drank. Mom didn't complain about picking up his discarded clothes now.

I pleaded with him to stay home but knew he wasn't going to when the flag went up on our house. Blue and gold star service flags hung from gold cords in the front windows of homes across the United States. They had fields of white bordered in red, and, in the center, a star. A blue one designated a family member overseas; gold signified that a father, brother, or son was killed in action.

Daddy's orders came: report for departure in forty-eight hours. I felt a thump of something inside, even though I expected the news. My face and hands became stiff, my body heavy.

"Don't look sad, you have such cute dimples when you smile." Daddy tickled my cheek, put on his army hat at the same angle as MacArthur's, speared a package of cigarettes with a knife, and thrust the knife in his mouth.

"I shall return," he shouted, with his arms flailing wildly.

We reached out to each other across our anxiety and hugged with the force of desperation, and I went to bed, slept for about an hour. Then my eyes flew open, and I climbed into my parents' bed next to Daddy. I could feel his breath along the side of my cheek. Not wanting to wake him, I lay there, loving the warmth of him, the sound of his sleep.

Later that day, he put jumbo olives on the ends of his forefingers and called them puppets named Punch and Judy. Then he took Mom shopping and bought her gifts she still has: a hand painted scarf, doeskin gloves, a pink silk robe trimmed with fluffy feathers, and silver knot earrings. She showed them to me, touching them hesitantly, and Daddy wrapped the scarf around her neck, arranging it carefully.

Forty-eight hours later, the morning sky shone pearl gray, turning the neighborhood walls creamy. I came into my parents' room, and Mom lay on her side with her legs pulled up and her head on Daddy's chest, while his arm rested on her in a protective gesture. His head bent over her face as if to reassure himself of her well-being. Frankie toddled in, we climbed into the bed and cuddled, even Frankie, who got into the spirit instead of wiggling.

Finally Mom went downstairs and cooked bacon and eggs for us, and I shared mine with Jeep, who wolfed down his morsels. While clearing the table, Mom began to cry and didn't stop. I started crying, too. "Please, Daddy, I don't want you to leave me. When will you be home?"

"I don't know, Little Monk." Then he stroked the back of my neck, "Everything will be OK," he said, but his usual appetite for life's richness waned, and a sadness shone in his summer blue eyes. Did I also see fear in them?

He went into the next room and produced a hidden arrangement of roses, lavender, and forget-me-nots, handed it to Mom. She set them in a vase, and, still weeping, got a pair of scissors and snipped off a lock of his hair that she put in a pink porcelain box.

We climbed into the de Soto and drove along, surrounded by the East Bay hills, the air overhead, glittering, infinite. Mom kept one arm around Daddy's shoulders as he drove, and with her free hand, she kept smoothing back her hair, her favorite gesture always, along with replenishing her lipstick. Heading for Ft. Mason, we parked along the Oakland estuary and climbed on the ferry to cross the bay. Seagulls wheeled overhead.

"Flying goats," Daddy said. "They'll eat anything from any picnic leavings to the eggs of other birds."

Mom tried to smile. My chilling dread deepened.

The rain let up, and along the horizon, the sun gave forth all it could; its path on the water widened, a bright path, golden. As we stood on the deck looking toward San Francisco, we watched the buildings grow larger, their reflections quivering on the water. The noises of the city sounded muffled, like remembered music.

The ferry pulled ashore, and the familiar scent of Hills Bros. Coffee greeted us. Sea lions barked their welcomes. When we reached the pier at Fort Mason, Daddy gathered us in his arms, said good-bye, and turned toward the troopship, moving with his usual grace. Even among all the other men, he looked incandescent. I squinted to see him better. People around us wept, and Frankie started crying too in the reflex way that toddlers do.

Daddy paused on the troopship, stood still, and, outlined in a soft light, raised his hand to us in farewell. The air glistened as if a telescope brought everything into unusually sharp focus, and I felt the salt breeze ruffle my hair, the moisture on my mother's hand. This is wrong, I thought. I wanted that ship to stop and let my father get out, go back to the beach with us. But it glided slowly away from us. Puffs of smoke rose from its stack while it headed through the Golden Gate into the hell that lay thousands of miles away. The ship became a speck, and the speck disappeared.

"I love you, Daddy," I called.

Mom swayed as she stood on the platform, watched the troopship disappear with an expression of despair mixed with intense love. Then she turned, and we walked away. Though surrounded by people, she seemed so alone; nobody ever looked more alone. I wanted to help her, but did not know how.

# CHAPTER TWENTY-SEVEN

OUR SUPER-COURAGEOUS AVIATORS scored again, this time flying the longest strategic mission of the war – seventeen hours from Australia to Borneo. They attacked the oil refineries and returned to a welcoming crowd singing "The Star Spangled Banner."

Enroute the Gilbert Islands, our marines and the allies paced the decks of ships, paced and listened to the hours passing before they assaulted Tarawa Atoll. There, the Japanese had built an airstrip, and Nimitz wanted it. An Imperial Commander bragged, "A million men in a hundred years could not take Tarawa."

Nimitz planned a new strategy, which set the precedent for the rest of the war: use amphibious tractors as troop carriers. He appointed Major General Julian Smith to lead the assault on Tarawa, and Smith decided it would begin on November 23, 1943. A coast watcher told him to postpone the attack for a month, when the tides would be more reliable, but Smith ignored him.

Not surprisingly, disaster awaited on landing day. The tide receded, exposing coral reefs, and the ships ran aground, forcing the men to wade through a killing rain of bullets and mortar shells as they moved forward to face the enemy.

A Tarawa beach photo reached the press. This, the first published photo of American casualties, created a huge uproar, as horrified citizens faced the sight of dead boys blanketing a beach, their flesh pierced with hellish shrapnel, limbs strewn over the sand.

Mom saw them and read in the Chronicle:

"Our men fell, and the gasps of the still living emanated in an eerie hum from the mass of bodies, the sound diminishing until it faded. In bitter silence, the survivors bade farewell."

After seventy-six hours, we took the atoll, but the Japanese killed nearly one-third of the allied assault force. The survivors demanded revenge, and they devastated the enemy who'd killed their buddies. Only seventeen of the forty-five hundred imperial defenders survived when the flag with its blood-red sun finally came down.

After Mom saw the Tarawa photos, she changed. A shark's fin of anger rose to the surface of her mind. How could old men far away in Washington DC throw away these young lives?

When Alice told her about a "deserter," a soldier who ran away, Mom offended her by replying that she didn't blame him.

I pretended to concentrate on a puzzle of a rabbit with a hen while I eavesdropped. What choice did I have? Secrets make children feel worse than the truth does.

To this day, Mom treats us to a stream of political "truths," but otherwise avoids telling her children too much. "I waited twenty years and then said one sentence," she likes to say. The sentences are perfect, of course, as she takes so much time to polish them.

That day, during the war, I thought about Daddy's assignment. The worst thing about having him gone was the mystery. What did he do in the blue Pacific that I saw from my window? He lived beyond the flat line on the horizon, the fine line that separated two worlds: mine and his.

I wondered about the "deserter" Mom discussed: why all the fuss? If the deserter kept running on one of those islands, wouldn't he just fall into the sea? And turn into a shark snack?

Often I got mad that Mom didn't tell me more about the war, but at the same time, I didn't like the way she discussed it with Aunt Lenore and her friends. She always ended up upset after these conversations, but they were part of a grand story, a story to fill the emptiness.

She phoned Aunt Lenore and talked about the Tarawa pictures for nearly an hour.

"Forget them," her sister replied. "Sometimes forgetting's a great achievement."

"That it is." Mom groaned.

* * *

After Leavenworth, Daddy's troopship returned him to the Guadal-canal garrison, and he found the men changed. He wrote in his diary:

"Guys who used to have laughing faces have developed that soldier's

122

stare. Waiting with hope becomes exhausting, especially when a man sees the jungle first thing in the morning every day for more than a year. Some have an insolent sluggishness, which probably means they'd rather provoke fate rather than remain here."

He wrote Mom:

"You're probably in more danger every day walking up and down stairs than I am here. I keep organizing football games. The men are great competitors – champions.

"Are you keeping up your diary? You'd better be, because some day I'm going to write about my war in the Pacific, and you'll be the home-front point man."

One night he dreamed he walked along a beach, and he wondered if he was on his own coast or a Pacific island. The sky blazed with bright sun that turned the sea a vivid blue, the sand white, and the horizon clear. The shoreline curved. Every cove became more luminous, and from the sky burst heavy light, like quicksilver. He looked up the shoreline and over his shoulder, but saw no one and heard no sound except the soft slosh of the surf. Still, he had the sensation he should watch and listen carefully.

His feet began to burn, but he saw the rocky coastline ahead. It loomed dark but for an opening in its base with a faint glow inside: a cave. As he moved closer, the glow became brighter and more radiant; it beckoned him, and he wanted to enter, but stopped, terrified. Something looked unnatural. The interior of a cave should be dark. Turning away, he tried to run but woke up with perspiration glistening on his neck and face.

\* \* \*

At home, a howling siren's shriek woke me up, and lights went out everywhere, blanketing me in an eerie darkness. Air raid. I dove under the bed. When the lights came on again, I knew it was just a drill, but pulled my bedroom curtains tight, for fear some light might seep out

123

and a hidden Japanese would see me and kill me.

The next morning, my friends and I, worried about bombs, ran to school fast, and neighbors, as usual, spread two fingers in the Victory sign as we passed by. Along the way, we saw quail and cotton tail bunnies vanishing into the shrubs of a vacant lot, and, near fishponds, frogs leaping into hiding places. A crow flew overhead.

In a brown bag, I carried pimento sandwiches plus carrots or radishes from our victory garden "for a balanced diet."

Today at recess I jump-roped the longest and played on the jungle gym. Recess made me feel so good, that the world was good too.

At home, Mom seemed gloomier than ever. As time went by, she missed Daddy more, not less. He was the powerful connection, and being without him again took its toll. Confusion burrowed in and marked a mood whose changing face kept her off balance.

She wrote in her diary:

"I think of my childhood as if trying to recall a book I read or a movie I saw. But Frank – I remember him with such intensity it sometimes makes me nauseous. Lately I fight a need to be alone. The thought of seeing anyone besides my family feels like staring into an overhead light. I try to keep my hope, since without it, I'd be on the next train to oblivion. I know that."

She shut her diary, interrogated me, and then Aunt Lenore arrived in a beige sweater set and skirt, plus pearls. After Mom poured some coffee for her, she began whining (like she told me not to do). "Pooksie just came home from playing jacks with the Grim Preacher's staggeringly spoiled Belinda, whom she now calls her best friend."

Aunt Lenore stirred some cream into her coffee. "Is Belinda as bad as the mother?"

"Need you ask? She looks like Shirley Temple – all dimples – but bursts into floods of screaming tears if I ever say no to her. Pooksie gives me these 'see what a nice child I am by comparison?' stares and tenderly takes Belinda's hand."

It made me mad when Mom talked about me, especially right in front of me.

Aunt Lenore laughed. "Little Miss Good Ship Lollipop. Pooksie will get tired of her, in my opinion."

No, I wouldn't. She had a pet parrot who could say, "Hi, there, Mama Kingfisher," and, in her back yard, a pond as green as Lake Merrit. More than that, we had fun playing together. Mom needed to learn to have fun. It would be good for her.

A week later, Mom peeled a green apple in one continuous spiral while Jeep curled up in a circle and dozed for a few seconds, moved a few feet away and dozed a while longer, then repeated the procedure. They waited for me to come home from school. I was late, and Mom began to feel ill from stress, as she often displaced her anxiety about Daddy onto Frankie and me. Finally, I injudiciously came in clutching a kitten, gray with white paws.

Mom raised her paring knife. "What have you done?"

"Belinda's mother gave it to me. Isn't she nice?"

Mom eyed the kitten with loathing. "Belinda's mother can take it right back. It has a sneaky expression on its face and will kill the birds in my garden if it has the chance. Cats are dreadful and the natural enemies of babies."

I said crushingly, "My brother's not a baby anymore."

"The cat's glaring at him. Besides, it will run away. They all do. Temporary shelter and food: that's all they want."

"It's just a kitten. And it likes me."

"You don't know what you're talking about. It will soon grow into a cat, and the cat will gain the upper hand with you. It would be underfoot all day, pouncing on all of us, shredding the furniture. And adult cats have bad breath, you know."

"I thought you said it would run away." Then, to negotiate, I added, "It can play outdoors with the two cats next door."

"It's a kitten; they would kill it in no time. Besides, Jeep would resent the intruder."

Jeep wagged his tail and began licking the kitten's fur. I smiled at Mom.

"OK, Pooksie, I'm the one who resents the creature, and we're taking it straight back to Belinda and her mother. Naturally, the Grim

Preacher couldn't consider tedious inconsequentials like my raising two children and a dog by myself."

"The kitten's a present for me. And I don't think you should call Belinda's mom the 'Grim Preacher.' "

Mom scowled and put her hands on her hips. "I'm sure Belinda and her mother will be enthusiastic about having it back. When your father comes home, he will deal with this sort of thing, but right now I have to do everything."

"Daddy will buy me a cat."

I began to cry, and the kitten began to tremble.

Mom wrapped it in a warm towel, spirited it with Frankie and me into the car, and drove to Belinda's. There, the maid approached the car, and Mom explained her mission. We waited while the maid tried to decide whether to take the kitten back or not. Then Mom got out of the car, the kitten escaped the towel, and we departed with the maid still chasing after it.

I glared at Mom. "I'll talk about you at 'share and tell' tomorrow."

"It won't be the first time." Her eyes looked inward, as if contemplating a riddle I knew nothing about. "Anyway, get used to it. I'd as soon own a rhinoceros as a cat."

The next day, while I practiced raising one eyebrow, she lit a Camel and telephoned Aunt Lenore as usual. Outside the window, the handyman, flecked with sawdust, banged his hammer, unhurried, as he built a sand box for Frankie.

Mom spoke while her cigarette developed a tenuous-looking ash. "Can you hear the hammering in the background? Is it driving you crazy?"

"No, not really."

"The handyman's eyes get shifty when I ask how long it will take him to finish. I'm paying him by the hour."

Aunt Lenore laughed. "Tell him you have so much money and that's it. Say if he can't build a sand box for that amount, you'll find someone who will."

"Right. There are so many carpenters around."

"Very funny, but there's no point letting him take advantage of you.

The few workers available have become insufferable."

"That's the truth. Didn't you go to a play last night? How was it?"

"Not bad."

"Something numbing or life enhancing?"

"The leading man tried to do everything much better than anyone else. It got boring. At one point he said, 'I can smell money from a mile away and find a lie in the quiver of a nostril.' What a dope."

"You should be a critic. Work for the Chronicle."

"My husband says the same thing, as a matter of fact."

"How is Billy Boy?"

"I'd prefer you to call him 'Bill.' "

She went on to explain that he'd started to study accounting books, deeds, debts, futures, and deductions, learning techniques which would someday give him title to all he surveyed.

Undoubtedly a masterstroke.

"That's good news," Mom said.

She later wrote that she marveled at her sister's gift for the inaccurate précis.

Eventually, stifling a yawn of boredom, Mom got off the phone and went to the window. The man building the sand box stopped working and slouched against a tree for a cigarette.

Mom diverted her angry eyes away from him, turned to me, and said I should apply myself more in school.

I had. I applied myself to jumping rope, the jungle gym, and crossing my eyes. Plus share and tell. "Let's write Daddy," I said, by way of changing the subject.

Mom let me dip the Venus fountain pen in the inkwell and squeeze the rubber pouch to fill it. I wrote:

"Hi, Daddy. I look out my window at the sea an wundr what you are doing. Love, Ann."

Mom wrote:

"In a couple of hours, we'll be feasting at Lenore's. The weather's amazingly warm, but I read about these horrible storms where you are. Try to stay dry, sweetheart.

"Went Christmas shopping in San Francisco last week. The guards around the bay have chased away the poor bird watchers. I guess they'll have to stare at inland species for the duration.

"Frankie's wilder than ever, and Pooksie runs to and from school like a small creature fleeing at the sound of a twig-snap – she's afraid of enemy bombs. Her friends are the same way.

"At the moment, she's drawing you a picture of Jeep. He's over his I-am-a-cat phase and has concluded he's a retriever. Hoards things in the basement, barks at the cats when they slink around. Lenore allows me to lean on her strength, which, though given freely, has its own sort of weight. I live for your letters. You live on a foreign island worlds away now, but I try to keep up my spirits. It's hard."

She sealed the envelope and stared out the window at the horizon, just like me. Missing her husband, she prayed for him. Then she fed and bedded Frankie and me, washed and stacked the dishes, swept, and organized breakfast so it would be easy tomorrow. Not a morning person, she wished she could arise around ten o'clock and have Daddy bring her coffee in bed along with her Chronicle.

As usual, she turned on the radio. Unbearable. On a few small Pacific atolls, men wore gas masks to disguise the scent of rotting flesh. Neither side took prisoners anymore. She preferred not to consider the alternative.

The week before Christmas, the aunties, Frankie, and I went to the "Nutcracker" ballet, while Mom helped at the Red Cross. Later she decided to visit Lake Merrit in Oakland alone and watch the ducks fluff their feathers and sail on serenely while the sun began to set. She loved it there, drove around a little before parking, and then walked through a grove of trees. The wind rose, and she felt a sudden menace. Her knees melted, but she had to get away. Turning around to go home, she looked into the evil face of a man closing in on her.

She began to run faster than she ever had before, afraid to turn, but hearing the man's footfalls, feeling him. Faster she ran, dizzy, out of breath, her chest burning, trying to get around the next bend, but his hand, a terrible hand, covered her mouth. She smelled his sweat and felt his breath, as he grabbed her purse and disappeared into the trees.

Desperate, she called out, and a policeman appeared. "Are you all right?"

Her voice shook. "He took my purse with my car keys and the keys to my house.

"Get in the squad car. We'll find him."

He caught up with the thief, handcuffed him, and put him in the front seat, with Mom in the back.

"Be glad I came along," the policemen said. "There aren't many of us around these days, what with the war. Most of the men have left to fight somewhere."

When Mom returned to Clarendon Crescent and the aunties brought Frankie and me home, Aunt Marie asked, "Have fun on your big day of independence?"

"Sure," Mom replied, and said good-bye. Then she called Aunt Lenore. "I hope you can stop by for a quick Manhattan." She got out the Four Roses whiskey.

# CHAPTER TWENTY-EIGHT

EMPEROR HIROHITO had a drawer lined in black silk where he arranged his rubies in rows, as the Chinese did their small jades. The Chinese would open the drawer and contemplate each jade to soothe the mind in much the same way Tibetans gazed at Tankas with rows of deities, each with a different color combination. Today the emperor followed the same ritual, gazing at every detail of his rubies as he tried to calm himself before meeting with his military leaders.

They arrived, took their seats, as wind chimes rattled on eaves, and dark clouds stole the sunlight from the sky. A servant appeared carrying a Satsuma plate decorated with blue, gold, and white waves; he passed the emperor's unworthy guests carrots carved into goldfish shapes and radish roses, and a second servant followed him with thin strips of white fish arranged between vertical rows of bean sprouts, grapes, grapefruit, and a confetti of chopped peppers. They rested on a jade plate from China inscribed with the words:

"Hard rocks are eroded by soft water, anger by a kind word, all of life consists of complimentary opposites from which derives its energy."

After eating their fill without apology, the emperor and his commanders moved to the map room, where they proceeded to disrupt his digestion by dishonoring him. Amid reports of defeats, they once more accused each other of blunders, as usual stopping just short of putting each other to the sword. On their faces hung forced smiles still; they continued to hide their true thoughts behind ceremonial ritual. Yet they tracked enemy progress with little red flags on maps with a dishonorable air of defeat, their eyes rarely connecting with the emperor's. Only bickering among themselves and pouting brought them to life.

The distinctly tight-faced emperor kept jumping up, stabbing the maps with his finger, and demanding explanations "to learn how to avoid future disasters."

Victory seemed ever farther away, like a glimpse of Mt. Fuji through a snowstorm. During today's meeting, several recommended surrender, rather than following the old custom of sitting outside the Gate of

Heaven, chanting apologies for their mistakes, and then committing seppuku by slashing their abdomens.

Tojo called them "calculating old women," while the emperor leaned over and rubbed his back, crooked from curvature of the spine. He said the word "surrender" made his back go into spasms; to lay down arms would be sacrilege.

After the meeting, he wrote in his dairy, "The commanders avert their eyes while I study them. Do any of them possess honesty when it comes to assigning blame?"

# CHAPTER TWENTY-NINE

THOUGH TEN MONTHS had passed since the Japanese evacuated Guadalcanal, many still lingered in the jungle to hunt and kill, so Daddy had some terrifying skirmishes. But he still felt a shadow, a sense that destiny eluded him. If he had to fight this war, he would prefer glorious assault battles, rather than combat patrol.

His brave, upbeat letters hid his nightmare existence, but his diary revealed more:

"Last night I tried chatting with a man who'd lost his buddy, but he turned his head and looked down. Then he raised his hand for silence, or to say it didn't matter; life was, after all, merely a foolish trifle.

"It's not. I know that, and I try to keep the enemy abstract in my mind. I don't wish real harm on any human being. Anyway, I gave up on talking to the man, went to bed, and dreamed of falling. The air whooshed by as I went down, and picked up speed, spinning, feeling the air, blistering at this velocity. I called out for help, a faint, fading cry that died in the wind. My mouth dried to sandpaper, pain scorched my eyes, and my chest burned as the speed advanced, heading for the moment when I would die before hitting the ground below. Resignation grew heavy, and I kept falling, trying to see something below, besides a dark emptiness.

"Awakening in the night heat, I tried to recall some aspect of the dream, but what? I needed to unravel something I sensed about it that wouldn't go away. All my loves, my dreams, my experiences have yielded knowledge, and this one contained knowledge as well, useless unless I could decipher it. Life has a way of watching and listening. My own life lies beyond the war if I can just get to it."

He digested another K-ration Christmas on Guadalcanal, listening to Tokyo Rose on the staff radio, repeating her usual phrases like, hey, GI Joe, why are you out here? You should be home at the farm walking with your girl and getting your chores done, then sitting down to supper. Or singing carols around the Christmas tree.

Again Daddy wrote in his diary:

"Charlie Harrington, of course, madly adores Tokyo Rose, talks about her day and night. She's kind of funny in a dark way, but some of the men here no longer respond to humor or hope, react only to the incessant jungle motion. I think of my little family. The idea of leaving them alone makes me fear death for the first time. I came here to protect them, not abandon them. It is love on earth that makes us unwilling to give up this life."

\* \* \*

Late in 1943, the submarine USS Lipscomb Bay sank in the Solomons. In Oakland, Thomas Sanchez, kicked inside his mother's swollen womb. He soon slid free from her birth canal at Oak Knoll Hospital. A Lipscomb Bay crewmember, Thomas's father, lay beneath the sea by the time the baby emerged into our world. The boy grew up to write "Rabbit Boss," described in the New York Times as one of the 100 best books of the twentieth century. He had war on his mind when he wrote in a different book, "Mile Zero":

"Ah! You are beginning to understand, beginning to see in darkness. My child, it is this simple: love will kill us all."

# CHAPTER THIRTY

IN THE US, WAR WEARINESS now spread a dangerous pall. Munitions factory workers went on strike, and Congress balked at more military appropriations, although the armed forces needed new recruits, double the number of nurses, and more equipment. Getting them became ever more difficult for Roosevelt; he needed to win this war fast. He knew it.

Mom and I didn't like the strikes; they made us mad, as Daddy needed all the help he could get. My friends and I weren't selfish like the strikers. We collected scrap materials and newspapers for recycling, saved pennies and nickels to help buy War Bonds, and prayed. Helping gave us a feeling of greater human worth and value; we played on the team, and pride in our cause made us proud of ourselves. Our buoyant optimism prevailed.

Around March 1944, I began cutting pictures of Elizabeth Taylor out of magazines, planned to change my hair color and style to match hers, as her beauty dazzled me. Mom did a pass on my hair dye plea, typically resisting my better ideas. Lucky Elizabeth's mom was clearly different. She even gave her daughter a horse.

I spent a lot of time wiggling a loose tooth. Belinda and I competed over who could blow the biggest bubble with Fleer's Double Bubble Gum. Whenever I got a double, she'd get a triple, but I usually got the best of her when it came to playing card trades.

Aunt Lenore bought me a Lanz dress, blue cotton with white lambs, hearts, and birds trimmed with rows and rows of white rickrack. Don't tell me clothes are as pretty today. I won't believe it.

Sometimes when Mom lunched with Alice or worked at the Red Cross, the aunties took care of Frankie and me. A series of crushes on movie stars gripped Aunt Nini. Right now she palpitated over Errol Flynn and George Raft. Still, she always prayed for Rudolph Valentino's soul, but by the time she died of old age, she'd replaced him with several others, including Cary Grant, and taken an interest in an attractive newcomer, Clint Eastwood.

Aunt Marie called cable cars "string boxes" and automobiles "contraptions." She spoke in a simple, direct way that made me find within myself the truth of what she believed. A great fan of Ralph Waldo Emerson, she often said, "You cannot do a kindness too soon, for you never know how soon is too late."

Uncle George cheerily recited the "good news," as he called it from the Pacific, glorying in the Allied invasion of Burma. I asked him if he'd ever fought in a war, and he lapsed into silence. He and the aunties lived their own private society with a code of silence; they asked Frankie and me about our lives but never discussed themselves.

# CHAPTER THIRTY-ONE

IN THE PACIFIC, Daddy received dangerous new orders. A troop ship, the USS Kota Barde, moved him toward a filthy beach of Cape Gloucester in New Britain Island. Time ticked away slowly. Days became hard to distinguish one from the other, and things that happened a day or a week before seemed equally distant.

The men in the hierarchy tried to snap to attention, saluting and clicking their heels on unsteady decks, and even when the sea roiled or the sky burst open to let rain gush down, these same men with the same soldiers' faces said the same things and performed the same duties. Every hour, every day they tried to believe they mastered their situation. If they harbored unsoldierly thoughts, if the troopship felt like a prison, they never said so. Daddy watched them and marveled.

He looked out at the endless sea, green playing fields with goalposts a distant dream. Brass bands, pom pom girls, cheering crowds in the bleachers – they began to seem unreal, as if someone else experienced them. War no longer felt like a football game; here some men in the end zone never got to their feet again. Win or lose had morphed into kill or be killed.

On April 23, 1944, he debarked in Cape Gloucester, where rugged terrain alternated with waters infested with swarms of disease-bearing mosquitoes that whirred around, eager to suck human blood. The insects bore malaria, typhus, and dengue fever, but if he swatted one, a lurking sniper might hear.

Garrisoned troops eventually turned sour. Victories brought elation at first, but the feeling diminished as the months passed and the white crosses thickened. Rumors of entire enemy squadrons encamped here and there made the rounds every day, and men returned from combat patrols drenched from wading through water up to their necks or ill from vector mosquito bites. Daddy suffered the dread; it burned in.

One night, bullets rained down, barely missing him, and he dove into the sea for safety, staying underwater until his lungs felt like fire. He pushed himself up to the surface and gulped the air. An undercurrent caught him, and he tried to swim, knew he could – knew he could walk, even, if his feet managed to reach the ocean floor below the undertow. Fighting the sea never worked, but he could try to float, trust its mercy.

Behind him, a great wave swelled up and washed over him in a kind of embrace, until he felt the sea become part of him. His thoughts blurred as he let it all go, gave up for whatever part of a second, maybe a whole one or two, and then he came back. Shocked, he found himself still alive in the sea.

A new wave pounded down, and water filled his tortured lungs. His leaden body needed a moment of rest, but his eyes became sharper, as if a pale moon shone through the evening fog above the surface. The tide turned and pushed him toward the shore again, and he no longer heard the sound of gunfire. "Thank you, God, for letting me live," he whispered.

He described the incident in his diary but didn't want to scare Mom by telling her, so instead he wrote:

"Our CO's regular army, a real finger snapper who believes the only way to succeed is to infuriate people. His eyes bore into us with a drill-like stare, and he always has purple patches on his face. They move around from cheek to cheek to forehead, sometimes neck. He claims to be fighting for humanity but hates people. He loves the thought of them, particularly those he's just met. Cockeyed. But I guess he's good at asserting his authority, a major game in the army.

"The insects bother us more than he does and seem far more worrisome than the Japanese, who must be recruiting strays they find in back alleys. The only samurais around look like antiques needing repair. A friend in intel told me they try to teach the cutting-bodies-in-half trick, but if the recruit gets impatient, he might stick his sword in the master's eye, or – I hate to think.

"They're still desperate enough to sneak around raiding our K rations. By the way, those have not improved. Maybe the idea is to make them so bad we become fighting mad. I'm so preoccupied with the things I want to eat when I get home that I'm writing a list. As of today, it's six hundred pages long. A few highlights: pineapple upside down cake, roast beef, and strawberry shortcake.

"We cleaned out Cape Hoskins Airdrome in less time than it takes to mow a lawn, and we have some new toys: bazookas – portable anti-tank rockets. Big and bad, you might say. We're making the Japanese leave hurriedly wherever we go.

"This morning I had a shave, a welcome respite.

"Some of our men are true warriors, and others should be home tending victory gardens. The sage counselor of our unit scares me; I'm afraid I'll find him lying on his face. He doesn't have a wife and children. I can't imagine living through this war (with the food, especially) without you, Pooksie, and Frankie.

"I look forward to holding you, the relief of being with you, my solace, in our house with its flower gardens, porch, and wonderful smells coming from the kitchen – our beloved home, over the hills from the bay, with its fireplace and furry blankets on the beds. You know how I feel about you. And I always will."

# CHAPTER THIRTY-TWO

IN JAPAN, Emperor Hirohito tried yet again to reason with his twisted mother. She continued to scribble inanely about peace, her latest haikus deploring the vast emptiness of war, the void, the blackness. One referred to him as riding an upside-down wooden horse. He should reciprocate by writing her a haiku about a hamster that thought she should be emperor.

He wished she would act like other mothers and busy herself marrying off relatives. However, she'd long since moved to Numazu on the coast, accompanied by her peace faction, whom the emperor regarded as toadies chewing on her hem. Her treacherous circle of adherents grew every day.

Today she claimed she acted for the emperor's own good — that the Americans would prevail and hang him if he protracted the war.

He tried to defend himself, pointing out that only a few years earlier, such famine ravaged Japan that farmers had to sell their daughters as prostitutes or factory slaves. Then he reminded her that he'd looked outward to survive, forming the Greater East Asia Co-Prosperity Sphere. But Roosevelt immediately interfered, instead of minding his own country's business. The meddling American president called the sphere "a long-winded way to say colonial empire." The irony! Caucasian colonizers leeched away Asia's assets for centuries without apology.

Ignoring these facts, the Dowager Empress called Japan a leaf in bitter winds and ruminated again about red blossoms of blood.

Though disciplined in public, the emperor threw tearful tantrums around his traitor mother when she fulminated. It happened again today.

After his mother left, his wife soothingly urged him to ignore her. Nagato drew him into a conversation about the old days, when she would don a white kimono and walk along the shore with him, gathering marine specimens from tide pools. Or they would play a round of golf on the palace course.

Lately she spent her hours writing letters of condolence to the families of the war dead. Unfortunately, the blunders of his imbecile commanders made it impossible for her to keep up, so she began sending printed cards bearing the imperial seal.

However, the emperor still believed his country would triumph as it had triumphed against Chinese invasion attempts throughout history. He led his people, while his brothers sat around indulging themselves. Except for Chichibu-san, a man marvelously adept at gathering real treasure.

Though she didn't deserve it, he loved his mother, needed her approval. If she didn't appreciate his life of sacrifice and service to his country, how could he go on?

\* \* \*

MacArthur moved his headquarters from Brisbane, Australia, to Lake Sentini in New Guinea. Under his leadership, the army covered an astonishing one thousand miles to cut off enemy supply lines, and the atmosphere calmed considerably. Scorched walls marred towns, but citizens hiding under rubble began to emerge.

MacArthur further refined his brilliant "Operation Cartwheel" strategy. Beginning April 24, his men would advance along the coast of New Britain, cut garrisons off from each other, and destroy Rabaul's supply lines. Meanwhile, Admiral Halsey's South Pacific Area units would move through New Georgia and Bougainville as they converged on Leyte and Luzon in the Philippines.

Daddy became part of New Britain's leapfrog operation. The samurai there reacted to the slightest movement, sound, or scent. One day a bullet flew closer than ever to Daddy's head. It seemed to approach slowly, and when it passed, he felt light, as if rising upward in the sky. Days seemed topsy-turvy to him, as he groped through the hours trying to find the enemy. He wrote in his diary:

"I'm doing my part. We all are, and by picking off these small garrisons, we're cutting off Rabaul's supplies. I hear the enemy's withering away there. Thank God for that much."

Operation Cartwheel succeeded so well that over 100,000 Japanese troops eventually "withered away" in Rabaul, a euphemism for starved to death, despite resorting to cannibalism.

\* \* \*

Today Mom and Alice would have lunch at El Prado again, but San Francisco seemed different than it used to. The palm trees and flags around Union Square remained the same, but seeing all women and no men in the streets felt creepy to her. Every lamppost sported a poster of Uncle Sam holding his forefinger to his mouth and saying, 'Loose Lips Sink Ships,' and from every building hung a huge American flag.

At lunch, Alice adjusted the little animals called stone martins that she wore around her shoulders and smoothed her beige suit. "FDR told the Joint Chiefs he needed to settle the key Pacific strategy issue: whether to advance on Japan's Home Islands from the Philippines or Formosa?" she said.

Mom nodded. "I gathered something like that was up when I read he'd he called a meeting in Hawaii for July 26, to discuss the Luzon — Formosa issue."

"Right. With the Pacific commanders – MacArthur and Nimitz. I hear that Nimitz and Admiral King, you know, from the JCS? Well, they took the meeting seriously, but MacArthur called it 'a political picture-taking junket.'"

Mom laughed. "Probably a little of both."

"Did Frank get the peanut brittle you sent him?"

"So far I haven't heard a word. As usual, I used the official address: Hdq. 40th Division Field Artillery APO40; Postmaster, San Francisco. I always ask why I can't send food direct, but the postman, officer, or whatever looks at me as if I were a lunatic. Maybe I am. At this point, it wouldn't surprise me."

"We're all ready for Bedlam at this point," Alice said. "Wonder how Roosevelt's meeting will go?"

\* \* \*

In Honolulu, MacArthur arrived half an hour late for the meeting, riding in Hawaii's "longest car," preceded by a shrieking motorcycle escort. He got out, waved at onlookers, swept up the heavy cruiser USS Baltimore's gangplank, and told the president that a commander belonged by the side of his fighting men.

"That's why I'm here, Douglas," FDR replied, knowing MacArthur expected to be called "general." The President asked Nimitz to speak first.

Nimitz and Admiral King wanted to seize Formosa, occupy the strait, and use the island as a jumping-off site against the Home Islands of Japan. Meanwhile, MacArthur would attack islands in the Southern Philippines. After securing Formosa, the navy would supply air cover while MacArthur moved northward to Luzon.

MacArthur sprang from his chair, described himself as a soldier who would hold a horse if so ordered, and then insisted on bypassing Formosa in favor of Luzon.

Nimitz retorted that invading Luzon first would be long and bloody. Too many soldiers would die without air support from Formosa.

MacArthur dismissed the "long and bloody" idea and swore that the battle would last no more than five weeks. He also promised that casualties would be "minimal." Then he raised his arms to form a "V for Victory" and reminded FDR he'd given the people of the Philippines his word that he would return.

Roosevelt replied, "The war should be prosecuted on your word, sir?"

This question prompted an extended MacArthur outburst.

Hours later, the meeting ended, and Roosevelt asked an aide to give him two aspirin, adding that in all his life, nobody had ranted at him the way MacArthur did.

# CHAPTER THIRTY-THREE

AT HOME, my schoolteacher made me stand in the corner twice this week for "disrupting the class," though I did the class a favor, in my opinion. When she phoned Mom to tattle on me, Mom took her side, as usual. I sat through her "importance of school" lecture, one I knew by heart, like her other favorite, "share with your little brother."

When she wound down, I considered my hair, started to wonder if I really wanted bangs anymore. Maybe Daddy would prefer my hair to look more grownup when he came home.

Early spring extracted new buds from barren branches, and across the bay from Clarendon Crescent, fresh flowers bloomed on Mt. Tamalpais. More than ever, I felt restless and angry that Daddy still faced danger in the Pacific when he should be with us. Me, especially.

And Mom's mood hadn't improved, quite the opposite. She constantly reminded herself that she could neither stop the war nor change Daddy, but knowing he did the only thing his nature allowed no longer strengthened her as before.

She wrote in her diary:

"During the past three weeks, a kitchen pipe broke, the vacuum shorted out, and the washing machine quit. My potted ivy's turned yellow, and I got a flat tire. Replaced it with my last spare. I'm worried. Tires are scarce. I called to place myself on the plumber's wait list – will have to stand by for weeks. I try to keep the house half way repaired, work on Frankie's ABCs, pick up after Pooksie."

Men worked on our roof, repairing damage from rain, and their laughter came floating down, along with occasional shards. The neighbor, apparently worried one would hit the Siamese cats, pleadingly coaxed the cats to "Come into the house right now."

They snuggled down on their perches and flicked their ears at each other.

Today, Saturday, Mom waited for the mail, stiff with hope. A letter arrived from Uncle Arthur, who wrote:

"Since Frank went overseas, mother can only feel despair, the end of possibility, and father looks away with an air of uselessness when I try to talk to him. They only show signs of life when I remind them to pray for Frank."

No sooner did Mom finish reading the letter, than Aunt Ruth called to describe a new love. To amuse Daddy, Mom recorded the whole conversation in a letter:

"Here's exactly what your sister had to say, 'One minute he adores me, the next minute he says he's not the type to be housebroken.' She sounded perplexed, like someone who walked through a door expecting a party and instead found an old violin with broken strings resting on a deserted floor.

"'He's a type,' I replied. 'A cliché, as your brothers would say. I'll bet his mommy thinks he's adorable.'

"Of course, Ruth had an answer, 'But, sweet Mary-Helen, he's such a good friend to his past loves. They um – call him – and chat about their new men as if he were a brother. Isn't that – you know – a sign of a nice person?'

"I told her, 'He may be good at talking to ex-girl friends, but he's an escape artist. Likes them because he's eluded them. Call him Houdini.'

"'Well, I had coffee with one of his old flames. She told me he's nice and considerate every step of the way, but then he disappears. Always. Should I listen to her? Or is she just jealous?'

"'Ruth, listen to her,' I said. 'If you don't, you're beyond my help.'

"'He's in the army, stationed here, but keeps saying he wants to go overseas. Does he want to escape me?'

"'All I know is, you should be the one to do the escaping.'

"'I go back and forth. I swing against him a lot, and each time the swing gets a little farther away. And it takes longer to catch up to adoring him again.' She paused. 'Mary-Helen, why does falling out of love take so much longer than falling into it?'

"'It's exactly like gaining and losing weight. A weekend in the country can pack on five pounds, and it takes months to get them off.'

"Your sister sighed. 'That's the truth. Sometimes he acts as if I'm a prize, and sometimes he acts as if I'm a threat.'

"'He pushes and pulls at the same time. Probably thinks of himself as unique and deep. You need to find yourself a good man like Frank.'

"'Mary-Helen, you and he have all the luck.'

"'Yes, we do,' I said.

"I miss you, my love."

Despite her beauty and endless lovers admiring it, Aunt Ruth could not grasp the simplest things about men. She never did catch on, but maybe she would have, if she'd lived longer. However, we didn't know her fate then.

After Mom wrote Daddy, she called Aunt Lenore to discuss today's news: our B-29 Superfortress bombers flew their first mission. Bombed Japan's Bangkok railroad out of existence.

Since Aunt Lenore sounded preoccupied when Mom tried to discuss the planes, she sarcastically asked, "How's Billy Boy?"

Aunt Lenore skipped her usual "call him Bill" and proceeded to, "His mother arrived yesterday."

"She did? I didn't know she was coming."

"Neither did I."

"How's it going?" Not that she needed to ask.

"Apart from her constant criticisms, she told me a man could have many wives, but only one mother."

"What did he say to that?"

"Nothing. He just looked nervous."

"He should stand up to her. He's so lucky to have you. If I'd a chance, I'd – "

"He was the most romantic man in the world until I married him. Well, sometimes he still, um, but his ulcer – . His mother hints I'm to blame for it somehow."

"I'd pack mother's bags for her. She's making you shaky on your pegs."

"I wouldn't dare do that. But come to think of it – I don't know how long she plans to stay."

"Why not give her a deadline? Like ten minutes from now."

"It wouldn't do any good. She ignores me or treats me like a servant who needs to please its owner somehow. Her other trick: reminisce sentimentally about his ex-girlfriends."

"Maybe you should tell him he's free to leave a marriage which does not meet his mother's impeccable standards."

"I knew you'd react by saying something stupid. I never should have spoken."

"Sorry."

Mom said good-bye, stretched out on the chaise lounge, and began picking at her sweater cuff, fraying it.

I lingered underfoot, counting red and blue stars in the food-rationing book while Frankie pretended to be a pilot, and his teddy, a copilot. We didn't speculate about worthless men nestling in safety while Daddy . . .

Mom knelt and encircled Frankie and me with her arms.

That night we prayed for Daddy and world peace, as usual, and then Mom sat at her mahogany desk with a cigarette and a glass of sherry, and wrote in her diary:

"The children seem halfway content, so I guess I'm an OK mother. But I seem to spoil everything else. Lately I've over watered plants, overfed Jeep, who bulges with fat, and I keep repeating myself in my diary."

Though phone calls were rationed like so many things, the next morning, Aunt Ruth called again. "Mary-Helen, I felt a lump in my breast when I took a shower this morning. Don't tell anyone, even your sister. I know that when your mother died, she stepped into her place, but I insist on silence. I don't want people to worry my family, especially Frank. Besides, I'm sure it's nothing."

# CHAPTER THIRTY-FOUR

"CANCER." That much I heard. Mom tried to keep her voice down when she talked to Aunt Ruth, but her tears gave her away. From Mom's end, I could tell that Aunt Ruth had refused an operation for her cancer lump, as she claimed all surgeons except the butchers inhabited the battle zones. She'd found a "doctor" who could get rid of lumps with herbs and things. Over and over again, Mom pleaded with her to try surgery. Finally Aunt Ruth hung up without changing her mind.

Spring arrived, expanded in its warmth and beauty. Alice came over, so she and Mom reviewed what they'd read in the Chronicle. Mom managed to say nothing about Aunt Ruth, but I knew she wished she could. Instead they discussed the Allied navy, which continued blasting away at the Japanese on the blue waters of the Pacific.

"We overran Saipan, Guam, and Tinian in the Marianas, and beat the Nips in the Battle of the Philippine Sea," Mom said.

"That was good, but mistakes? I hear both sides made so many the battle could have gone either way. Still, two hundred Allied ships fought only sixty-four Japanese."

"How do you suppose the Nips keep their spirits up now? I mean, considering . . . "

"They fight with 'Yamato damashii,' a spiritual strength they feel will defeat us merchants. Spirit Warriors, that's what they call themselves. Ha. Monsters, more."

On June 19, 1944, the Allies ran out of patience and shot down nearly three hundred Japanese planes, losing only twenty-nine. One of our jokester pilots called the sortie, "The Great Marianas Turkey Shoot," and the name stuck.

Mom and Alice laughed as they discussed it, and I smiled "from ear to ear," as the aunties said. Shooting turkeys sounded much safer than battles with people. I could not have been happier. All my eavesdropping when Mom and Alice described the hideous battle conditions in the Pacific unnerved me. Once Alice shook her head sadly and talked about eager young men who imagined sunny, unknown lands, seas of glittering beauty. She spoke of their "courage, enthusiasm, and, most vital, their love of life."

Mom had replied, "But this nightmare war cuts them down; their lives drain away on these dumb little islands," and then they both started crying.

Now that the subject had turned to turkeys — at last, good news — maybe we could have turkey at Christmas again. I hadn't thought much of Aunt Lenore's venison, no matter how many fake "delicious" toasts went round the table last year.

I would weave turkeys into my share-and-tell stories at school. Some kids just brought an ordinary wishbone or something and told boring stories, but I made up mine. They involved an elf whose personality mimicked Frankie's, except that it included feats of magic. When an evil emperor or big bad wolf pierced the veil of his magic, the elf sometimes hid among the birds in my plum tree until the enchanted quarterback came to his rescue.

\* \* \*

The Turkey Shoot devastated Japan's air power, but the lords of the imperial navy found fresh inspiration from a pilot's act of courage. The pilot took off from the carrier Taiho, saw a torpedo heading for it, and dove into the torpedo, trying to save his ship.

The idea of asking pilots to sacrifice their lives had occurred to Admiral Yamamoto when he planned the Pearl Harbor strike, but it remained an idea only.

Admiral Takijiro Orishi taught teenagers how to fly the glorious katamici kogeki, one-way flight, or kamikaze mission. Divine wind, like the typhoon that prevented Kublai Khan's invasion fleet from reaching Japan from China. Kamikaze pilots donned hissos, "victory," bandanas, and "thousand-stitch belts." A thousand women each took one stitch, symbolically uniting with the pilot's sacrifice.

The pilots flew light, stripped-down planes loaded with explosives and crashed into targets, certain of rebirth as kami with places in the sun.

The night before his mission, a sixteen-year-old fondled his ivory

netsuke carved with a crane and lilies for luck. A small toggle, it originally attached to the cord binding of his grandfather's inro, a small red
lacquered wood container for carrying medications. Then he wrote his
mother a poem that has become a classic:

"My dearest mother, I am an empty dream
Like snow left on the mountain in summer.
I feel my warm blood moving inside of me
And I am reminded that I am living.
My soul will have its home in the rising of the sun.
If you feel sad, look at the dawn with all of its beauty.
You will find me there."

# CHAPTER THIRTY-FIVE

ON NEW BRITAIN ISLAND, Daddy thought, what will we do with all these islands and atolls we've captured? Put them on the yellow brick road to democracy? Never mind. The nations in the empire of Japan had to be liberated. He wrote in his diary about one wild day:

"A snotty second-guessing type got us into a trap, and when the shooting started, a couple of men dove like prairie dogs into the nearest ditch. Jake threw up on my sleeve. And we had the wrong damn maps. It's happened before. When it gets tough, everyone's on a first name basis. And no saluting. Nobody complains about outrages against Army Regulation 123 (re: the salute).

"The heat! Ridiculous. I turned into a sweathog. 105 degrees feels balmy, so now my brain switch can turn halfway on."

He received a letter from Mom:

"I'd like to be there with you instead of sitting here helplessly. What wouldn't I give to go out and kill the enemy myself? I often dream I enlist and find myself posted with you. Lenore could take care of Pooksie and Frankie. Yesterday I called the army recruiter, just to ask, but he treated me as a nuisance, the type that makes his long days longer. He almost suggested I get a hobby, so I gave up and went back to my Red Cross."

Daddy wrote back:

"My precious, we're managing without you, welcome as your presence would be. No. You would distract the men, and the enemy would take full advantage.

"Remember the name Chuichi Nagumo? Nip Pearl Harbor Commander? Plus Midway? Some of the guys trapped him on the southern tip of the island, so he led his staff into a hut, one of his henchmen set it on fire, and then they all shot themselves. Nip honor.

"We celebrated the news with some sake we found when the Japanese dashed off terrified and left it behind. For the first time in far too long, I have a hangover this morning. It takes practice to drink that stuff, but last night it really got me going on my jokes, and everyone laughed.

Ace comics like me need drunken audiences.

"The emperor must be in a rage and probably will soon order the rest of his commanders to follow Chiuichi's good example. Or maybe he should put them all to the sword himself. Apparently the big Japanese businessmen moan about financial losses. Those guys I described – Two years ago? Kuramakus. HRH emperor must think that they're cur-like snivelers. Many of his people plead for surrender, and some of them want him to step down. Imagine! A Son of God kicked out of office. I thought he spent his time sitting around drinking sake while people kowtowed before him with ceremonial greetings and asked if they had given offense, and if they should commit seppuku? But apparently not any more.

"Enough about warm and inspiring enemy comraderie. Probably due to last night's sake, I fell asleep and had a dream: you and I climbed up a narrow staircase in a lighthouse. The staircase had no handrail, and as I watched you move, I realized we weren't on stairs, rather a steep hill, part of a ridge, sort of. Below, little boys ran around playing some kind of unfamiliar game, and I asked you what it was. Then I woke up.

"I felt happy after the dream. Maybe I saw our future grandsons playing a new game. My love, we're going to hold each other soon. I'll see to it."

We knew that he would, and we expanded our victory garden, saluted the little flag in our window every morning. Sometimes Mom would let me help her roll bandages for the Red Cross.

\* \* \*

In Washington DC, a mirror-like murk glazed the Potomac, and the air crackled and quivered with heat. FDR, however, couldn't worry about the weather; he had to resolve the Formosa versus the Philippine strategies. Finally, he and the Joint Chiefs decided to let MacArthur attack the Philippines before Nimitz hit Formosa. Southwest Pacific forces would invade Leyte in the Philippine Islands on October 20, 1944, and Nimitz's third fleet would supply naval support. However, the air support Formosa could have provided would not yet be available with this timetable.

MacArthur had won in the end. In his map room, he studied the seven thousand islands of the Philippine archipelago dotting a thousand miles of sea. For the invasion, he would assemble the largest assault force of the Pacific war: two hundred thousand men from the Sixth Army under General Walter Krueger and the Eighth Army under General Robert Eichelberger. He couldn't transport them all at once, so they would debark every two weeks through January and February.

Before storming Luzon, he would land in Leyte, his first active duty post after West Point. Capture bases on Mindoro for air cover and lure the Japanese to the south while the Sixth Army landed on the long beach at Lingayen Gulf on Luzon, an island the size of Ireland.

Crosswinds often whipped the gulf, causing huge swells to rise, and behind the beaches stretched a maze of rice paddies and leech-infested swamps where swarms of vector mosquitoes hovered.

General Walter Krueger wrote later in "From Down Under to Dai Nippon" that MacArthur wanted to march into Manila in time for his birthday. Others confirm this assertion. He planned his quick advance on Manila, claiming the Japanese had 120,000 troops on Luzon when actually they had 262,000.

Daddy would be among the first to wade ashore, to face the largest force the Japanese had amassed during the Pacific campaign.

\* \* \*

On Clarendon Crescent, yellow butterflies rose, fluttering into the roomy places of my imagination. They could not charm me for long because I had heard Mom and Alice say that every time "our boys" went ashore in the Pacific, they won, but some Japanese troops always stayed behind to hide and kill.

Besides, their empire still stretched from China through the Kuriles, the Home Islands, Philippines, and Dutch East Indies.

As Mom and Alice discussed the still-huge enemy empire on the phone, I eavesdropped, as usual. What choice did I have? If I tried to ask

Mom anything, she told me to go out and play.

Later I sat on the porch and ate ginger snaps, washed down with minted lemonade. The citron yellow sky faded to lilac at the horizon; the garden trees cast violet shadows. Frankie's third birthday. Mom and I gave him what he wanted: model warplanes. Flying Fortresses, Mosquitoes, and the stellar Hellcats, which reputedly won twenty engagements for every one of the enemy's, and the Corsair, that the Japanese called "Whistling Death."

Frankie jumped up and down in eagerness to open them and vowed he would be a plane when he grew up. Not fly a plane, but be a plane. Daddy wrote him a birthday letter containing a story about Greenie the Toad going about his frog business until a fly came along, and the story became an action-adventure piece in which the wily fly avoided becoming Greenie's dinner.

Then Daddy went on to other subjects:

"I hear you play with toy soldiers for hours, lining them up in facing rows, and that your Daddy always wins. Great! But you don't need to learn to fight, because war will never happen again, and this one's almost over.

"The one thing I like about being here is the planes, and your wonderful mother collects models for you. Do you own a TBM-3E Avenger? It made history at Midway, but isn't the only plane in the sky. Here in Guadalcanal, the Douglas SBD-5 Dauntless does its fair share, too.

"Speaking of war, your mother tells me that you and Pooksie fight over Batman – that she tries to relegate you to the Robin position, her justification being that she's the elder. My pal, I can sympathize; your mother always did the same thing to me, even though I'm the elder. I made you a scorecard on the next page, and you and Pooksie can put down an 'X' whenever you are Robin. Your sister probably wants to be Even-Steven but just loses track.

"Take good care of her and your mother until I come home. They can be handfuls, I know, but right now you're the man of the house."

While Mom read the letter, I thought of Daddy's warm, low voice, his firm touch, and dark hair, thick and curly. Every day without him deepened my sadness. He and I had missed so many good times together that we would never get back.

Frankie flew the planes, "r-r-r-r-r!" and then let them crash onto the rug, "ka-boom!"

Mom retreated into the den for one of her hush-hush conversations with Aunt Ruth. I listened through the keyhole, as usual. Mom always ended up in tears during these talks, because she couldn't talk Aunt Ruth into finding a surgeon to remove the lump.

Later, a red-eyed Mom and Juanita took Frankie and his friend, Buzzy, along for ice cream sodas at the St. Francis Soda Fountain in San Francisco's Mission District. Aunt Lenore picked me up after school, as I didn't want to spend the afternoon with babies.

Mom wrote detailed descriptions of the day – partly in her diary and partly in a letter to Daddy. The rest she still remembers. She says she drove down Dolores Street with its rows of giant palm trees, and in the Mission District, the pallor of war evaporated. She inhaled the scent of chilies and watched men in curl-brimmed hats of straw roll their tacos and squeeze limejuice on them. Outside the St. Francis Soda Fountain, a norteno trio sang. Juanita and her gringos went in and ordered chocolate sodas, and Frankie said, "Let's bring my Daddy here when he comes home."

Juanita's eyes filled with tears, and she made the sign of the cross. A chill touched Mom, but she tried to shrug it off.

Next, they took Frankie and Buzzy to a park where they could blunder around on swings and slides. Mom could really feel summer coming on. It was in the dust off a dirt path, a girl in blue shorts lying on her stomach at the top of a rise, flexing her leg back and forth.

Frankie kept trying to climb a tree and falling down while Mom begged him to stop. I can picture her terrified face and Juanita's look of a magistrate as she announced, "Only he who does not mount, does not fall," and added, "The horse gets fat when master keeps an eye on him."

The following day, Mom bought a copy of Munro Leaf's "Safety Can Be Fun" and read it to her son. She decided to mail Aunt Ruth a copy as well.

# CHAPTER THIRTY-SIX

IN THE IMPERIAL PALACE, Emperor Hirohito listened to more dishonorable reports of the enemy's victories. Outside of the palace, afternoon yielded to evening, and a few desolate people walked the crooked and broken streets in silence, remembering their dead warriors.

The emperor tried to restrain his rage. Instead of apologizing, his commanders whined that the Americans had new tracked amphibious craft that waddled across coral reefs until islands seethed with their fighters. In 1944, the barbarians' pace had picked up, seriously undermining the Greater East Asia Co-Prosperity Sphere.

Hirohito kept demanding his commanders find some way, some place where Japan could win a real victory over the Americans.

By way of reply he heard stories of spirit warriors sleeping on corpses for warmth or stacking them like logs as barriers against the surging scourge Allies. And worse.

At today's meeting, a kempeitai intelligence officer described the upcoming Allied Philippine invasion. MacArthur, he said, possessed a devious talent, though he talked too much for a commander.

The emperor agreed and added that Roosevelt talked too much for a head of state. It seemed the Americans couldn't rush to the microphones fast enough. But one clear fact emerged: the loquacious MacArthur would have a large and well-equipped force. Only Yamashita could fend him off.

Premier Tojo, enhancing his reputation for consistency, opposed his old enemy's appointment. Moreover, he had the nerve to hint the Son of God should step down from his throne. Shocked, Hirohito contemplated accusing him of mutiny and treason, but decided on simply removing him from office. A member of the Yamato family would be better as premier.

In a matter of weeks, Saipan fell. The first prewar Japanese territory to be lost, it provided the excuse for Tojo's ouster. He "resigned" as premier on July 18, 1944, and Yamashita accepted the command of the armies in the Philippines.

The emperor sent him a golden silk sash embroidered with his

Yamato family motto that had shaped Dai Nippon for centuries, "A warrior should adhere to the Way of the Warrior, that is, death. It means selecting death, given a choice between life and death."

Next, the emperor followed the good example of the Nazis and deposited more Golden Lily funds in Swiss banks, ones that ranked in Zurich's then super-secret establishment. Even though Hirohito thought of Swiss moneymen as just soulless instruments of chicanery, they did business properly; in return for large deposits, they gave honorable pledges of silence and kept them.

He wrestled with the problems of meeting his payroll, which can make a man feel more like a seal balancing a ball on the tip of its nose than an emperor. He paid his traitorous mother a huge allowance, which he needed to cut back. She could learn to see the beauty in everyday life rather than extravagance. He visualized the flurry of haikus she would send about a starving old woman betrayed by her son.

He decided upon further economy measures: Imperial Commanders needed to eat rice gruel instead of beef teriyaki, and they needed to turn the comfort women loose to seek clients in the streets. POWs would have to starve, as most of them had become weak and useless, anyway.

\* \* \*

On New Britain Island, Daddy's 40th Division moved to Arawe to relieve the 112th Cavalry Regiment. With virtually no trails, he and his friends managed to push the enemy to the Gazelle Peninsula. The sun heated his metal helmet until touching it produced blisters, or rain trickled down, soaking his uniform. Sometimes he thrilled to the moment, the high level of endeavor. Other times he did not. He wrote in his diary:

"I see Mary-Helen glancing in the mirror to check her face as she walks by in that place and time before I was called up when everything we ever dreamed might be possible lay in front of us like airplane tickets to Paris."

On New Britain, Greer, the officer who stood on the bluff at Cayucos, fought with him side by side. One bloody afternoon, he suddenly shouted, "I'm getting out of here! I can't stand this rotting filth another day. Not another hour!"

Daddy patted his shoulder, "It's OK."

Greer fell silent and pierced Daddy with eyes reflecting the hollow confidence of the condemned. Three days later, an enemy mortar shell slaughtered him, and he tore at his uniform, begging God for mercy as Daddy held him and tried to console him. Greer calmed, adopted a mildly concerned look, and died mumbling a last jumbled phrase. It might have been about Pearl Harbor day - the ride from Cayucos to Fort San Luis Obispo when he and Daddy had such optimism.

Daddy removed Greer's dog tag, telling him his dead buddies would show him the ropes in heaven. Then he retrieved the bloody last letter in his pocket, rewrote it for the widow, and watched as the medics carried his friend off on a litter with an army blanket over his head.

"Mary-Helen, oh, God, Mary-Helen." Daddy said it aloud.

* * *

At home, the aunties invited Frankie and me to dinner. They filled their elegant mansion with dishes of candy and spoke of the Holy Family as if they were relatives. For guiding me, they possessed an abundant repertoire of "old sayings" which they quoted as the situation demanded. They covered their mouths when they laughed or whispered secrets to each other, and carried lace-trimmed handkerchiefs in case something made them cry.

Busy cultivating African violets, Uncle George rarely ventured beyond his potting shed except for horse races. Though no supportive evidence existed, he considered himself a superior judge of horseflesh. He had a huge mop of hair by pre-Elvis standards. As the hair would creep over his collar, the aunties would nag about cutting it. His hair's length became one of my preoccupations.

Tonight a pale linen cloth covered the table, laden with silver as if we were royal guests, not children. An epergne in the center overflowed with grapes, ivy leaves, and hydrangeas; the Aunties glowed from their Pond's cold cream regimen and avoidance of the sun; if they went to the garden to pick a rose, they wore hats with veils and gloves.

A maid named Hilda served dinner, responding whenever Aunt Marie rang her round silver bell. Hilda pulled her silver-blonde hair into a tight bun, and had an air of peeking over spectacles, even though she wasn't wearing any.

"We must clean our plates, considering rationing," Aunt Nini said, "we are using up a week's rationing tonight." Au courant with Hollywood make-up fashions, she wore smoky eye shadow. Aunt Marie kept glaring at it.

Uncle George nodded at Frankie and me. "You're good children to put up with my bossy sisters."

"George, you don't know how to talk in front of children," Aunt Nini said, and Aunt Marie agreed. "That's right. Let me, please, handle the conversation."

"I will handle it," Nini replied.

With care, Uncle George examined his cuticles, then smiled at Frankie and me and asked, "Aren't I a patient man to spend my life cooped up with two sisters who quarrel all the time?"

Beneath their circles of pink rouge, the Aunties' cheeks burned.

"We never quarrel," Aunt Marie insisted.

"That's right," Aunt Nini agreed.

Uncle George leaned back on his chair, an amused smile flickering on his lips. Then he gave me a serious look. "I know you worry about the war, Annie-girl, but it ended when we got rid of Yamamoto."

"Then why isn't Daddy home?"

"There's still a little clean up to do. But Yamamoto was the king of morale even more than the emperor. Japan held the largest state funeral for an admiral since Britain's for Lord Nelson after Trafalgar. Every mobile Japanese in the country attended except the emperor and Yamamoto's geishas."

"What's gayshas?"

"Women different from my sisters."

"How do you know?"

"A friend's son went to Harvard with Yamamoto. Said he could stand on his head for hours and do Japanese folk dances. Everyone liked him."

"I want to see your friend."

"Not possible. He's in heaven now. I heard all this third hand."

A third hand? I didn't ask.

Uncle George wiped his mouth and leaned toward me. "What do you want to be when you grow up?"

"An army nurse, but first I want a horse, a cat, and an airplane."

He shook his head. "Planes, no. They're dangerous. I know little girls equate Flyboys with movie stars, but don't fool yourself. It's best to keep your two feet on the ground. Same with money. Put it in something you can stand on, not a piece of paper."

The Aunties changed the subject to our table manners. The first challenge: teach us to curl our pinky finger when using forks and spoons. I worked on it, but Frankie banged on the table with his knife. The creator did not design any little finger of Frankie to be curled.

Aunt Marie raised her arched eyebrows at me. "When you chew, be sure to maintain a rosebud mouth, as if you were saying prunes and prisms."

"And when you use your napkin," Aunt Nini added, "just wipe lightly three times or less, and don't forget to keep your little finger curled."

"I'll have more soup," Uncle George said.

Ignoring him, Aunt Marie pursued her primary topic, "When you speak, Ann, you must be sure to modulate with pear-shaped tones." She sat tall in her chair and used her hands gracefully in conversation.

"My soup!" Uncle George repeated with emphasis.

Aunt Marie finally rang for Hilda. Between courses, the Aunties sat with straight backs, hands folded, and ankles crossed.

After soup, we dined on leg of lamb with victory garden roasted potatoes. I didn't object to the cramp in my little finger. It's just that I cared more about being brave than table manners.

After dinner, Uncle George drove us home, and I put on my white flannel nightgown decorated with little pink hearts and went to bed.

Soon I tiptoed out of bed and opened my window to look at the stars, the same stars my faraway Daddy saw at night. I sent him my love through the air, while downstairs Mom wrote him about her day as usual.

* * *

In Manchuria, the sky heaved, its dark clouds bottomless, when Yamashita, the Tiger of Malay, heard the long-awaited news. He would fight again. Tojo's excoriation had banished him from the action, but now, buoyant, he would serve his emperor as a man should. In Malay, he'd inspired strong loyalty and affection in his men, wading ashore with the first wave and facing the same risks of combat they did. Underneath his courage and tactical skills lay a will driven by intense belief.

At six feet two inches, he towered above most of his countrymen. His thick face and neck did indeed resemble a tiger's. He had a reserved dignity and eyes full of secrets and ambiguous history. His narrow nostrils and sharp features emanated a chronic disdain. Reports of his comments indicate he saw the defense of Luzon as a kamikaze mission, but he intended to tie up Allied troops as long as he could. If he could not save Japan, at least his strength in the Philippines could serve as a bargaining chip in the inevitable surrender negotiations.

He boarded a plane for Manila to replace General Rai Huroda, who would give him a two-day briefing on the situation there. Yamashita arrived without incident, and the heavy, frangipani-scented air felt thick when General Huroda greeted him. His contours conveyed softness, while Yamashita's body contained no excess flesh to ameliorate the hardness of bone and muscle. One look at the bleary-eyed warrior convinced Yamashita that Huroda's present state hadn't resulted from a half-hour of drinking. He'd been at it since lunch, or maybe breakfast.

Huroda said intelligence sources indicated MacArthur underestimated the size of Japan's Philippine force. Besides, the emperor would produce fourteen hundred planes for the Philippine struggle that MacArthur didn't know about.

Yamashita nodded. He planned to surprise MacArthur with both the aircraft and the method of deployment. They would launch from Formosa.

After the meeting with Huroda, Yamashita paced the floor in diagonal criss-cross patterns when he concentrated, his movements showing as much of the tiger as the man in their poised tension. He had little more than six weeks to create his strategy, and portents looked cloudy. He made his plans, then bowed to the small bronze Shinto idol he always carried with his belongings.

The Philippine flatlands held too many guerillas. A woman in a straw hat bending weaving a basket, an old man smoking under a banyan tree, or a teenager chewing betel nut might be a commando in disguise, so Yamashita would station his troops in the mountains. He would let the Allies ashore unopposed, surround them, and rain down fire, withering fire from above that would scorch their very souls.

He planned to split his troops into three groups: the Shobu, north of Baguio would track the rodents on the plains like, well, tigers; the Shinbu would protect Manila, and the Kenbu, in a mighty chain along Sacobia Ridge, would bombard Clark Field. Unlike the enemy, his men knew the terrain and would use his night fighting methods. They would swallow their prey.

Besides his own Luzon force, about 2,500 naval ground troops divided themselves between Manila, Clark Field, and Legaspi, under the command of Vice Admiral Dedshichi Okochi, a weary man who knew he'd launched a performance that would become irreversible as time went by.

Yamashita could be sure of one thing: the admirals would be as common as sea urchins around Leyete, and would greedily siphon off troops and supplies needed to defend Luzon. The navy planned a Shogo victory operation extending over more than six hundred miles of sea, and Yamashita knew flexibility counted. Unfortunately for him, however, the custom-worshipping admirals froze when it came to on-the-spot decisions. Still, they had some fancy gadgets: star shells like fireworks that illuminated the night, powerful searchlights, flashless gunpowder.

Yamashita carried two swords with him, one large and one smaller.

The single-edged blades, curved and tempered from steel, stood as the most lethal cutting weapons known to man. They shimmered in beauty from the tempering process by which men repeatedly folded the steel into thousands of thin layers. Sword sheaths looked like works of art, exquisitely wrought in gold, silver, and other precious metals. Only the most respected artists in Japan designed, fabricated, and decorated them with largely religious depictions.

Like MacArthur, contemplating a battle gave him a rush. The fever gripped him: the unbearable longing for victory, however impossible it might seem.

# CHAPTER THIRTY-SEVEN

PROUD OF KNOWING how to count, I kept asking how many days until Daddy came home. I turned the page of my calendar: October 1944. Halloween would come, and I would dress as a witch. Speaking of, I might add a new witch costume to my Christmas list when it came time to write Santa.

The list could be on the long side, as I'd been good, at least at home, this year. Sometimes I sneaked cookies between meals and did a few other wrong things, and I learned to put my foot down with Mom: no more cod liver oil and no more "Peter and the Wolf" at the children's symphony. After a big effort, I trained her to braid my hair. Belinda's mother stopped rolling her daughter's hair in metal curlers to achieve the Shirley Temple look and now braided it instead, but Mrs. Wilson, being a true artist, did a better job than Mom. When I said so, hoping she would try harder, Mom scowled. "I can sing 'Gaudeamus Igitur' in Latin and 'La Marseillaise' in French."

Although I found my braids imperfect, I still liked them and in-sisted Mom take my picture of them to send Daddy.

She did, and then every day I wanted to hear how he liked them.

"What? He still hasn't written back?" I would ask.

When no letter arrived, Mom's face assumed a deadly, level calm, as if she sensed that a wind could rise, felling trees, shaking foundations. Still, despite her loneliness and fear, she always looked immaculate: manicured, brushed, shining, her auburn hair pressed into finger waves, the gray of her eyes heightened with powdery black mascara applied with a small brush dipped in water.

Not realizing Mom's grooming constituted a small act of courage, I asked her why she fussed over herself so much, and she replied, "Don't you remember your father saying a quarterback needs to look the part when he leads his team onto the field?"

The next day, fog slowly burned off while she sipped her coffee and read the morning Chronicle:

"In the Marianas, we advance inland on Saipan . . . Our battleships shell Guam . . ."

Then she went to the globe, as usual, to try to find the spots, after which she walked aimlessly through the house, opening and closing doors, straightening ashtrays, and pinching dead leaves off house plants with sharp, disconnected motions.

She called Aunt Ruth in "secret" and had her usual pleading, sobbing conversation with her. As Aunt Ruth remained resolute, Mom called every nun and priest she'd ever known and asked them to pray for Aunt Ruth as well as Daddy. She lit three candles in church for her.

Aunt Lenore called. She'd given up malted milk in her quest to get pregnant, substituting a cup of green tea with every meal. Billy Boy had competition now: a dachshund puppy from Jeep's breeder, whom Aunt Lenore named Tinsa Bella.

Mom smirked, picturing Billy Boy indignantly hovering in the background while Aunt Lenore raved about the dog, making no mention of her husband's health, his eating habits, his accounting studies.

The father of the puppy, Jeep, brought over his leash, and gave us the stare. Mom scratched his back, but he resentfully waved the leash at her. Confident and correct, he led us on a walk for a block or so, his hindquarters wiggling. He made slow progress, as he stopped to sniff every tree, every female canine, every shred of paper, and whenever he spotted a male, he lunged until Mom jerked him back by his leash. Sometimes he paused to chew grass like a calf.

He began straining to be set free. Mom gave in, and he ran to a mud puddle and rolled in it, followed by Frankie, who splashed in it. He and Jeep always tried to see who could bring more dirt into the house. Once home, Frankie pointed at his father's photo and said, "That's my daddy," and banged into the table knocking the picture over.

I stuck my tongue out at him.

Pointing at me, he said, "Mom!"

"Tattle-tale." I made donkey ears over his head, then got Daddy's football and said, "I can make it spiral, and you can't."

I demonstrated, breaking an English porcelain vase in the process, and Mom said, "Pooksie, look what you've done! Stop and think. You must learn to stop and think."

Later she settled down at her desk, but the overhead light bulb pinged and fizzled out. After replacing it, she wrote Daddy:

"My darling, what do you do, how do you feel in the solitude, the damp tropical air? When I think of you stranded off in some dangerous jungle, my eyes moisten and my throat constricts.

"Every time we pass a phone booth these days, Frankie wants to go in and turn himself into Superman. He will be a star athlete like you one day, I can see that much already. So can everyone else. He runs around, climbs up trees. He's all smiles, giggles, and dimples, a boy born for singing his way through sunny mornings and lazy afternoons. You are, too. Soon, my love.

"I'm beginning to feel old now that Frankie's running around as fast as Pooksie. Why couldn't I have one placid child who liked to sit? Could the reason lie in my choice of husband?

"Pooksie's friendlier than ever with the Grim Preacher's daughter, Belinda. By the way, she showed up with renewed rows of curls today, so I may have heard the end of the braids.

"Every night I dream now. Every night. One way or the other, they're all about you, my precious. Sometimes I'm happy in them, sometimes terrified. Terrified, mostly. Usually I can't really understand them. They're always disconnected and irrational – fragmentary and unclear. Last night's was extraordinary. I saw footprints on a dark path in an elegant, straight pattern like a dancer would leave. Certain they were yours, I followed them, but they disappeared, and I woke up feeling your lips on mine. Truly. But only for an instant. I've never before had this exact experience of feeling a touch."

After finishing the letter, she turned on the radio and listened to the music, but the song, "As Time Goes By," depressed her. She switched the radio off and began writing in her diary. Her entries got longer and more replete with detail as she tried to comfort herself. She described the carrots from her victory garden, then the garden itself: lizards scuttling, chipmunks scurrying to the rhythm of her rotating sprinkler. Then she called Aunt Ruth again, but no one answered.

* * *

At the same time, the emperor insisted that the War Ministry in Tokyo issue a directive for the "final disposition" of prisoners, known as the "Kill Order." Showing a less than jovial side of the leadership, it told the prison staffs to guard POWs carefully until officials completed preparations for the final disposition. The POWs might die from mass bombing, poisons, drowning, or decapitation – whatever fit the particular situation. None must escape, and no traces should remain. The spirit of the order: be thorough.

# CHAPTER THIRTY-EIGHT

DADDY WOKE UP one October night, and not a foot away stood a lizard. It acted brazen, curious, and he began to love that lizard, all the lizards around. He tried to catch them and make them into pets when the action slowed. Soon he could tame them, let them sit on his arm or run around his room, tails swishing, or flexing up and down in that little push-up motion.

He received orders: he would be in the front lines, rather than the rear guard, when we invaded Luzon on Strike Day, code-named S-Day. He and 30,000 others from the Sixth Army would land on Lingayen beaches to face 250,000 Japanese troops. In the following weeks, an additional 170,000 Allies would land. Daddy's 40th Division would go ashore first as part of Lieutenant General Oscar Griswold's XIV Corps, establish a beachhead, capture the Central Plain, then join the Eighth Army arrivals for an assault on ground transportation and Clark Field. Next, Manila.

Fortunately, he didn't know how outnumbered they would be when he wrote home, "Kiss the children for me. I'm on my way to the big battle."

# CHAPTER THIRTY-NINE

ON CLARENDON CRESCENT, Mom read and reread Daddy's words, "I'm on my way to the big battle."

Every day fog rolled in, thick and heavy, like a man's wet sweater. For me, the distant Pacific turned a melancholic dark blue, and the caw of seagulls sounded like weird cackles. Food had no taste. We three lived in nervous symbiosis, Mom somehow trying to reassure us, as we huddled together waiting.

Today she went to El Prado for another lunch with Alice, and according to her diary, Alice looked composed, but Mom sensed an edge in her, the way a person senses a dentist's tool against an anaesthetized gum.

Mom said, "I wonder how we can bear it. I feel like an animal tied with ropes, caught with Frank in a trap." She reached into her purse and produced her latest snapshot of him. Before boarding his troopship in the invasion fleet, he sent her a photo of himself and his friend Wally Nickell standing by the troopship. Daddy still had his athletic slimness, his infrangible quality of poised tension.

Alice smiled. "Frank still looks like the quarterback."

The Philippine menace erased their spirits as darkness does day. Alice cheered Mom by calling Halsey's carrier strikes in the South China Sea "easy—breezy," but she didn't know about the Japanese plan to deliberately save their air force for the Philippine and maybe the Home Island invasions.

Mom and Alice could not really eat, so they pushed their Waldorf salads around on their plates and discussed what they read and heard. "The Okinawa raids? They're going well," Alice said.

Mom felt queasy. She stared at her salad in silence, realizing her husband would go ashore while imperial troops threw hand grenades and fired machine guns, with bullets making blunt sounds as they entered flesh, sending up fountains of blood. Sand would billow up, hitting men in the eyes and choking them.

No. She couldn't stand the thought. She shuddered. For a moment, she saw herself before the war, carefree, laughing at her husband's jokes.

"I wonder if any of us will be the same when the war finally ends?"

"In time. You know? It takes time. MacArthur? He lost fewer men during the past two years then we did at Anzio in Italy." Alice spoke as if that settled everything.

Mom nodded. "You know, I've had insomnia ever since Frank went to Fort Lewis in 1942."

"I know what you mean," Alice replied. "A nice snoring form next to you is reassuring, even when the form rolls over and takes the entire blanket."

The waiter brought a poached pear dessert, which remained un-eaten, and soon the two friends left the restaurant and headed for a green and white flower stand with yellow tubs filled with dark red roses, white chrysanthemums, and orange marigolds. Mom bought roses, gave them to Alice, and said, "Here's to seeing our husbands soon."

When she arrived home, she looked like someone who'd left her keys in a departing cab. She sat Frankie and me down and asked us to tell her about our feelings. My worries about Daddy deepened, as I heard and understood more about war casualties, so I told her we should just tell Daddy to stop fighting and come home now. Period. She tried to reason with me, then pulled herself together and made us a dinner of macaroni and cheese. I said, "I'm sick of cleaning my plate."

"Remember the hungry children in England," Mom replied, as she always did. "What wouldn't they give for your good food?" They could have it, as far as I was concerned.

The next day she had a Halloween party for me, as I decided to save my birthday party for when Daddy came home. I dressed as a witch, borrowing a black skirt from her.

Before the guests arrived, I asked, "Will Daddy come home for my party today? As a surprise?" I was tired of parties without him.

"We'll have fun," she replied, but she got that look on her face as if I'd strayed into a forbidden area, one too charged with feeling.

The party began. One friend hid under the pumpkin table, nearly knocking it over, the puppeteers had an alcohol-infused jocularity, and Belinda's mother arrived before the party ended, sauntering in with the loping stride of a dog, with amber beads dangling from her prominent chest. Belinda burst into tears and ran to her.

Mrs. Wilson turned her huge eyes toward Mom and fixed her with a hostile stare.

Mom said, "Belinda's crying because she came in second instead of first in the apple bobbing contest."

"I'm astounded you would say that's the reason."

"Her tears and the apples aren't unconnected," Mom replied. "In any case, I hope Belinda feels happier soon."

"I'm appalled," Mrs. Wilson replied, Flaring her nostrils dramatically, she turned and stomped out still holding her sobbing daughter's hand.

Aunt Lenore wanted to miss the children's party, and I could see why. When it wound down, she dashed in bringing two goldfish in a round glass aquarium. A mother-of-pearl mermaid rested on its bottom, and a strand of green sea plant wafted around her. Serious and tranquil believers in life, the fish swam round and round, mesmerizing me.

Later, Mom read me Daddy's letter, which had just arrived:

"I hear you're celebrating Halloween, little angel, and that you now have lead jacks and a sponge rubber ball, plus Fleer's Double Bubble Gum. I'm still an old-fashioned Wrigley's Spearmint Gum guy.

"Your mother also tells me you plan to be an army nurse who saves lives some day, so be sure to practice bandaging your brother and Jeep, provided they behave like good patients. Stroke their heads, hold their hands (or paws), and sing them songs. Do they know the words to 'The Sturdy Golden Bear?' I love you, my little angel. Soon we'll be together."

After hearing the letter, I felt better, so Later I wrote Daddy back decorating my letter with a drawing of Frankie with a pumpkin head. Next, I changed into regular clothes, went outside, and roller-skated.

Mom called out, "Don't go too fast on the slope. Try to show a little normal caution."

I laughed and sped along, as if I could go faster than the winding axle of time.

Later, Mom wrote Daddy:

"Your daughter skated into a tree. She's lucky to have survived in one

170

piece. Billy Boy says she needs discipline, that I should teach her who has the whip and chair (me) and who has the tail (Pooksie). I suppose he's right, in a patronizing way. I have to admit he's a more cheerful and friendly person since he started the accounting. And he's crazy about Frankie. Really good to him and a big help."

After she finished her letter, she turned on the radio and waited for the news, just as she waited for the mail, and waited for Daddy to come home. Her life: waiting – waiting, living in the past, living in the future, and finding the present unbearable. The news controlled her. The war controlled her. Was this freedom? She felt more like her country's slave.

In memory, she heard Daddy's youthful laugh, felt his nurturing devotion, relived their honeymoon, when, unhurried in the fragrant darkness, they made love.

Then, late at night, she called Aunt Ruth yet again. She hadn't been able to reach her for too long, and fear had morphed into panic. I remember hearing her say, "Ruth, your voice sounds so weak. I beg you to save yourself and go to a doctor. I contacted everyone I know in Southern California, and I have three recommendations of good ones who can take proper care of you."

Aunt Ruth apparently made her usual comments about "butchers" and turning into "a maimed freak."

Mom pointed out that millions of men fell in love with women who had mastectomies, but it seems Aunt Ruth didn't buy into this, as the conversation ended shortly.

Mom went to the kitchen for a cup of Ovaltine to help her nod off while Frankie and I tossed in our beds. Once standing at the sink, she wondered why she'd come to the kitchen? Oh, yes, Ovaltine, but it wouldn't really do any good. She complained to her diary about how forgetful she'd become and then wrote Daddy for the third time that day:

"My darling, God will be with you. I know it. Pooksie, Frankie, and I pray for you every night, and salute the flag every morning."

Aunt Ruth wrote letters in a faint scrawl and enclosed old photos:

Daddy riding his hobbyhorse, digging in the sand, and waving from his first car, the "Blue Flyer."

But one day, in her thirty-three year old beauty, Aunt Ruth drew a long last sigh and died.

At the time, no one told me. Uncle Arthur, by then Assistant Editor of the San Diego Union, kept her death out of the press and forbade Mom to tell anyone. She agreed. The memorial service and obituary could appear after Daddy returned. In the meantime, the tragedy would demoralize him, as he adored his sister.

Whenever I asked Mom about Aunt Ruth, she began to cry, so I sought other sources, such as Aunt Lenore and the aunties. After endlessly hearing standards about "little pictures," "pains in the neck," and "let us pray," I gave up and just stuck to my Hail Marys and Our Fathers. But my stomach felt queasy, and I didn't laugh much anymore.

I kept thinking of the last time I saw Aunt Ruth. She wore a luscious lavender sweater set and a gray skirt with a kick pleat front and back, but her clothes could not disguise the changes in her, the shadows within. I remember what she said to me, "Keep your life unpredictable, Pooksie. That way you'll have more interesting memories when you look back."

CHAPTER FORTY

Though fatigue stalked the Allied troops, they raced toward the Land of the Rising Sun, gaining territory in Burma, India, and some parts of China. After four years in the nightmare, some managed to retain their patriotism and hope, while others developed a contempt for people, for the world, for heaven itself. A man never knew when something would destroy his hope, and his best self would slip away.

\* \* \*

During this time, MacArthur and Yamashita became obsessed with each other, bound by a tie as strong as love. Each believed he conducted a sacred mission, possessed the heart and spirit of a conqueror, and understood the mind of the other.

If celebrity was MacArthur's natural milieu, quietude was Yamashita's. He would tell his troops to fight each moment as if it were the last. If they thought they had another chance to try, their minds slackened. The moment became all, especially that instant when the opponent made his move.

Alone at night, both generals heard the loud caws of birds in banyan trees, the buzz of insects, and the croaks of frogs in the humid, close heat. Fireflies lit dark skies. Each man's thoughts implicated the other, and each man focused on his enemy, deepening the bond between hunter and prey.

Yamashita flew to Manila, and MacArthur boarded the flagship USS Nashville. Their ultimate confrontation would be in the spirit of the laws of the jungle: equal contenders, both on their feet and on the same ground.

\* \* \*

Gripped by a brittle expectancy, Daddy and his friends joked, "Have a last smoke," when they passed around the cigarettes. As Daddy blew his smoke rings, he visualized the clean line from Mom's chin to her waist and the willowy body of her youth. She stretched across his imagination, and he could almost detect her delicate breath, feel her cool pearl earring grazing his cheek.

He wrote her:

"My feelings about the Philippine invasion are strange. I'm not a bit excited yet; it seems just like another tactical question on an exam, only this time I will know whether or not the solution works. The answer will be short and sweet, as the Japanese don't have many men or resources left. MacArthur says it will only last a couple of weeks. He may be (censored) but he's bright.

"You write that you worry about my safety, but I'm safer here than you are at home; I carry calm with me. And Luzon will be more like home. The Philippines don't really belong in East Asia; everyone's Catholic and has a Spanish name. One joke is that the country was part of South America that blew to Asia during a storm across the Pacific.

"In a few days, this year will be over. In the New Year, I'll see you and hear your voice. Mary-Helen, you make the stars appear in the daylight for me. I look at my snapshots of you and the children every minute, to remind myself whom I'm fighting for.

"The aunties send me prayers every week, short ones printed on little cards adorned with Holy Virgins, roses, lilies, the cross. I share them with the guys, and they carry them into battle. You write so faithfully, and, believe me, I appreciate it. Some of the guys greedily stare at photos of Betty Grable with a slathering desire because they have no letters. How do they endure it? They have so little and I so much – it's unjust. A man needs to feel he's not alone in this war, that somewhere someone's waiting, someone whose spirit watches over him. I keep my diaries with all my letters from you and the children in my footlocker. It's my treasure chest."

# CHAPTER FORTY-ONE

TOWARD THE END OF OCTOBER, enemy destroyers bobbed in and out of sight on the wind-streaked black water as legions of Allied forces convened in Hollandia, New Guinea. They would voyage twenty-one hundred miles to Leyete, whipped by killer storms. On the troopships, they passed their days watching the rain, its sheets deepening the solitude of those facing death. They tried to believe that after the war, they would have all the time in the world to make up for these days. The world with its music and dancing, movies and fine wines awaited. Their careers would flourish, their war records affording promotions or plum civilian jobs.

At the first light of dawn on October 20, 1944, the Sixth Army's armada moved into the emerald waters of Leyte Gulf and proceeded to its tip. The landing craft formed lines of assault waves, and the mother boats raised the assault flags. MacArthur watched from the Nashville, as waves of troops waded ashore, then donned his scrambled egg cap and trademark sunglasses, and waded ashore himself.

With a flotilla of newsmen gathered round, he stood atop a radio truck, grabbed a waiting microphone, announced he had returned, and rallied Filipinos to his side.

* * *

Yamashita gloated. MacArthur had behaved as predicted, and now the navy's Shogo operation would divide and conquer the US Third and Seventh Fleets at Leyete Gulf.

However, two nights later, in Leyte Gulf, history's last ship-to-ship gunnery duel ended with the virtual destruction of the enemy's Shogo fleet. The imperial force of four carriers, two battleships, five cruisers, and six destroyers virtually disappeared.

Admiral "Bull" Halsey wasn't there. The Japanese tricked him away from Leyte. He had a vital mission to protect the San Bernardino Strait, but the enemy lured him into abandoning the strait to pursue a decoy.

Nimitz radioed him asking for his whereabouts and adding that the world wanted to know.

When Halsey realized the enemy had duped him, he threw his hat on the deck and started sobbing. According to an aide, he resembled a walrus tangled in a fishing net more than a bull.

The Sixth Army went ashore and thundered across southern Leyete, an island drenched with rain and blood, until on December 1, only pockets of enemy resistance remained. Around Ormoc and the San Isidro Peninsula, the boisterous Americans lost twenty-two hundred men, the enemy, twenty-four thousand.

After seven weeks of continuous warfare on land, sea, and air, the Allies secured Leyete. Unfortunately, MacArthur miscalculated the strategic importance of an airstrips there, which did not, in fact exist, and, amid rivers of rain, could not be built.

\* \* \*

On New Britain Island, the Australian 5th Division relieved our 40th, and Daddy wrote Mom:

"Believe me, being bossed around by the regular army isn't anywhere near as enlightening as taking orders from you, as the brass lack your brains. So do I, for that matter.

"Today, the Aussies sashayed in, and they looked darn good to me. They're optimists, always saying, 'Things'll come right, mate.'

"They've got this gift for understatement. One told me we fight pretty well for American isolationists. If you're wondering whether we compared K-rations with the Aussies' food, the answer is yes. Their food tastes better. I volunteered to be a waiter if they would share, but no go."

\* \* \*

Occasionally, at two or three in the morning, the phone would ring on Clarendon Crescent, and the operator would warn, "Do not say anything to give aid or comfort to the enemy," indicating that the caller was Daddy. The ring always woke me, and I raced to Mom's room, lunged for the phone.

"Hi, Daddy," I'd say, and after sending my love and kisses, returned the receiver to Mom. We heard his voice, familiar and human, though distant and muffled, and we tried to discover from its tone how he felt. He'd speak to us for about five minutes, telling us that he loved us, and that we need not worry. Then the operator would cut us off.

Shortly before November 23, 1944, the calls stopped. Daddy and Allied troops from all over the Pacific converged at Borgen Bay, New Britain, for the invasion of Luzon. Dark clouds covered the sky, and ships stretched to the horizon like small black islands. In its immensity and solemnity, the scene awed Daddy, as his ship moved across the sea with the others, gliding in a long, brave stream. He never felt so small and overwhelmed. He wrote Mom:

"A seagull lay nearly dead on the deck, and when I picked him up, his tiny head fell deep into my hand; his breaths turned into shudders. I fed him water from my canteen, and soon he began to peck at my K-rations. We stuck together for a while, and next thing I knew he began to chirp and flap around. He's still my friend, flies near me, roosts on my shoulder, and flares his tail. Likes me to scratch his neck. He reminds me of my friend the Oahu parrot."

Daddy's ship moved via Huon Gulf, New Guinea, and the Manus Islands toward the Philippines. Kamikazes blasted ships in the invasion convoy, and Daddy saw the explosions, fires in the blue, flames rising higher, still higher, until the blue swallowed them.

As he waited, he saw scenes from his past, remembered his nervous excitement when, as captain and quarterback of tiny San Diego's "wonder team," he waited for the finals against Los Angeles. San Diego won, the first little village to cop a state championship. Yet now he felt as if he had always stood on this deck, waiting and watching. His past lay far away, beyond this ship, this vast blue sea.

\* \* \*

Stateside, Mom and I listened as reports of the Pacific War blared on our radio. A few years earlier, the broadcasts combined outright falsehood with grotesque understatement; now they sounded more honest. We heard phrases like "fierce opposition," and "heavy casualties."

Newscasters described a typhoon in the Philippine Sea, "high winds and giant swells . . . battleships pitched as high water broke over their massive forecastles . . . the long guns vanishing in the spray. Destroyers sunk . . ."

"Isn't Daddy in the Philippine Sea?" I asked Mom.

"Oh, no," she replied.

Liar. "He is too in the Philippine Sea. I heard you telling Aunt Lenore. You think I'm too young to understand. I hate that."

"Go out and play," she replied as usual, looking frustrated, close to defeat.

In our garden, white poinsettias blossomed; Mom didn't like the red ones. An esthetically definite person, she gave a thumbs-up or thumbs-down to every detail of her world. She tried to prepare for Christmas, while I wrote Santa, saying that he didn't send Daddy home last year like I asked, and would he please pay more attention this year? I didn't care about toys. He could give them to the starving children in Europe.

Frankie drew a picture of a model plane as a hint. He played with his collection every day, morning, noon, and night.

However, it just didn't feel like Christmas nearing. No amount of writing Santa or singing "O Little Town of Bethlehem" made the spirit come alive for us. The rain fell silently for days, obscuring the horizon, making the sidewalks wet, the streetcar tracks gleam, and the sky sullen.

Indoors, we listened to the splatter as heavy drops hit our windows. Mom assured me this would be my last holiday without Daddy, but I felt she called across a vast gulf.

"You're so young," she added. "So very, very young."

"It's OK, Mom, I'm old inside," I replied.

"Me too," Frankie said.

I glared at him. "You are not. You're nothing but a baby and a true tattle-tale."

"Worrying about Daddy makes you sad," Mom said. "Don't let your worry turn into anger."

Ignoring her, I went outside to jump rope. Jeep ran after me, tongue and ears waving. The neighbor's cats perched on the fence averting their eyes.

Later the mail came, and Mom got a letter from Daddy:

"I think of the curve of your eyebrows, your slender legs in silk stockings that flash as you move. I love our children and will call up their faces on Luzon. A physical longing to touch them gnaws at me."

She wrote back:

"It's hard to start this letter because by pooling the various bits of news, we believe that you will soon land in the Philippines. May God take care of you. I have a queer sinking feeling someplace deep inside. Christmas will be a tough hurdle, but I'll try to do it anyway for the children's sake, it all means so much to them. We'll do our tree all by ourselves. The three of us don't feel like sharing that with anyone, somehow."

Well said. We only liked to huddle together, with Jeep.

One night I had a dream I remember in detail because it returned and returned over the years and still does occasionally. In the dream, I walked through a high, arched doorway into a strange building. Inside, I saw Daddy's back as he walked away from me.

I followed him, and he hesitated, but moved on, his back still to me. Then he vanished, in one of two directions. I turned to the left, but couldn't see him; so I doubled back to the right, found him disappearing around a partition, and woke up, still trying to follow him.

I couldn't get back to sleep, but wanted to sleep for a year, I felt that tired. The clock showed six-thirty in the morning, so I got up and pulled open the curtains. Fog covered the sky, turning the Pacific horizon the color of pewter. As I said my morning prayers for Daddy's safety, I visualized the tilt of his head, his blue eyes radiating through his eyelashes.

In her bedroom, Mom threw on the clothes still draped over the chaise lounge from the night before, and emerged to nag me about brushing my teeth thoroughly, bathing without kicking and splashing, and picking up after myself.

At breakfast she jabbed her half-grapefruit with her spoon and pushed a toast wedge around on her plate. One of her eyes twitched now, and I thought it looked weird, wished she would make more of an effort to control it. Sometimes I practiced the twitch in the mirror. I could do it and then stop. Why couldn't she?

After breakfast, my friends and I ran to school, and when we arrived, Donnie made a plan for ending the war. He said, "We'll call, 'Come here, Japanese,' in nice friendly voices, and then when they come, we'll hit them as hard as we can." Then he gave his idea further consideration and shook his head. "No, we need to blow them all to pieces with a cannon."

He found a stick and brandished it like a sword, yelling, "Death to the Japanese."

With his freckled face and dimples, he didn't look as fierce as he intended.

Mom had the house to herself now, so she wrote Daddy:

"Enclosed find a picture of your new niece, Andrea. Isn't she beautiful? A cross between Virginia and Ruth. Arthur's mad for her.

"You and I must trust God. Trying to, but needing more information, I turn on the radio for the news, and then turn it off again.

"When you come home, the shower will be yours, and I'll buy you a waterproof songbook. I'll be all yours, too. I already am, have always been. For me there is you, and no one else, and never could be.

"I live for your next letter. The years you and I spent together are reality; all the rest is play-acting. I've relied on you so much. Where do I leave off and you begin? Our love gives me strength I never found before."

"The paper calls the Luzon invasion 'imminent.' No comment from Headquarters yet. It terrifies me; I keep wondering about you and am afraid to even consider. Oh, darling, never think you're not important; I feel that all four of us face deadly peril, not just you. But you have strength, courage, and intelligence, and these things must count. When you come home, you can have and do anything you want. Better keep this letter for proof. You're my whole world, and I don't like having you roam around in strange places. If only I knew what you do and think. My devotion will last as long as I do."

One night I woke up from a dream I could never remember, and I cried out, "Don't get off the boat, Daddy! Don't!"

Mom dashed in to reassure me and let me come into her bed, where I lay awake and offered God good deeds in return for Daddy's safety. I would give more clothes to the Bundles for Britain so the children there would not freeze, would clean my plate so they would not starve, even if the connection still seemed a little unclear to me. I would turn off the radio when Mom wanted, try harder in arithmetic, love all other people, even my teacher, smile at strangers to make them happy, and be kind to Frankie, even if at times he was the king of nuisances.

\* \* \*

Frightened and homesick, Daddy spent his loneliest Christmas in 1944 as his ship moved through dark water under a charcoal sky. He wrote in his diary:

"When I was ten, the circus came to town. The sound of calliope music hung like haze, and I ate cotton candy, the spun sugar melting on my tongue. I saw a booth with wood framed mirrors hung on panels, and I looked for myself as though in a picture of many people. I found another man's legs, the hips of a woman, and a confused-looking face – mine. I felt unsettled. Nothing seemed secure, nothing definite. It's the same here.

"I study Mary-Helen's photo, imagine her face framed in the window as she looks out, her elbows on the sill. Maybe that's my strongest memory: her youthful face in a succession of front windows along the road to war."

\* \* \*

Emperor Hirohito and Empress Nagako decayed in the airless bombproof shelter underneath the palace, using it as a conference room and sleeping there overnight. Darkness fell in every direction. He didn't understand why, after he was so gracious and progressive. He'd allowed visitors to stand on their feet after kow-towing, rather than remaining on their knees, especially if they brought him jewels. But only a few of the rubies he'd acquired remained.

Now his relatives claimed his mother was right all along; Japan never should have fought the Americans. She followed every sentence with, "You have destroyed your family and your country. If only you had listened."

His wife, Nagato-san had withered; her face thinned, lines deepened at the corners of her mouth, and a blue blood vessel throbbed in her temple. Her hands trembled and her voice quavered. Instead of practicing Christianity in private, she prayed aloud to Honorable Holy Jesus in front of everyone, holding endless one-way conversations with the God of the Americans. Worse, she sounded like his mother now, accusing him of behaving like a night driver without lights, no longer knowing how fast or where he was going.

The emperor felt adrift, never fully in the moment – any moment – embroidering the edges of life, no longer fully living.

The luxurious imperial palace and the bombproof shelter where he and the Supreme War Guidance Council now convened was a study in contrasts. At the palace meetings, they enjoyed light repasts of sashimi with miso sauce, pleasantly chewy octopus, and tall marinated bamboo sprouts, suggesting a rise to great heights. Now the emperor could not even offer guests water in his dim, claustrophobic new residence.

Continuing to fiddle in his fashion, he said the public must not know the truth about Leyete, though he did write about it in his diary.

His staff bunkered his diaries and records for safekeeping. Now they wanted to spirit him away to the Matsushiro Bunker. The three sacred Shinto relics – Amaterasu's mirror and necklace, the sword – should go as well, they said.

One kami plucked the sword from a dragon's tail for Amaterasu, and another gave her the necklace to wear for strength while giving birth to rivers and trees, birds and flowers. A third used the bronze mirror to tempt her out of her cave so the world would have light.

The emperor intended to remain in the shelter and keep the sacred objects with him. He often looked in the mirror, but it reflected back a blur, rather than his face.

# CHAPTER FORTY-TWO

ON NEW YEAR'S DAY, 1945, Daddy felt an unusual sense of peace, a belief that whatever fate lay ahead had been there all along, waiting. He wrote Mom:

"Happy New Year, precious. May this year mark the end of our separation. Censorship rules have been relaxed here; it will be easier to write.

"We've been at sea some time now, and I've had my fill of ocean voyages. On a ship, time seems unbending. Stopped in the Admiralties for several days. Every afternoon we gathered at the Navy Officers' Club to catch up on our long drought during Christmas and New Years. We had a wonderful time – first time in years we've gotten together and really let down our hair.

"Then we did a few days of amphibious training in New Guinea, and now we're on our way. We form a good-sized convoy, and for once the safety precautions, blackouts, and drills seem vital.

"Despite the blasé attitude we all assume, there's a feeling of tension. I trust Nimitz; his navy has performed remarkably over here. But nothing's perfect, and I'll be glad when we reach the 'far shore.'

"One feels so insignificant in an operation like this, but when the shells start to fly, it will be a very personal thing. And the stakes are about the highest I've ever played for. Remember that I love you, and I'll take care of my part of us.

"Think of the Philippines as bright islands where yellow frangipani grows and the nights turn navy blue.

"This will be my last letter until after the first act of the show."

His troopship moved through the South China Sea and Central Philippine Islands, but this time he experienced time as racing by, unlike before; it raced with increasing speed, never halting or allowing for a glance behind. He wrote in his diary:

"I sit for hours, while the nights become mornings and the miles fall away. Water, oblivion, sky, and water. Time seems more abstract now, the past more distant when I look back. Luzon. How much will blind me? Evade me? I've fought in combat patrols, but training's not a promise.

"The sea, the sky enlarge with time, and I shrink. My buddies and I are passengers on the same ferry, bracing for a ride, knowing we will fall off at different points. I see Mary-Helen hovering near me. Her image looks bright to me as a desert noon, and I want to reach for it."

A kamikaze hit a ship right next to Daddy's, and flames seared the night with bright red and gold. The scene assumed a monster configuration as men tried to survive, their bodies specks of black against the maddening glow. The smell of smoke and metal filled his nostrils, and the odd idea came to him that even Mom's perfume would never rid him of it.

He kept silent, feeling a sudden oppression; death could touch him soon. He would try to elude it, to fight, to fulfill whatever promise he had, but he could never have imagined anything like the sight of Luzon when it appeared on the horizon.

The island lay at the northernmost tip of the Philippine archipelago, and the island stretched about 450 miles north to south. Birds wheeled and hung above its hamlets, inlets, and deep green rivers, or called out from trees. The flowers, the leaves, and the sparkling waters caught the full light of the sun, as natives guided boats through gorges hacked out of the forests or tended rice paddies. At least half of the men stood ready to join the Allied troops.

"Strike Day," January 9, 1945, dawned with a light but broken overcast sky and regular, gentle swells whose great beds of foam broke against the white sands of Luzon's coastline. The guns of Allied naval fire support vessels bombarded the landing beaches, and then the lead troops waded through the swirling waters to the shores – among them, Daddy.

They seized the Lingayan Airfield, and General Krueger descended the gangplank of the flagship USS Wasatch to take command of the Sixth Army ashore. Immediately reporters infested the region. Krueger brushed their questions aside, "I would much prefer you drop the matter."

At sundown, Daddy, a euphoric man, wrote Mom:

"Well, my pet, it's the end of the first day. Strike Day began with the thunder of naval bombardment – harrowing and beautiful to watch. I saw the whole show from the bridge of our ship.

"I waded ashore about noon. Since then, the battle has been like a map plan at Leavenworth, but with sound effects and real ammunition. The Japanese apparently decided to withdraw and live to fight another day. Wonder what happened to their 'invincible spirit?'

"The Filipinos acted overjoyed to see us, and very hungry. Guerillas come out of the hills and fight with a strength and fury born of living under Japanese domination. They're a ragged band, some arriving unarmed and barefoot, their teeth stained with betel nut. Among them are well-trained soldiers with names like 'shooting squid' or 'blood angel.'

"All of them help and will dig a foxhole for a GI in return for a cigarette; the GI just sits and enjoys it.

"MacArthur smuggled arms to the guerillas right along, but the Nips purloined half of them. No matter. It won't do them any good. They're beat, and they know it.

"Never saw so many kids in all my life, cute and happy little tykes. It's been interesting to watch the natives returning to their simple homes. They fled to the hills when the battle started, taking the few possessions they could carry on their backs. The large families return, loaded in the carts. It's a pitiful sight; in most cases, their thatched houses have been reduced to ashes.

"Late in the afternoon, during an air raid, a shell fragment fell about ten feet from my hole. My friend Jim Williams worried a lot more than I did over that.

"Well, my precious, I'm happy and busy. Writing will be spotty for some time, but I'll do the best I can. Working about eighteen hours a day, but it's fun."

\* \* \*

Mom read Daddy's letter aloud to Frankie and me several times, laughing and crying, then phoned Lenore. "I never felt as relieved and thrilled in my life as today. Frank wrote that nothing's really happening on Luzon. My beautiful man will be safe."

"The Japanese have turned into paper tigers, in my opinion," Lenore replied.

"True! Now I really can face how scared I've been."

"Me too. You're a brave sister."

"Thanks. If something happened, imagine not being with your husband. You know – "

"When he died. Yes. That would be the worst part. But you don't have to worry about Frank."

"I would feel like I had died with him."

"Forget that kind of talk. He's fine, and so are you."

"I'm going to hang up, call the aunties and Alice and so forth."

Mom talked on the phone for hours, and that night felt so happy she let Frankie and me stay up late, playing and listening to the radio. We bounced around, as thrilled as she was, partly on our own, and partly because intense happiness is contagious.

Remembering the officer standing on the Cayucos bluff, Mom reentered that moment and wondered what her life would have been without it. What burden would the war pass on to her children? What questions? If the past four years yielded any wisdom, she did not know what it was.

At midnight she sat at the mahogany keyhole desk and wrote:

"My darling, your letter made our hearts rise in celebration. Whenever I pick up the paper or listen to the radio, tears come to my eyes. I'm saving all the articles in the paper and in Life Magazine, and Time too covering Luzon for when you come home. You'll be fascinated reading them and can fill in the details for me.

"Even though you will be returning any minute, please still drop me lines, just a daily sentence, so I know you're still safe. That's all that worries me and all I think about, even now, with the end in sight. Everything else in life has blacked out, and I pray only for your safety."

# CHAPTER FORTY-THREE

ON THE "BRIGHT ISLAND where the frangipani grows," Daddy crossed over into another experience. After an unopposed landing, the Americans faced devastating bombardment, as Yamashita's troops opened fire. Mortar shells blew the tops off palm trees, ruined roads, filled the air with steam and dust. The deafening sounds of weapons enlarged the grand and terrible events.

The screams of the wounded combined with the "banzais" the Japanese shrieked at the top of their considerable lungs, and sometimes they shouted taunts: "Hello, hello. Where are your machine guns?" or "Surrender, surrender. Everything is resistless."

Daddy said, "Give me a moment, and I'll think up a swift, incisive reply."

He tried to keep his friends alive with humor, joking that he'd seen MacArthur at battlefields riding in a jeep with Eleanor Roosevelt by his side. In his diary he wrote:

"Ammunition's running low. Strikes in the ports hamper transportation and unloading. Oxen-drawn carts loaded with pigs or chickens help move weapons, and water buffalo tote signal equipment for our field artillery units. A flu epidemic rages, but I won't catch it. I never get sick. Guns, blood, noise, and heat. Will I ever again be able to experience a day without dread? In battle, men learn who they are and what they can do. The chaos and exhaustion deranges some of them. Their teeth chatter, they scamper around aimlessly. One burrowed into a cave and got blown up. You figure they've gone beyond little lectures on the dream of peace."

Night fell, and he climbed into his foxhole with Jim. Feeling the warmth of a good man next to him made it better. They rotated eating, sleeping, and watch in four-hour shifts, saying nothing. One word, and a Japanese might hear and toss a grenade or satchel charges, incinerating them. Fires were forbidden, so they lit cigarettes with special black lighters and ate cold K-rations: cheese, crackers, lemonade powder.

After breakfast, Daddy gave the men a pep talk to muster extra enthusiasm. "Strength under siege," he would say, "it's important, and you men have it."

His words energized them but could not offset the sight of the crosses that sprang up every day.

A week after landing, they moved west under heavy artillery and mortar fire, crawling along, staying clear of each other as if contact represented danger. Daddy prayed. He kept moving.

One morning the firing subsided for a few minutes, and he wrote home:

"Thank you for saying the shower will be all mine. I'm sick of not being able to sing in one. When I return, I'm going to sing until the hot water runs out, wait for it to reheat, and sing again. I plan to shower and sing for a year. And hold you, my precious. How long it has been?

"We're rolling right along. It's amazing. There's hardly a Nip standing around here.

"Today the gulf kicked up, and one LST (landing ship tank) broached; we lost some pontoon bridge materials, and the rough surf made unloading impossible. Do you think that slowed us down? Never.

"We secured the Manila railroad and the strategic Route 3 from Bambam to Mabalcat, sealed off Bataan. Ready to slow down and take a rest? Not us. We seized Calumpit, crossed the Pampanaga River twenty-eight miles from Manila, and, to the west, secured Subic Bay. I don't mean my battalion did all these things at once. The Sixth Army does have other battalions, but we're the toughest.

"As the Seventh Fleet glided into Subic Bay, Filipinos planted Old Glory on the shoreline, and a brass band played the Philippine and American national anthems. Filipinos gave the GIs cowrie shells as tokens of esteem. Remember when Montezuma gave them to Cortez, along with some feathers? Cortez was so disappointed he arrested Montezuma and kept him incarcerated until he came up with some gold. Sounds like something Hirohito would do.

"You're probably wondering if our K-rations have improved. No! Tonight's arrived in rain—drenched cartons that turned the 'food' into soggy mush. Whoever devised them preferred a life of making mistakes to a life of idleness. Maybe he was a spy. Some day I'll die of overeating, but not here.

"Speaking of, Jim Williams told me the food planners 'noodle around with ideas.' Ideas? How to prevent weight gain ranks first. When I get home, I'm going to eat like a starved elephant on a peanut farm.

"We're winning, but revenge is not as sweet as advertised. It's more enemies wronging each other, leaving behind hatred. I keep my sense of humanity by holding to my memories of home: the small beige owl in our garden, poppies dancing on spring green hills, the pale color and fine texture of your skin.

"The sky turns from blue to lavender to pink in the sunset. This time of day always makes me homesick."

The next day Daddy rode the Bambam River boat, a ride from hell with Japanese bullets whizzing by the entire time, killing men right and left, knocking them overboard until they turned the water red.

# CHAPTER FORTY-FOUR

ABOARD THE NASHVILLE, MacArthur waved his corncob pipe at General Krueger and famously hollered, "Go around the Nips, bounce off the Nips, but go to Manila!"

Krueger told him that Yamashita wanted a mad dash to Manila. It was premature and could unnecessarily cost lives. He explained the logistical problems: the need for support troops, improvement of communication facilities, railroad and bridge construction, supplies, and reinforcements.

"Nonsense," MacArthur replied. He demanded Krueger divide his artillery battalions between Clark Field and Manila with no further argument. Most, of course, would head for Manila for MacArthur's birthday celebration. Krueger insisted the insufficient Clark Field troops would outrun their supplies, since the enemy destroyed all the relevant bridges. Outnumbered and surrounded, they would die from pulverizing enemy artillery fire.

Later, in "From Down Under to Dai Nippon," Krueger wrote that MacArthur "did not seem very impressed by my arguments . . . He did not take seriously the danger of our troops' overextension."

MacArthur pulled rank and commanded Krueger to obey him. With sadness and foreboding, Krueger sent a large group in two "flying columns" on the road to Manila, and, on January 24, he ordered a few battalions, including Daddy's 143rd, to change the axis of their attack ninety degrees and advance toward Clark Field.

Here the wide, patterned farmland fell away; mountains, inflexible in their demands, continued for miles. Their rocky crags remained constant and yet never the same, and their jagged peaks surrounded Clark Field. The dangers Krueger feared proved all too real. Imperial General Tsukada, a devious tactician with an onion-shaped head, arranged the Kenbu defense along the ridges, some a thousand feet high. His machine guns, mortars, and heavy artillery lurked in caves on the high ground. The pillboxes, some three stories high, contained within their concrete walls 150-millimeter mortars, 20-millimeter, 40-millimeter, and 90-millimeter cannon. The Japanese could look down at Americans struggling along and open fire.

Stranded, outnumbered, our men fought against overwhelming odds. From above, the Kenbu group pinned down Daddy's battalion. Heavy artillery fire from the far side of the Zambales Mountains slaughtered our men in the rear lines. Roaring masses hit them, and they felt agonizing bolts of pain run through them, saw blood, their blood – everywhere – their bodies ripped like pieces of cloth, and they writhed, begging God to stop the pain. Some kept feeling it as they cried out, kept feeling their pain and their heartbeat and their breath, and the metal and the fire, and then nothing.

Our men on the front lines took more blasts from interlocking fields of fire anchored in pillboxes and connected by trenches to well-placed machine gun nests. The barrage raged twenty-four hours a day. Heavy Kenbu artillery blazed over the terrain, shredding men with shrapnel. Tracers blazed arcs of flame that illuminated the mud and blood of the mountains, and their fire bound itself to soldiers, consuming them. Glitters from flamethrowers burst against the blue sky of day or the black of night, gold arcs streaking and blossoming into more yellows and vermilions.

# CHAPTER FORTY-FIVE

ON JANUARY 29, 1945, Krueger's first cavalry division liberated POW camps at Cabanatuan, Muntingulpa, and Santo Tomas. At Santo Tomas, MacArthur strode in and greeted the POWs with his, "I'm a little late, but I finally came."

General Robert Eichelberger's paratroopers landed in Manila. Their famous motto: "Yea, though I walk through the valley of death, I will fear no evil, for I'm the meanest sonofabitch in that valley." They established a toehold, but, when questioned, Eichelberger said he'd rather find a rattlesnake in his pocket than speak to the press.

MacArthur, however, assembled his photographers and announced that he had secured Manila.

The general's comment proved a bit premature. Six gruesome months later, the US finally did secure Manila, a city reduced to rubble, its streets littered with the dead, in what became one of World War II's most atrocity-plagued battles.

\* \* \*

Reading the paper, Mom realized the Japanese on Luzon had just waited to open fire. I reacted to her increasing fear and my own by escaping to my garden corner – my secret place where I went to daydream, run my fingers through grass, find pebbles for Daddy's homecoming collection.

My secret corner became my touchstone, a place that separated me from the shadow of war. I liked crouching down and hiding in the bushes, watching Mom's legs as she walked by, not knowing I was there. I imagined myself flying above the topmost branches of the cherry tree, a soaring bird, immersed in reaching higher and higher into the sky. Sometimes I just relaxed and sniffed the flowers like Ferdinand the Bull or picked a Cecil Breuner rose and tucked it behind my ear.

Mom liked to do that: tuck flowers behind her ear. Occasionally in my garden, I drank a Coca-Cola from a clear glass bottle tinged with blue or ate popcorn.

Today the sun shone, so I worked on a daisy chain while Mom sat on the porch writing Daddy:

"After all your years of training, you now fight, and even though I dread the deadly peril we all are in, I know you wanted action. I hear the 40th is doing a marvelous job, and we're all proud of you. I constantly think and plan for your return. We know it will be this year. A glorious thought. It has been a long war, but my hope is reborn. I'll see you soon. You are my beloved.

"Pooksie's still whining about wanting a cat. Can you imagine? After I bought her a dog? I can't stand cats. The aunties had a fat gray one for years - the most conceited creature I've ever seen. During its three or four wakeful hours each day, it either sulked or glared suspiciously, and it had an insane phobia about both the vacuum and the sprinkler. I'm telling you, I never saw that cat look pleasant once, even though Aunt Marie always talked about it 'purring contentedly,' (her imagination).

"You know how I worry about you, and you don't want to make it worse. Typically wonderful of you. All my thoughts are about you and how much you mean to me and what adorable children we have and how grateful I am, because we have our real and enduring love. When I tucked Pooksie into bed tonight, she said, 'I want my Daddy back.' I told her soon we'll all be reunited. Take care of yourself, my darling."

She sealed the envelope, opened a can of tuna, creamed it, made some toast, and poured herself a Four Roses. After dinner, Frankie and I looked at comics: my favorite, Little Orphan Annie, plus Nancy and Sluggo, Gasoline Alley, and Archie, the cockroach who loved Mehitabel the cat. "Toujours gai, toujours gai," Mehitabel would say, and I reminded Mom of the kitten she sent back to Belinda's house.

Frankie ran and hid when Mom wanted to tuck him in at night, and as usual, I checked the closet and under the bed for hidden Japanese. Then I peeked through the blackout drapes, to be sure none lurked in the garden.

Jeep curled up in his basket without complaint.

"You're so nice, Jeepie-dog-dog," Mom said.

One night she heard me turn on my new bedside radio, though I was supposed to turn it off at bedtime, I sneaked it on and began listening to Marlene Dietrich sing "Lily Marlene." Someday I planned to look, talk, and sing exactly like her. Elizabeth Taylor became a fallback.

Mom marched into my room. "You must think I'm stupid and deaf," she said.

"No, just bossy," I replied.

She took the radio away, ignoring my tears, and shook her head as if to say: will I last until Frank comes home and does something about that girl? And her brother? "You become more impossible every minute," she said aloud.

So did she, and she just did not comprehend what an amazing, wonderful person I was. I could do so many things, like saying "supercalifragilistic-expialidocious" faster than any of my friends.

The next day, she went to the hairdresser's and ran into Belinda's mother, who, with a smug light in her eyes (according to Mom), began talking about war atrocities. Plus mistakes. "The navy can't figure out the right place to land supplies," she said, "and one guy just left our troops on an island to starve rather than risk his ships."

Mom returned home, and wrote in her diary:

"I wish the Grim Preacher would move to Tokyo where she belongs. Not only is she unbearable, her cat-like Belinda is a bad influence on Pooksie . . . Lenore says I either hover over the children, trying too hard to reassure them, or withdraw into a silent stoicism. She's right. I should try to be steadier for their sake."

# CHAPTER FORTY-SIX

ON LUZON, THE JAPANESE fought without letting up, their numbers swelling as imperial seamen whose ships sunk found themselves now reassigned to Yamashita's infantry. In February, 1945, an American commander said to tell Admiral Halsey he'd found the enemy sailors he'd been looking for at sea right here on land.

At Clark Field, Daddy fought side by side with the dying, feeling a heartbreaking connection. He wrote in his diary:

"Days pass like black coffins in a procession. For the first time, I feel as if my fingers could slip off the fire escape. Life is fragile, and if I'm not alert, mine could be gone. We fight and joke and refuse to give up. I've fought so hard and so long that I can't remember when I last ate, but I keep going, because if I falter, I won't come home. I have to keep trying. If I just keep trying, I'll make it. Exhaustion has set in. I pray that re-inforcements will arrive."

On February 5, he inched along through the molten metal to cover one thousand yards, while men chewed by fire fell.

At night he wrote Mom:

"I spend more and more time with Rapp. He always asks about Frankie, since he's the godfather. Despite the K-rations, Rapp's packing on the weight: Meaty Rapp, the he-bear. How can he do it on these K-rations? He's a great general, a man of action, rather than a peacock enmeshed in egocentric complexities like (censored). He gives me cigarettes. That's what I like about rising in the army: the higher you go, the more cigarettes you get. He's still a cigar man, smokes them in huge gulps, holding them with two fingers on top, thumb below.

"Every day brings me closer to home. My precious, I can't wait. Meanwhile, I read your letters about the aunties and Billy Boy and my sister to the guys, and we all laugh. My pet, you keep us going."

\* \* \*

A velvet breeze circled our house as Mom began her daily chores.

The weather improved after weeks of overcast skies and flat, cold winds; today, a weak sun deemed it safe to appear. "A day of goldenness and flowers," the Chronicle weatherman wrote, "Morning fog along the coast, burning off by noon."

"Goldenness and flowers" was right. The letter of our dreams arrived just after noon, and of course it came from Daddy:

"I'll soon be coming home. I feel it. It's fifteen months since you and I said good-bye at Fort Mason, and I'm burning to see you and the children. Rapp Brush says our elements of the 40th definitely will head home when we wrap up Luzon. In some areas, the Nips have given up and divide their time between retreat and burning down their installations so we can't get them.

"When I come home, people will call me Idleness Ribbel. Tell my little blonde angel that I'll be holding her soon, and Frankie that I'll race him. I'm counting on seeing an unspoiled son. Will I? If you've been too soft on him, you'd better toughen up quick, so his father doesn't have to do it.

"Am focusing on my first breakfast at home – bacon and scrambled eggs, hash browns, toast, orange juice, and coffee. You and the children by my side.

"Last night Jim and I pooled our K-rations and had quite a supper. We even found a ripe mango and some tasty tiny bananas. He has become one of my best friends, and I'm sure it will stay that way all our lives.

"He's made some key reconnaissance flights here. Once he puts on his flying suit and headgear, he's a serious man – confidant, indestructible, an excellent pilot with a keen eye. He has taught me about planes in combat: use of the radio, navigation aids, codes, how to recognize enemy planes at a distance.

"I'll tell you one thing: he will never be shot down. I'm sure of it."

A tidal wave of bliss swept over us as we hugged and cried and laughed and hugged some more. Mom made a homecoming to plan, especially for the moment Daddy saw her again. On the mirror-covered vanity stood an array of faceted crystal bottles and jars filled with scents, powders, and creams. Pearl and colored bead necklaces hung on the walls beside old post cards of Venice and Portofino. Maniacally she rattled around trying on her necklaces and patting things on her face, her hands – everywhere. Did she share with me? No, but I didn't care.

We agreed on important matters. Mom wanted my hair curly instead of in pigtails, so she shampooed it with Breck, "the shampoo of beautiful women," rolled it up in rags and tied them, and, then after comb-out, added a fluffy white taffeta bow. When Daddy came home, I'd wear my pink dress from Aunt Nini decorated with embroidered merry-go-round horses. Mom would wear a Hattie Carnegie yellow dress with white polka dots, collar, and cuffs, mother of pearl buttons.

One day I watched her snatch away spare eyebrow hairs with her tweezers. "Why do you do that?"

"You're just a little girl, but I'll tell you right now: men see better than they think."

Her thoughts reached backward to her honeymoon, Daddy resting in the sun, his warm flesh speaking of his well-being. She immediately began preparing the house for him, singing about the "boogie-woogie bugle boy from Company B," skipping up stairs two at a time. Aided by Juanita, she cleaned – really cleaned – and polished every surface. Every day she arranged bouquets of fresh flowers because she didn't know his exact arrival date.

She parted her auburn hair in the middle and swept it up into French twists on each side. Standing in front of the full-length mirror, she held up sweaters, dresses, and belts, trying color combinations, getting ready to pull Daddy into her arms.

She slept more, and her appetite returned, also her strength. It had been waiting for her to find it again, hidden but not entirely lost. She felt a vivid elation.

Time to get ready, because Daddy could arrive any time without notice: pick pear and cherry blossoms, arrange them in vases, have the gardener remove brown leaves from the wisteria that grew along the pergola, sugar coat walnuts, make strawberry preserve, put the picnic basket and thermos on the kitchen counter. When Daddy came home, we'd picnic at Lake Merrit with stuffed eggs and salmon, for sure. On the

Sheridan buffet in the dining room stood two champagne glasses for the celebration.

I was eight years old now, my brother, three. Super-coordinated like Daddy, he not only could run and throw a ball, he climbed on top of the garage roof. I'll never forget Mom coaxing him down, her white face, trembling voice, her hand holding a lollipop aloft like a peace flag.

Later, over a Manhattan, she said to Aunt Lenore, by way of understatement, "I'll be so glad when Frank comes home and can chase after his son on roofs."

"At least you have the satisfaction of knowing the only time you can change a man is when he's under four years old."

The next day, Aunt Lenore invited me to play, since it was unseasonably sunny and warm. Her glorious garden grew along the hillside; hedges of snapdragons bordered beds bursting with tulips, peonies, and bells of Ireland. Gardenia bushes lent their scent, and, on a level area, a separate rose garden grew surrounded by hedges. Beyond the rose garden stood an orchid-laden greenhouse with a white wrought iron table and chairs in the middle.

Billy Boy sunbathed on the porch. He smelled of cocoanut tanning cream and looked sweaty. His toned, sculpted body had turned the color Tan in a Can, though it didn't exist then, and his hair looked extra fluffy and brown. "Would you be so kind as to get me a glass of ice water, my dear?" he asked Aunt Lenore.

She scurried into the kitchen, and he addressed me, "I'm surprised you aren't helping your aunt with my ice water, after all we've done for you."

I sensed then what all adults know: some things never change.

Aunt Lenore rescued him, presented the ice water; she'd adorned it with a sprig of mint and a paper umbrella from Chinatown.

"Thank you," Billy boy said. "This is just what I need to cool off." He took a taster's sip.

Aunt Lenore took my hand. "Come inside so your uncle can rest." I thought of bumping Billy Boy's ice water so it spilled on him. I didn't.

* * *

In the Clark Field area, Daddy still fired his artillery into the smoke and flames of the war. In a moment of respite, he wrote in his diary:

"I fight each day, wait for the last flare. Say good-bye to friends who fall. Their dead eyes stare: Why me? A bullet for your life, good-bye, now."

On the night of February 10, he dreamed he stood alone at night, lost, and he felt worried; his men would wonder where he had gone. He heard noise – a siren, voices – someone must be hurt. He needed to work his way back and see if he could help; its importance weighed on him.

Though he couldn't remember how the dream turned out, according to his diary, he woke up feeling peaceful for the first time in years, despite the usual roar of gunfire.

\* \* \*

General Rapp Brush called frequent staff meetings to debrief and revise tactics. He, Daddy, and the others met in a secured headquarters area behind Allied lines. On February 12, Rapp said, "We've got to find the artillery positions on the reverse side of Sacobia Ridge; the heavy, concentrated fire there's raising hell with our troops, but you know that first hand. Chewing up our armored vehicles. We need to send Jim Williams up on a reconnaissance flight with a spotter."

He paused, studying faces, then nodded at Daddy. "Assign the job to someone in your unit."

"I'll go, myself," Daddy said. "I think I know where the heavy artillery is."

"No. Send one of your men."

Daddy stood up. "It's not a kamikaze mission. Jim can really maneuver planes; they dance with him."

"I want you to delegate this. There's a lot of anti-aircraft fire in the target area."

"Is that an order, sir?"

Rapp hesitated.

"Then Jim and I will go."

The decision made, Daddy wrote in his notebook: "Feb. 14, 5:30 p.m., Hangar K."

# CHAPTER FORTY-SEVEN

Did Daddy sleep the night of the 13th, or did he struggle with himself, stemming fear, as he faced the thought of his mortality? Open-eyed and surrounded by sleeping buddies, did he feel alone as never before? Did he suffer through the darkness as the feeling of isolation, deep and implacable, stalked him? And the question: would he ever see his family again?

On the 14th, Valentine's Day, the sky cleared except for a few high cumulus clouds drifting by, until finally the horizon turned that tangerine color it becomes right before the sun disappears.

"Easy living's only a few weeks away," Jim said to Daddy, "and then we'll become professional lounge lizards. We'll concern ourselves with the cut of our blazers, the wax on our cars, and the question of who's minding the yacht."

Daddy wrote Mom describing Jim's words and adding:

"All's well here, though we still have a few Japanese to be disposed of. Am about to go into the objective area and look things over. In a war, you need your nerve and your sense of honor, and I'm fine – better off than in the jungle.

"How's Pooksie? Last night her face kept appearing before me.

"All my love forever, Frank."

He had never signed a letter "forever" before. He must have known. In any case, he consumed a K-ration dinner, smoked three Fleetwood cigarettes, and immediately before taking off, wrote another letter and put it in his pocket, as was the custom among soldiers when in peril:

"All my training has prepared me for this great moment. This is the biggest mission of my life. Now I am in God's hands."

He would head for the hostile mountains and face antiaircraft fire with his life, his only life. He donned his helmet, flying suit, parachute, and seat pack, and strapped on his pistol, his hunting knife and extra ammunition clips. Next, he filled his pockets with cigarettes, a lighter, and a picture of Mom, me, Frankie, and Jeep standing under our plum tree in the garden.

He would have his mind on the target. Jim could call the plays on maneuvering the plane. Right before takeoff, they would do a last inspection, as all those about to face the enemy in light aircraft did. They had to secure everything, or it could be lost upon bailing out.

When they finished, Jim asked, "What do you say, Frank?"

"I'm ready."

Friends gathered with the radio operator, Charlie Harrington, at ground control. "Happy landings," they said.

Daddy and Jim told Charlie to pay attention to them rather than trying to pick up women on the radio, gave their friends the "V for Victory" sign, and walked toward the reconnaissance plane to inspect it. An L-4 Grasshopper, it was a typical light, unarmed two-seater that flew only 120 miles per hour. Its maneuverability enabled the pilot to zigzag to avoid enemy fire. As the spotter, Daddy, would read the compass and radio in the latitude and longitude when the enemy started firing at the plane.

He and Jim moved around the Grasshopper, their steps in cadence, climbed into the cockpit together, and strapped themselves down. Of course, they went through the steps to check the instruments and start the engine. Run your fingers over the switches, test the pedals with your feet, rev up the engine until the frame vibrates and smoke shoots backward.

Soon, a long roar filled the air. The plane quivered, its rudders flicking slowly from side to side as it began to roll, slowly at first, and then quickening as it taxied, its hard tires jolting on the concrete. Now, the moment. Concentrate. Mistakes kill.

The plane reached the end of the runway and rose into the sky.

Daddy and Jim climbed higher, at full throttle, disappearing into their lonely mission. They flew over the invisible line that demarked enemy territory – Sacobia Ridge. Legendary, imposing it stood, with black lines weeping down and rocks shaped by centuries. Now the sun finished setting, erasing the faint gold afterglow against the violet evening sky.

At ground control, static and Japanese transmissions jammed the radio, but Daddy's voice came through, constantly describing their compass location – the latitude and longitude – so when he found the artillery, the radio operator would know where it was. Suddenly Daddy's voice exploded with excitement. "We've spotted artillery!"

The radio operator heard an explosion and called, "Williams, Ribbel, do you read me?"

Silence stretched until Jim replied, "Roger. We're taking fire."

"Do you still read me? Are you hit?"

"We're hit. Mayday. Mayd – "

Silence.

The radio operator called again, "Do you read me?"

Daddy cut in. "Roger. Jim's unconscious. I'm wounded, losing blood, but will try to steer the plane into our territory. Have an ambulance meet us at the emergency landing strip. We can't make the main airfield. Altitude's falling away, but we're on course." In his voice, hope vibrated.

He flew with the controls gone, the airspeed winding up higher, the dark earth rushing to meet him. He'd experienced danger before. He could do this.

\* \* \*

At ground control, Charlie felt like he hung in the air himself, until the plane appeared over the emergency landing strip and started dropping in a long, shallow trajectory.

"We made it to the emergency landing strip!" Daddy's voice soared in exultation, and the men around the radio cheered, slapped backs, and held each other.

"Good show!" Charlie shouted. "Great show. Great, great! Bring that bird down, and you're home free. Ribbel, do you read me?"

"Roger. I'll do a soft crash landing. Here we go."

The plane hovered for an instant and smashed onto the landing strip with a roar. As the men watched in horror, flames billowed up – bright leaves that scorched the air – rose higher, still higher, a roaring fire, a glowing fire that the night couldn't swallow.

Daddy unbuckled his harness and extricated himself from the plane before it exploded, then crawled for almost one hundred yards, the length of a football field. Probably he focused on his love for Mom and his children - so young, and so vulnerable – probably believed he could make it to safety, so we could live happily ever after. Did he begin to understand: this was the end? Behind him lay his life, ahead the remnants of alternatives, once thriving, now laid waste?

Perhaps for a moment, he imagined victory scenes of the future, scenes with rhythm and beauty, part of a large and potent drama with his family at its center.

But his blood leaked his life away. At age 35, he had made his last end run.

# CHAPTER FORTY-EIGHT

ON VALENTINE'S MORNING, Mom woke up feeling a confusing dread. She didn't want to get out of bed. Fog from the Pacific moistened the windowpanes, making her bedroom look dim, and when she rose, her knees shook and her stomach felt queasy.

She dressed, cut toast in heart shapes for breakfast, and sent me off to school. I couldn't stop smiling, because I'd made wonderful Valentines for my friends. A few years earlier, my Aunt Ruth taught me to press flowers so they dried in full color and then arrange them with cut out hearts, paper lace, tiny satin ribbons. I had become famous for my collage Valentines.

By noon, the fog lifted, and the winter sun burned in silence, as, with a bright white light, it moved along the arc of the sky.

Piled high on my desk, Valentines from bunches of boys waited invitingly. My favorite, from Donnie, showed Donald and Daffy Duck kissing. "Roses are red, violets are blue," it said, "sugar is sweet, and so are you."

After school, when Mom opened the door for me, the sunlight scalded her eyes, and they slammed shut against the glare, stinging. She perspired, panted; she couldn't see the potted rose trees on her porch; they blurred.

I revived her with cheerful tales of sugar cookies and apple juice, and showed her my valentines. After dinner, she and I played Old Maid, and I kept winning. Then she put Frankie and me to bed and listened to her Glen Miller records for a while, finally climbing into her own bed.

Jeep followed her, as she sometimes allowed him to, but he would not settle down. His eyebrows and whiskers twitched; he parted his lips. He began kneading the bedding like dough instead of nestling beside her.

I fell asleep and dreamed about lying in a strange place. I hated it. Mice scuttled about. A stranger with an empty birdcage gazed at a flock of ugly black crows flying above, while another chased a turtle with a plate-sized shell crying, "come back." A little black-haired girl hummed

205

and whirled her skirt, moving as if in a trance. Men I couldn't recognize gathered around her, and I tried to read their eyes, but I awoke, and Daddy stood by my bed in his uniform. "My Pooksie – I'm sorry," he said.

He looked ethereal, and his voice emanated from uncalculated depths. I tried to see into his eyes but found a great empty space between him and myself. My heart quavered, and I reached for him, my spirit pulsing, I reached expecting to touch him, but he became a blur, and paralysis seized me as he flew, and he disappeared.

Something like panic revved in my spirit. Where had he gone? I went and told Mom that Daddy visited me, but she said no. You had a dream. She lay in her bed without moving, the blanket drawn over her against the chill, listening to the sounds of night outside her window: the hoot–hoots of the beige owls, the distant moan of foghorns.

Sometimes the line between dreams and waking life blurred, I knew, but Daddy's image remained intensely present in my mind. Outside the window, the stars reformed in their constellations, and the Milky Way became phosphorescent as the night deepened, but he never reappeared. I didn't sleep, even when the city passed out of night, and one by one the street lights turned off, leaving a fading moon quivering in silver paleness.

# CHAPTER FORTY-NINE

THREE DAYS LATER, Mom climbed out of bed quite early and decided to take a morning bath. She stretched out in her white tub and sank into the small bubbles, felt the texture of the washcloth against her skin. Outside, the sun grew brighter, but neither its buttery morning light nor the scents and bubbles could offset an uneasy nausea. She felt cautious, sure she'd overlooked something by chance forgotten, or perhaps never known.

When she dressed and examined herself in the full-length mirror, she saw pretty colors reflected: the pale blue of her soft silk blouse, the rose taffeta curtains in the background. She remembered her dream of Frank with happiness. Perhaps it meant he would come home this week.

Soon she would eat breakfast at the walnut kitchen table with a clay pot of red geraniums in the center. She loved the kitchen with its blue and white Portuguese tiles, herbs spilling out of porcelain containers, the pots of chives.

The doorbell rang. I slid down the banister, and she smiled at me. Early morning sun slanted through two tall windows flanking the front door, creating an arc of gold light along the rim of its brass knob. Mom turned it and opened the door.

Two uniformed men stood with a folded flag and a telegram.

Mom said, "Yes?" and paused.

The ivory painted hall became silent except for the ticking of the clock. Determination set the officers' features, as, with a sad dread lighting his eyes, one asked, "Are you Mrs. Mary H. Ribbel?"

Her body went cold. More real than any moment of her life, this one imprinted itself in her mind down to the last detail, the moment frozen.

"Yes," she said.

The officers stood at attention. One moved forward and handed her the telegram:

"Casualty Message Telegram. The Secretary of War desires me to express his deep regret that your husband, Major Frank E. Ribbel, was killed in action in defense of his country on fourteen February on

Luzon. Confirming."

Her face screamed without a sound, and she took three steps backward, closed her eyes, and dropped her head forward as if fatally wounded. Then she whimpered, "No. Please, no. No."

The soldiers presented her with a folded flag and started talking in clear, chilling tones, their words sadly given and relentlessly concrete, but she shut them out. No. No. Not death. Not the destruction of her love. No. She wanted to tell these men to stop talking, but shock closed her throat, robbing her of air and the power of speech. Her heart stopped, and her voice returned. "I must see him," she cried, "I need to hold him." She called him, as if he could hear, "Frank. Frank, I love you."

Her call shattered her ears, and her mind tried to run from what was too terrible to consider, and then the uniformed men murmured indecipherable words. They had to leave. She closed the door behind them and curled up like a diver mid-somersault, clutching the top of her head with her hands, her face washed clean of all expression.

I wanted to help her, but felt an isolation, could not reach beyond it. Fragmented I stood, no longer inside life, but a spectator.

# CHAPTER FIFTY

"A Japanese 20mm shell hit Williams and Ribbel's plane while re- turning from a reconnaissance flight over Japanese lines. The last message radioed in was "I'll do a soft crash landing. Here we go."

These few tragic words represent the finest in the American soldier who takes what comes with his chin up and the guts to face whatever is in store for him. The performance of the 143rd Battalion during the past thirty days of the Luzon campaign has been splendid . . . The toughest part of this campaign has been given to them . . . They have done the heavy fighting."
– Col. Wallace Nickel interview in the Los Angeles Times

"Freedom lives, and through it he lives in a way that humbles the undertakings of most men."
– Franklin Delano Roosevelt
    letter to Mom

DADDY HAD succeeded in locating the enemy artillery before he and Jim died, and his friends fired on it until they wiped it out. On February 23, they ascended Sacobia Ridge, where the Japanese shot him down. Up and up they went, through the rain of blood, faster, higher, up, up, up, firing artillery, throwing grenades, not caring what happened as long as they fought in the battle. They captured the ridge and hoisted the flag in Daddy's memory.

MacArthur and the Joint Chiefs named the ridge "Ribbel Ridge," and he sent Mom a letter about the designation, as well as a large map showing its exact location.

Rapp Brush wrote Mom:

"The Nips held Ribbel Ridge for many days, and men caught hell taking it. Everyone wanted in on that assault. They will not forget it. You can be very proud of Frank for what he did. We, his brother officers, feel proud to have known him.

"Frank was a dear friend and respected officer in my command, and

he possessed unique qualities of character, intelligence, and courage . . .
I speak in reverence and with love for one of the men closest to my heart."

* * *

The aunties' priest held a church service in memory of Daddy. He seemed to be engaged in a secret, crucial effort as he recited the litanies. The chapel had a dank smell, and candles flickered in tall brass holders, iridescent in the light from the stained glass windows. Veiled and dressed in black, Mom sank to her knees, closed her eyes, clasped her hands, and tried to pray, reciting the litanies with giddy willfulness, wondering if God ever heard.

She yearned to touch her husband one more time, and for an instant she saw him, happy and bright, sitting in the pew and watching as the priest mounted the hard stone steps leading up to the altar, cracked a wafer, and raised the wine chalice above his head. Daddy disappeared, but she would hold his image in her heart, deep, where it would always shine.

By now, I knew for sure: the telegram was a mistake. Daddy was missing in action, not dead, and he would soon find his way back to his battalion. Then he would come home, stand on the front porch, and I would feel the familiar closeness and recognition when I opened the door, and he walked through it. "I couldn't leave you, Pooksie," he would say.

Mom and the priest should be praying for his safe return rather than eternal rest.

After the service, the University of California Band played "The Sturdy Golden Bear" and "God Bless America" in the church courtyard.

We went home, and Mom greeted people, her eyes two open wounds, her spirit dead. Aunt Lenore couldn't stop weeping. "Not Frank," she kept saying. "Not Frank. He always burst with life." She hugged Frankie and me, Billy-Boy dangling by her side; sad but unused to offering consolation, he just stared at the ground.

The aunties clutched Bibles, reminding people of "The Good Lord in his infinite wisdom and mercy," while Uncle George stood with stiffened shoulders and immobile eyes, repeatedly saying "Amen."

Daddy's family held a separate service in San Diego, due to wartime travel restrictions.

At our house, his college football stood in the corner undisturbed, and he smiled from his silver frames on the side tables In the dining room an array of watercress, egg, and shrimp canapés awaited the guests.

Mom's friends came forward. "He died for his country," they said, "fell on the field of honor," was "a symbol of all democracy stands for."

Alice's heart hung naked as she whispered a few words to Mom, "On Luzon? They gave Frank a full military funeral. The battle? It continued. They had to pause and honor him, no matter what the cost. The men? They all came, and none of them could hold back tears."

I tugged on Mom's sleeve. "Daddy will come home, Mom. You'll see."

Friends bent down to kiss Frankie and me, telling us to help Mom. Juanita, dressed entirely in black, kept picking up guests' glasses and wiped rings off the tables. I decided to help her, because I felt as if a glass wall surrounded me, and I didn't want to talk to people. After a while she said, "Be proud. Your father knew how to die. In heaven, the brave get coronets of flowers."

She didn't understand. I shook my head.

Aunt Lenore's godson, Ed Heafey, brought me a feather fan bright red with three long, curling plumes and a tortoise shell clasp. It had the magic, so I could wave it and make Daddy appear.

The priest began circulating. "Frank was always so completely true to himself," he said. "I will pray for his soul every day."

Mom froze; for an instant she gave him a look that seemed to say, "Pray to Whom? A God who would do this to us?"

My little brother ran around smiling, waiting for his presents. If this were a party, it must be for him. After a while he got bored and began pulling Jeep's ears. I hated it when he did that.

As they said good-bye, people looked at me with a terrible grief, and I did not know how to answer their eyes.

# CHAPTER FIFTY-ONE

ON THE NIGHT of March 9, Major General Curtis LeMay directed his B-29 bombers to hit Tokyo from an altitude of 7,050 feet, instead of the usual 25,000. "Scorch the earth," he said.

Residents named their blazing houses "flowers of Edo," as entire neighborhoods vanished, leaving behind only smoking black squares. One night raid alone killed 100,000 people, and within a few days, pigeons with iridescent feathers roosted in the corners of burned out buildings and buried their beaks in their wings for naps.

\*     \*     \*

In Manila, MacArthur reinstalled the Philippine government under President Osmena. Yamashita declared Manila an open city and sent written orders for his troops to withdraw, then moved his headquarters into the mountains. The Americans could assume the burden of feeding the million starving Manilenos, and he would use the fortress island of Corregidor to defend Manila Bay.

However, Imperial Admiral Sanji Iwabachi remained in Manila to destroy all port facilities and gave orders to fight to the last man. If Filipinos died, so much the better. How many of them had been truly loyal to the Emperor during the occupation?

Combat proceeded from house to house, building to building, turning the city with its polo fields and pleasure palaces into a killing field. Over a hundred thousand civilians died, sometimes slowly, cut by cut. Beheadings occurred hourly, and frequently imperial navy men marched down the street slicing off hands or ears or breasts.

Allied forces closed off all exits. The hidden alleys became so crowded that people crumpled together in piles, everyone's legs on everyone else's, children trying to decide where to fit themselves in. Starving troops resorted to cannibalism, and their uniforms bore the filth of years. What a change. At home, self-respecting Japanese spent hours in steaming bathhouses, to be clean.

The imperial navy stragglers burned down MacArthur's Manila apartment right in front of him as he, his staff, and his photographers walked toward it.

In the mountains north of Baguio, the Tiger of Malay and his remaining staff ate small portions of rice and boiled snakes, fighting to the end with rats scurrying by and dogs sniffing the garbage piled up nearby.

MacArthur's "five-week" liberation of the Philippines lasted more than six-months, ending on June 30, 1945. His "minimal" casualties totaled 62,413 fighters. Over 100,000 bystanders perished in Manila alone, more civilians than any other battle in the war.

# CHAPTER FIFTY-TWO

STATESIDE, Mom kissed Daddy's photo every night and thought of how much he gave up for so many people he would never meet. Next to her bed stood a framed photo of him after a University of California football victory with a news clipping quoting his coach:

"A great athlete has died; he was not only a champion, his life was lived for his fellow man."

During the next days, her world shifted as if a leaf turned over, and she lived on its other side. She looked into the dark seaside cave of memory, a cave with flickering torchlight to show her, in shadowed inlets, images from long ago. When she slept, she dreamed of a wrecked room with Daddy crouching in the corner, his face charred so badly she could only recognize his perfect teeth. She would wake up crying with Jeep licking tears off her cheeks.

In the mornings she pulled her stiff, sore body upright, touched the cold rug under her feet, fed Frankie and me, and resumed her chores like shopping or filling the car with gas, unaware that tears dampened her cheeks.

I returned to school but no dictums of good breeding hid the shock in eyes or stopped the whispers. Everyone else had a place, but I spoiled the symmetry. I wanted to see my daddy, tell him how much I loved him, and I would. He would come home someday. He'd come home, toss his football up in the air, and make it spin again. It still stood in its corner.

Congress awarded him the Purple Heart. In Memorial Bell Tower at Valley Forge, men placed a bronze plaque in his honor, as he died in battle and was descended from a Revolutionary War fighter.

One of Uncle Arthur's letters said the school superintendent closed San Diego High for a day in memory of its "greatest quarterback," and the City Council named a grove of tall pines in his honor. My uncle added:

"When Dad heard about Frank, he began panting like a puppy, and when Mother tried to massage him with cocoa butter, he turned his head toward the wall, said the smell made him sick.

The Department of War advised Mom that it would send home Daddy's footlocker containing his insignia, notebooks, personal effects, and saved letters – his "treasure chest" footlocker. The message did not say when.

Looking back from the distance of years, Daddy seemed vulnerable right along, and I wonder if he knew he would die at age 35. Why did sign his last letter to Mom, "All my love forever," instead of "All my love," as before? Men often sense their destiny; I still wonder: did he sense his?

# CHAPTER FIFTY-THREE

AT HIS WARM Springs retreat, Roosevelt sat for a portrait by Elizabeth Shoumantoff, while Lucy Mercer Rutherford lingered nearby, watching. April arrived with its velvet air and spirit of hope. Suddenly FDR said, "I have a terrific pain in the back of my head," and slumped forward. Without regaining consciousness, he died on April 12.

* * *

In his Tokyo bomb shelter, Emperor Hirohito tore up a message from his mother saying he'd destroyed Dai Nippon and failed her as a son. At least she refused to see him today, so her beady old woman's eyes couldn't penetrate his mind.

His head ached, and he couldn't stand the smell of food anymore. Nothing, he believed, could cheer him, but in the Chinese yin-yang of complementary opposites, brightness followed darkness. A messenger brought the news, "The depraved enemy of Japan, Franklin Delano Roosevelt has died."

The emperor's delight over FDR's death proved to be as brief as one of his mother's haikus. On May 21, 1945, one of our napalm raids on Tokyo set fire to the Imperial Palace compound, destroying two-dozen buildings, including the residences of Dowager Empress Sadako and Crown Prince Akihito. A copper colored sky blazed with new light from the rising fire.

In an odd way, the emperor welcomed the destruction of the palaces. It felt like a sacred ceremony, one that united him with his people, people caught in the dark brocade called life. His people would take consolation from their emperor sharing their fate and stop calling his reign's name 'Showa,' a dour irony.

Mostly, the emperor missed his son, who had fled Tokyo for safety's sake two years ago. He wrote to him, accusing his commanders of underestimating the United States.

The crown prince replied, saying he believed he should study harder from now on.

In Washington DC, FDR's coffin moved down Pennsylvania Avenue, surrounded by military officers and a riderless horse, the traditional symbol of a fallen leader.

Vice President Harry S. Truman took the oath of office.

* * *

On Clarendon Crescent, when I mentioned Daddy to Mom, the shocked tears that she could not control showed me the cost of her years of optimism. "Everything will turn out right," she used to say, and, as the wife of a winning quarterback, she had believed it.

Every day more friends wrote, making him sound mythic, ineffaceable. But his heroism lacked reality for Mom; she only remembered how she felt around him.

She did not hoist up a new flag with a gold star signifying the death of a serviceman. Instead, she took the old flag down and threw it away.

Aunt Lenore worried about her, fussed over her, tried to help. "Mary-Helen, you act like you're no longer alive."

# CHAPTER FIFTY-FOUR

ON TINIAN IN the Marianas, Colonel Paul Tibbets ran up the engine of his bomber, Enola Gay, named for his mother, and carried the atomic bomb to Hiroshima. The date: August 6, 1945.

Initially nicknamed Thin Man for Roosevelt, the designers renamed it Little Boy when they downsized it.

Tibbets dropped his payload, and a ball of fire half a mile in diameter rocketed up into the heavens at a speed of twenty thousand feet a minute. It generated ten million degrees of heat until the flame died out and turned into a mushroom-shaped cloud, an image that children of the war saw again and again in dreams.

On August 9, Major Charles Sweeney, piloting a B-29 named Bock's Car, headed for Nagasaki with a fatter and more powerful plutonium bomb nicknamed Fat Man for Churchill.

"Bombs away," he shouted, then corrected himself: "Bomb away."

A mass suicide notion still pervaded Japan, and over a million of the emperor's finest warriors awaited. In an invasion, an estimated one million Americans, primarily from the Eighth Army, might have died.

Like Daddy.

# CHAPTER FIFTY-FIVE

NOW, THE MOMENT. August 1, 1945. The Cabinet of the Empire of Japan and its War Guidance Council entered his air raid shelter for an unprecedented event: a meeting in his presence without a unanimous decision. Single file, the twenty-four most powerful government and military leaders walked down the damp stairs and through the twelve-inch door to seat themselves at two narrow tables. A gold brocade cloth embroidered with thirty-six scenes of Mt. Fuji covered it, and, at the head, a single straightbacked chair stood before gilt screens painted with the Sun Goddess Amaterasu rising above tidal waves at Kanagawa.

When the screens parted, the emperor, in full military uniform and white gloves, walked to the chair, his face impenetrable, as all the men bowed.

Newly appointed Premier Kantaro Suzuki apologized to him, then reviewed the Hiroshima and Nagasaki news and the proposal to surrender. Hirohito later said that he heard Suzuki's words distantly. He began to sob, and the men in the room openly wept. Once rival commanders collapsed in each other's arms.

The emperor went to a radio facility and now announced Japan's surrender, ordering his subjects to lay down their arms and "endure the unendurable and suffer the insufferable . . . "

Most Japanese had never heard his voice before and found its sound confusingly human.

The Imperial seal was affixed on the fourteenth day of the eighth month of the twentieth year of Showa, Peace and Prosperity.

\* \* \*

On September 2, 1945, the sea around Dai Nippon looked flat, and a band of gauze covered the sun. The battleship USS Missouri glided into Tokyo Bay bringing allied leaders, including Nimitz and MacArthur, for the formal ratification of the peace treaty.

Next, MacArthur would take over as shogun. Though the emperor believed in seppuku for dishonored warriors, he did not for himself. He donned his favorite suit and top hat and drove in his maroon Rolls Royce to meet MacArthur, only to find the triumphant warrior wearing an open-necked shirt and khakis with no medals or decorations. The general posed for pictures with the diminutive, overdressed emperor, who looked like a frightened baby with the tall American towering over him.

Hirohito, though not photogenic, held an ace. He had stashed away an immense treasure, and he knew where to find it. His attitude has been described as, string me up, but the buried treasure map resides in my mind; lose me, and you lose the Golden Lily riches.

For decades US and Interpol agents have tracked down assets the Nazis stole and returned them to their rightful owners. Why has nothing been done officially about the far greater trove of Golden Lily?

In 1945, our Congress and the Allied nations unanimously favored a war criminal trial for Emperor Hirohito; however, MacArthur quickly convinced the politicians that communism had become the new threat, especially in China. Japan needed to be an ally. The dowager empress's antiwar clique survived, even Hirohito's brother Prince Konoe, who called Hirohito "the major war criminal."

Dr. Ishi survived as well, and the US forced liberated American POWs to sign documents stating they would not tell what happened in the Japanese biological warfare and slave labor prisons. If they did, they faced Court Martial.

Why? I asked Joe Martin. He explained that certain men wanted the research records for whatever scientific breakthroughs they could glean. The deal: secrets for silence.

This conversation with Joe made me reflect on the differences between men who make heroic choices and those who make pragmatic ones. Who were the better men? Yamamoto, Yamashita, or those who decided we should learn from Dr. Ishi's "work?" And if I were a quarterback, who would I prefer to have on my team?

# CHAPTER FIFTY-SIX

MOM SURVIVED the delirious VJ day celebrations and the songs like "Happy Days Are Here Again," stumbling through the hours without anything left inside, except the knowledge that the worst things did, in fact, happen.

She kissed Daddy's photo every night and thought of how much he gave up for so many people he would never meet.

Every day became more painful, and her fatigued lack of focus did not help. She would forget something at the grocery store and have to return, or check the stove three times to be sure she'd turned it off, but she could not give up – would not. I went to victory parades and searched for Daddy's face, waving at soldiers I thought I recognized as him.

Frankie still loved the teddy Daddy had given him, though one eye fell out, and its fur dulled. If it split at the seams, Mom would sew it up; if anything happened to that bear, Frankie would probably never again sleep. One day he carried it over to a picture of his father, pointed, and said, "My Daddy."

One day Mom decided to take us for a walk. She put Frankie in his brown tweed jacket with a velvet collar, me in my gray coat with a velvet collar, and Jeep in a little red sweater. She wore a camel-colored "skimmer," a three-quarter-length coat, over a gray sweater and skirt, and her pearls.

I avoided stepping on cracks so I wouldn't break my mother's back, and Jeep, on his leash, tugged and strained, eager to run around in circles. Frankie kept trying to climb up trees. "Let him," I told Mom. "Don't treat him like a baby. Daddy wouldn't like that. He doesn't want to come home and find a fraidy cat."

Mom's eyes filled with tears, "Pooksie – "

I ran ahead again so she wouldn't repeat her words about Daddy being in heaven, words I still did not accept and didn't plan to. She caught up with me, and we headed back home. My stomach clamped down, and I shuddered without knowing why. The terrible sadness came again, but I managed not to cry.

Turning the corner, we walked along our block, and could see that something stood on our front porch. As we got closer, we could discern the familiar khaki color. Daddy's footlocker, clearly stamped "US Army." It arrived while we walked, and could signify only one thing: there had been a mistake after all, and Daddy had come home. My spirit ascended up, up, up, and in that moment I felt happier than ever before. How could I have believed he was dead?

We raced up the front stairs, but Mom froze when she saw the other side of the footlocker. The full horror of the war overwhelmed her again, as she knelt down, almost falling over the footlocker, her hands hanging loosely at her sides. She laid her forehead against it, his "treasure locker" stamped in black letters:

DEPARTMENT OF WAR
MAJ. FRANK E. RIBBEL
DECEASED.


We opened Daddy's "treasure chest," saw our letters, his officer's notebook and diary, his uniform, the flag that draped his coffin, and a copy of his memorial service. It also contained letters we'd sent that were unopened and stamped "Deceased" – letters he did not live to read.

I finally faced the truth: Daddy had left, and I could not follow him. I began to sob and thought I would never stop.

The seasons came and went. During the war, people had given blood until they became groggy, shared their homes, cars, their tools. They served the defense effort day and night. Now they became selfish and striving upward again, but Mom lacked the emotional energy to blaze forward; she could barely endure to live. The aunties continued to pretend that everything was "lovely," and Aunt Lenore planned outings for us. One day she took me to Chinatown and bought me a little round tablet to drop into a glass of water. The astonishing tablet turned into a pink paper flower that quivered in its tiny pond.

Aunt Lenore also took me to the circus and bought me a small chameleon with a pin strapped to its small tummy and affixed it to my pink dress. The lizard couldn't quite manage to turn that particular shade. It didn't look happy, so, once home, I set it loose in our garden.

We braced for the nightmare of Christmas without him, of a lifetime of Christmases we would spend without him. Mom remained beautiful, with her long, elegant spine, the tuck of her small waist above the flare of hips, her slim ankles, but she had a drawn and lifeless look. She regarded Frankie and me with a tender expression, but the rest of the time her stare appeared flat with occasional flashes of puzzlement.

"Let's make ornaments for our tree," she said to me one day. She spread a table with red, green, and gold beads, colored tin foil, ribbons, and tiny gold pinecones. I sat at the table and glued things together like an artist, a giver of beauty.

When I finished, our tree reflected to infinity in two large mirrors, and Jeep leapt cheerfully at the ornaments. On the mantel stood a crèche: shepherds, animals and birds, and, dressed in silk robes, the wise men. Red and green packages with candy-striped bows hid in the closet.

I knitted potholders for Mom and made collages for the rest of the family. Belinda might get one of my trading cards, not the best, but a very good one. We both prized Petty and Varga pin-up girls above all. I kept debating, my generosity ebbing and flowing. Also, I practiced wrist and finger contortions, as Belinda was double-jointed, and I wanted to be, too.

Mom embroidered linen hand towels. We worked by a window, the winter sun hanging weightless above the horizon, and the porcine Jeep watched, carefully following the sun's rays as he curled up in circle after circle.

The day before Christmas, Aunt Lenore called (as usual) and said, "I know how difficult this holiday must be for you – "

"And the children." Mom's voice broke. "I'm just trying to raise them for Frank. I can't do it alone."

She said the same thing every day, even when she and Aunt Lenore eagerly played their new favorite card game, Canasta.

After hanging up, she shook my shoulder, because I was gazing out the window at the far Pacific that swallowed Daddy, wishing I could see the place where he lay in the silence that would surround him forever.

"Do you want to play Old Maid?" she asked.

"No, thanks, Mom."

"How about going outside and jumping rope?"

"I don't feel like it."

Frankie appeared and clutched her skirt. "Is Santa going to come?"

"Yes, he will." Mom smiled at him.

"Maybe he won't."

"Why?"

"He'll forget me."

"You've written three letters to the North Pole," I said. These were revisions, less greedy each time.

"And tried to behave well, truly tried," Mom added.

"But he might not come." Frankie started sucking his thumb.

I put a protective arm around the little boy who no longer seemed like a brat to me. "Don't worry, Frankie. He'll come and bring you your presents."

Frankie went outside and picked a poinsettia, brought it to Mom. He pointed to her ear; she tucked it behind, and smiled with something like genuine happiness.

Mom patted the top of his head. "Well, this has been the worst year of our lives, but we were brave. I'm so proud of you children. It's Christmas, and we'll try to be happy again. I have a plan."

An odd suspicion came over me. I studied her with care.

# CHAPTER FIFTY-SEVEN

MR. GWYNN. Friends introduced him to Mom. Tall, blonde, divorced, he liked to play golf, fish, dance, and hunt ducks. In fact, the highlight of his life came years later when he became the cover boy on a national magazine called Ducks Unlimited. The caption: "Charlie Gwynn, the Legend of San Francisco Bay."

When he and I first met, I thought, not a hero like Daddy. And what, exactly, was he doing in our house making Mom giggle in that dumb way?

One day the two of them went "clam digging," whatever that was, and they brought home a bowl of live ones in salt water. For three days they sat in their bowl spouting water at intervals, and I became quite fond of them.

Next thing I knew, Mr. Gwynn came and murdered them in a horrible way, by tossing them in boiling water. Then he added a bunch of junk, while Mom gave Frankie and me her do-what-I-say-or-else smile, simpering, "You'll love Mr. Gwynn's clam chowder."

I held my nose, stuck out my tongue, and pretended to throw up. As punishment Mom sent me to my bedroom, which could not have made me happier.

She had further punishment in mind: marriage. She tried to calm my tears and protests with nonsense: "We'll all have fun together, you'll see."

The priest visited and said the Church could not recognize a marriage to a divorced man; therefore, she would be living in sin.

"Fine," she replied, sounding more like Aunt Lenore than herself. I did realize she was mad at God over Daddy, and couldn't really blame her, not that it excused the Mr. Gwynn business.

She finalized her wedding preparations in her usual manner: endless trips to I. Magnin for long, boring fittings that involved both of us. At home she curled up with her decorator, a younger version of Uncle George, and planned her new house: floral chintz in the living room with pale aqua walls, fern patterned wallpaper for the foyer, gray French wallpaper with touches of silver and white in the dining room. She would create a deck off the living room in the latest fashion: terrazzo from our new good friend, Italy.

I began to make plans of my own. I called Aunt Lenore and asked her if I could live with her. She owned a home, and I could just move in; Billy Boy would get used it. If he didn't, and fumed about all his hospitality, I would just do as often advised by the aunties and "rise above it." But instead of joyfully welcoming me, Aunt Lenore spouted old sayings about a daughter's place being by her mother's side. She sounded like the aunties.

At least I had Belinda and our crank calls. I'd dial the Leamington Hotel. "I'm Belinda Spankingbottem, and I need a reservation." Or she'd call Claremont Country Club. "I want to plan a huge tea party." We honestly believed no one detected the youthful sound of our voices. We read comic books and went to movies. I remained loyal to Marlene Dietrich and Elizabeth Taylor, but The Lone Ranger assumed the position of quarterback.

I discovered him on the radio. The program began with the "William Tell Overture," the sound of a galloping horse, and a man's ringing voice, "Hi-yo, Silver!" The Lone Ranger's fighting spirit and loyalty to his kemo sabe, Tonto, proved he was a great American like Daddy, and I followed his every valorous deed.

One morning Belinda said, "Your Mom plans to marry again."

"Liar!" I replied, and we argued the rest of the way to school. In the cafeteria, I poured my milk into her grape drink to teach her a good lesson. Later she covered me with chocolate ice cream.

After school, as we walked home, I saw a hose. We had a duel for it, but I won and doused her until she soaked.

How could such close friends part without an explosion of frustration? I would soon move to a different school district, which in Piedmont translated to a different solar system.

A couple of weeks later, she and I cried and hugged good-bye, and then I sat in my beloved plum tree for the last time, feeling the deepest loneliness I had ever known. Apart from Daddy, my best friend, and my home, the clam killing Mr. Gwynn would soon take Jeep away from me. His huge German Shepherd, Boris, would kill my little daschund and probably eat him.

Our family moved into a big house with Mr. Gwynn, his sixteen-year old son, John, his maid, Hilda, and, as I feared, Boris. To my surprise and relief, my Jeep terrorized the hulking German Shepherd with his aggressive yapping, so Boris kept his place.

Allow me to summarize the rest of the picture: Juanita came four times a week, whereupon Hilda would retire to her room with a shrug of contempt. Frankie adjusted to the change by constantly throwing things out the window, sometimes breaking the panes of glass. Mr. Gwynn had a married daughter, Pat, with sleek long fingers, red nail polish, and a tendency to glare at me with scary eyes when she visited. Billy Boy, ulcer-free now that the war had ended, sulked because Mr. Gwynn basically ignored him, but we could live with that.

My stepbrother, John, like all teenagers, considered our house a foreign country and in his did not welcome Mom's advice, which usually parroted the aunties' old sayings. Neither did he express eagerness to hear them repeated by the aunties themselves, who would visit once a month.

On his bureau stood a photo of a girl in a strapless tulle gown wearing a gardenia corsage around her wrist: his true love, Dionne. Behind her, I could see a crystal bowl that undoubtedly held Hawaiian punch with pineapple chunks. When he talked to her on the phone, I listened on the extension.

"My Little Slim," he would gush, and I laughed until my side ached.

The day after my birthday, I went into my bathroom and found something horrifying. I ran screaming to Mom, who had stretched out on her chaise lounge to read a novel about an 18th century English governess living in the ghost-ridden castle of a widower aristocrat.

I managed to gasp, "There's a huge, fat snake swimming in my bathtub."

"It's an eel. Your stepfather will be cooking it tonight, and he wants to be sure it's absolutely fresh."

"I'm going to throw up. I will not eat that thing."

"It's for Vic Bergeron. Your stepfather gave him the loan to start

Trader Vic's, and they cook dinner for each other sometimes."

"If eel is what he likes, I'm never going to his restaurant. And I'm never going to take a bath in that tub again." To underscore my point, I went to bed without a bath that night.

The next morning, Mom gave me one of her "little talks."

As if my life weren't bad enough, she decided I should stop sitting alone drawing dogs and horses, stop making up stories, and to become normal – read gregarious. I told her exactly what I thought of that plan, whereupon she replied, "Pooksie, you need to learn to be a good sport."

Livid, I retorted that Daddy was a good sport, a great one, and she wasn't. Neither was Mr. Gwynn.

She forced a fake smile. "You need to make new friends."

"In my dumb new school? Why?"

"Because life can be difficult without friends."

My life wasn't difficult now?

Aunt Lenore "dropped by," and said, "Ann needs a few laughs."

That made me remember how Daddy would stick raw cauliflower in his ears to make me laugh.

Mom had long since stored Tinesey and Leilani, since I'd outgrown them, but today when I came home from school, she'd packed more recent acquisitions and stashed them somewhere. "It's time for you to grow up," she commanded.

I walked away from her, thinking about Daddy. Loving his memory always made the flags dance for me. But I did decide to grow up, by reading Herb Caen's column in the Chronicle. He taught me important concepts: never call San Francisco "Frisco," never feed the pigeons, and never eat Velveeta instead of cheese.

* * *

In 1995, when I visited The American Cemetery in Manila, Daddy's grave, a white cross, stood straight and proud, like he once did, and around it stood row after row of other crosses. Under each one lay the body of a father, brother, or son. On a grassy rise not far away stood the cemetery chapel, a soaring neoclassical structure with these words carved into the marble wall:

Take unto Thyself, 0 Lord, the souls of the valiant.

Overwhelmed by finally kneeling where he lay, I placed roses on Daddy's grave, and the box filled with secret treasures I saved for him as a child, plus photos of his now enlarged family. Then I silently told him all about what had happened since he left, and said the colorful seashells he sent me from Hawaii sit in a crystal bowl on my nightstand. They glisten with memories and remind me that the sea recedes and returns eternally.

In my mind I could see him – how brightly shone the image, how clear, and I could hear his warm, happy voice. He believed that studying history had value; it's an irony that this peace-loving man became part of history in such a tragic way.

Later, flying back to San Francisco with my husband, I thought of Charlie, the kind stepfather I once refused to call anything except "Mr. Gwynn," and decided he, too, was a hero. After all, he married a woman with a wild son and a daughter who carried a torch for her dead father. How many men would have the courage to take us on? In that moment, I grew up.

# CHRONOLOGY

## From Pearl Harbot to Tokyo Bay

### December 7, 1941

Japanese attack Pearl Harbor. The strike force, called First Air Fleet, was formed eight months earlier. The operation's chief planner, Admiral Yamamoto believes secrecy is the key, and the Japanese pilots will succeed, as they did against Russia by besieging its fleet at Port Arthur in 1904. Yamamoto is described as bold and ingenious in battle, and swift and sarcastic in argument. In concert with the Pearl Harbor strike, the Japanese bomb Guam, Wake, and Midway, with 353 aircraft attack warships and aircraft. Prior to the attack, General George C. Marshall receives a decrypted message from Tokyo instructing the Japanese Ambassador to break off diplomatic relations "At 1:00 p.m. on the seventh, your time." Marshall sends message to army commands in the Philippines, Hawaii, Panama, and San Francisco. All are received except the one to Hawaii, where atmospheric conditions and heavy static temporarily block the wireless channel to Honolulu. A Western Union telegram is sent, and a messenger on a motorcycle delivers it to General Walter T. Short's headquarters at Fort Shafter, but he receives it sixteen hours after the attack.

### December 8

FDR asks Congress to declare war. Congress declares war on Japan with a single dissenting vote, cast by Jeanette Rankin, who also voted against World War 1. Douglas MacArthur announces he expects a Japanese attack on the Philippines around January 1, 1942. Churchill famously says, "So we have won after all . . .the Japanese will be ground to powder." Emperor Hirohito declares war. "We . . enjoin upon you, our loyal and brave subjects: We hereby declare war on the United States and the British Empire."

### December 9

Japanese bomb the Philippines, destroying aircraft on Clark Field. MacArthur requests more troops to fend off an invasion, but only 15%

of available forces are assigned to the Pacific at this time.

*December 10*

Japanese occupy Tarawa, mount air attacks on Luzon.

*December 12*

Japanese troops invade Luzon in the Philippines.

*December 15*

Admiral Chester Nimitz appointed Pacific navy chief.

*December 23*

Japanese capture Wake Island. In Washington DC, a man chops down four Japanese cherry trees, which prompts the Central Park Zoo staff to change the Japanese deer sign to "Asiatic deer."

*December 24*

7000 Japanese reinforce forces on Luzon; MacArthur again requests reinforcements but does not get them. The Pearl Harbor and Wake Island carriers Akagi, Kaga, Shokaku, and Soryu arrive in Kure on the Inland Sea. Every carrier receives an ovation for having "delivered a mighty blow for the Emperor." All over Dai Nippon (Great Japan) wild sake celebrations last through the night.

*December 25*

Hong Kong surrenders.

*December 30*

In the Philippines, American forces reach their last defensive line on the Bataan Peninsula.

*December 31*

Japanese occupy Manila, capital of the Philippines. Churchill, now visiting the US, says, "We have not come his far because we are made of sugar candy.

*January 1, 1942*

In Washington, DC, at the Arcadia Conference, a Declaration of Intention is signed by 26 nations, who will combine resources to defeat the Axis Powers. This presages the post-war United Nations.

*January 7*

President Roosevelt signs a budget to manufacture 125,000 aircraft,

75,000 tanks, 35,000 guns, 55,000 anti-aircraft guns, and eight million tons of shipping by the end of 1943.

*January 11*

US carrier Saratoga attacked by Japanese submarine, I-6, near Hawaii. Japan invades Dutch East Indies. (Japanese submarines were called "I Boats," German submarines, "U Boats.")

*January 15*

Japan starts major offensive in Burma

*January 23*

Japanese land in New Britain, Borneo, New Ireland, and the Solomons. They focus on Rabaul in New Britain Island where they will commence work on a large naval and air base, to cut US-Australia supply lines and anchor the southern end of their defense perimeter.

*February 1*

US naval forces attack Japanese naval bases in the Marshall and Gilbert Islands. However, the Empire of Japan extends eastward to Wake, the Gilberts, Solomons, Marshalls, New Britain; south to New Guinea, Indonesia, Malaysia, Hong Kong, Singapore, the Philippines; west through most of China and Burma; north to the Aleutians.

*February 15*

The "Gibraltar of the Pacific," Singapore, surrenders its garrison of 85,000 British troops to a Japanese force of less than 40,000.

*February 18*

General Walter Krueger appointed commander of the US Sixth Army, "Born of War." He forms Divisions including the Fortieth. It becomes a Triangular Infantry Division. Some of the men had been serving under General Joseph "Vinegar Joe" Stilwell, who now becomes Commander of the CBI Theater (China, Burma, and India).

*February 22*

Col. Wendel Fertig inspires US troops to follow him to Mindanao and charms Filipinos into joining his 30,000-man team. With brio and tenacity, they liberate the island and hold it.

FDR commands MacArthur to leave the Philippines for Australia; MacArthur brings along staff and friends. He is appointed head of SWOPE, the Southwest Pacific Area: the Philippines, New Guinea,

233

Australia, and Papua. Admiral Nimitz controls the Pacific Ocean areas from the Solomons in the southwest to the Aleutians in the north; he assigns the southernmost sector (Guadalcanal) to Admiral Robert F. Ghormley. Col. "Vinegar Joe" Stillwell will command CBI – the China-Burma-India Theater. No overall theater command exists, which causes friction.

*February 27*

In the Battle of the Java Sea, a US-UK-Dutch-Australian fleet fails to halt Japanese invasion of the Dutch East Indies. British bases in Ceylon are bombed and a hundred thousand tons of shipping sunk. Remnants of the British Far Eastern Fleet head for North Africa, the Royal Australian navy to its homeports. The US Pacific Fleet has not a single functioning battleship. Japan's eleven battleships, six large and four small carriers, and thirty-eight heavy and light cruisers are untouched.

*March 1*

US begins internment of Japanese Americans, called Nisei. Subsequently, some Nisei fight in the US armed forces.

*March 7*

Japanese enter Rangoon, capital of Burma.

*March 9*

Java surrenders to Japan. US formulates a Pacific policy, codenamed "Watchtower," with three phases: secure Guadalcanal and the southernmost Solomons, rid Papua of Japanese and proceed up the Solomons toward Rabaul, launch from Papua to New Britain Island.

*March 10*

US carriers Yorktown and Lexington arrive off New Guinea to send aircraft against Japanese ships in the area.

*March 11*

MacArthur leaves the Philippines vowing, "I shall return!"

*March 12*

Japan in control of Solomons, but US building up Pacific naval presence; US troops land in New Caledonia to build base.

*April 3*

Renewed Japanese bombing offensive on Luzon forces US withdrawal to Bataan.

*April 5*

Japanese planes raid Ceylon.

*April 9*

US troops surrender on Bataan.

*April 10*

76,000 Allied POWs begin Bataan Death March to a POW camp 60 miles away. Heat, hunger, thirst, beatings, and disease claim 5,000 American lives along the way.

*April 18*

Doolittle raid on Tokyo. B-25 bombers are used, the first time they are launched from a carrier, the Hornet. Lt. Col. James Doolittle hits Tokyo and other cities, then he and his men crash land in China.

*April 29*

Japanese reinforcements land on Mindinao and attack Filipino garrison; shelling on Corregidor continues.

*May 2*

Japanese invade New Guinea and head for Port Moresby. A group of Australian nurses massacred by Imperial troops in Singapore. Admiral Nimitz sends ships to defend Australia. The Japanese send invasion forces from Rabaul to Port Moresby and Tulagi, but the US deciphers the naval code, JN-25, and rushes a task force to intercept the invaders. The Battle of the Coral Sea begins.

*May 4*

US aircraft from carrier Yorktown attack a Japanese seaplane base at Tulagi in the Solomons. FDR creates the Women's Auxiliary Army Corps.

*May 8*

In the Battle of the Coral Sea, the Japanese suffer their first reversal in their advance across the Pacific. For the first time, carrier-based aircraft do the fighting. Though the engagement is minor to the Japanese, it inspires the Imperial command to speculate about where the expected US counterblow will occur.

*May 14*

The US effort to crack Japanese codes is called "Magic." Code breaker Agnes Meyer Driscoll learns of planned Japanese invasion of Midway.

*May 20*

Japanese complete Burma conquest, invade New Guinea, and head for Port Moresby.

*May 25*

Japanese begin moves against the Aleutians to try to divert US attention from Midway.

*May 26*

Imperial Admiral Nagumo leaves for the five-mile long atoll of Midway.

*May 30*

Japanese send four submarines to Pearl Harbor vicinity to delay US departure for Midway, but we have already left.

*May 31*

Lt. Matsuo, a co-originator of the midget submarine attack, had wanted to lead the Pearl Harbor strike. He volunteers to attack Sydney Harbor as a diversion to Midway, but his ship sinks.

*June 1*

US sends 25 submarines to vicinity of Midway.

*June 4*

Battle of Midway begins. Horyu is badly damaged by US aircraft from Enterprise and Hornet; within 24 hours, Japanese lose four of their carriers. Japan's eastward thrust decisively halted.

*June 5*

Imperial Admiral Yamamoto withdraws from Midway – the first Japanese defeat in almost three and one-half centuries.

*June 10*

US Fleet enlarged with the battleship North Carolina, carrier Wasp, and cruisers and destroyers from the Atlantic Fleet.

*July 31*

US bomb Tulagi and Guadalcanal.

*August 7*

US Marines land on Guadalcanal. Four cruisers lost to the Imperial Navy in subsequent battle of Savo Island.

*August 24*

Naval battle in Solomons; US carrier damaged, Imperial carrier Ryujo sunk.

*August 28*

Imperial Admiral Tanaka's supply destroyers, known as "The Tokyo Express," reach Guadalcanal.

*September 8*

US Marines reinforced on Guadalcanal. Heavy fighting resumes.

*September 10*

Japanese floatplanes drop incendiary bombs on Oregon forests. News suppressed at the time.

*September 15*

Japanese sink carrier Wasp off Guadalcanal; battleship North Carolina and destroyer O'Brien also hit.

*September 16*

American and Australian ground forces with US air support halt Japanese advance across New Guinea mountains 40 miles from Port Moresby.

*September 27*

British launch offensive in Burma.

*October 13*

Imperial battleships Kongo and Haruna bombard Henderson Field in Guadalcanal; Tanaka lands 4,500 more men and equipment.

*October 18*

Admiral William "Bull" Halsey takes command of US carriers in CINPAC. He answers to Admiral Chester Nimitz.

*October 26*

The battle of Santa Cruz, Guadalcanal, begins. Japanese sink USS Hornet.

*November 3*

Japanese land 1,500 more troops on Guadalcanal.

*November 12*

Admiral Nimitz announces repair of many ships damaged at Pearl Harbor. Congress lowers the mandatory Selective Service registration to 18 years of age.

*November 15*

Tanaka lands 4,500 more troops on Guadalcanal. South Dakota damaged; carrier Kirishiima sunk.

*November 17*

1,000 Japanese troops land at Buna, New Guinea.

*December 9*

General Patch arrives at Guadalcanal with the Sixth Army's XIV Corps, including the 40th Division, to replace the First Marine Division.

*Janary 2, 1943*

Allies take Buna in New Guinea

*Janary 10*

Final US offensive on Guadalcanal begins.

*Janary 13*

Japanese retreat from Sanandan, the last and most heavily defended position on the Papuan coast.

*February 1*

Japanese begin evacuation of Guadalcanal.

*February 8*

In Burma, British and Indian troops commence guerilla operation.

*February 9*

US secures Guadalcanal; Japanese complete evacuation. Col. Alexander Patch radios Admiral Halsey that the Tokyo Express no longer has a terminus on Guadalcanal. Cruiser Northampton sinks, bringing the total of US cruisers lost in Guadalcanal to five. Imperial Admiral Yamamoto realizes that although many US ships went down, they won the land and naval battles of Guadalcanal. Dai Nippon's air superiority has slipped, and its position in the Southwest Pacific is becoming untenable. The US has made its first forward thrust.

*February 21*

9,000 US troops land in the Russell Islands, part of the central Solomons. These and other small islands – the Shorts and Treasuries, for example – stand near the tip of Bougainville, useful for airstrips and

PT Boat launches.

## March 2

The Battle of the Bismark Sea banishes the Japanese Navy from southern New Guinea waters. New American aircraft debut, including the twin-tailed, twin engine P-38 Lightening. Low-level sweeps by mid-sized bombers carrying fragmentation bombs replace high altitude bombing by B17s. US air coverage leaves Lae impossible for the Japanese to defend, and it falls to MacArthur within a few months. Yamamoto plans 'Operation 1' which begins with naval raids at Tulagi and Guadalcanal.

## April 16

A captured Australian physician, Wheary Dunlop, takes care of his fellow prisoners, but one day he breaks a rule, and the guards tie him to a stake, leaving him in the blazing sun. Once untied, Dunlop's legs collapse beneath him, but he gets to his feet and says, "And now, if you will excuse me, I will amputate the Dutchman's arm; he has been waiting all day." He does, and the Dutchman survives.

## April 18

Yamamoto killed when US P-38s shoot down his aircraft over Bougainville. Charles Lindburgh, lone conqueror of the Atlantic, helped plan the mission, called operation Vengeance. Those who carried it out were Major John W. Mitchell, Lt. Besby T. Holmes, and Thomas G. Lamphier, jr. US troops attack Japanese at Attu in the Aleutian Islands.

## June 20

US Sixth Army establishes its headquarters at Milne Bay, New Guinea. The island is shaped like a bird, with its head to the west, tail to the east. Rabaul is at the head, and between it and the tail stretch mountains and jungle. This landing begins MacArthur's taking of the other end of the island with the eventual goal of cutting off the Japanese from supplies. The next series of operations in the vicinity form parts of a strategy called "Breaking the Bismark Barrier."

## June 30

US retakes Attu, one of the Aleutian Islands. Nobody wants to be up in the Bering Sea and most of the Aleutian conquests are propaganda efforts for one side or the other. In fact, when the Allies capture one island, no Japanese remain.

*July 18*

US troops get a new portable anti-tank rocket called a "bazooka."

*August 1-2*

15 US P-T boats block Japanese convoy in Solomons. John F. Kennedy's PT-109 is sunk, and he tows a wounded crewman to an atoll. Though many are injured, only two die.

*August 2*

Japanese leave New Georgia and move to Kolombangara Island in the Central Solomons.

*August 6*

US destroyers sink three Japanese destroyers enroute to Kolombangara. Japanese defeated in naval battle of Vella Gulf, Solomon Islands, by Americans and New Zealanders.

*August 15*

US troops occupy Vella Lavella in the Solomons and land on Kiska in the Aleutians. Halsey prepares Vella Lavella as a forward base for his landing on tip of the largest Solomon Island, Bougainville.

*August 25*

Allies occupy New Georgia and recapture Lae-Salamaua, New Guinea.

*September 21*

Japanese evacuate Arundel and Sagekarassa in the Solomons, and US forces land on Cape Gloucester. MacArthur has leapt from New Guinea to New Britain Island, as envisioned in the "Watchtower" strategy.

*October 5*

US attacks Wake Island in the Central Pacific. This maneuver and several later ones surround the Japanese at Rabaul, New Britain, and cut off their supplies.

*October 12*

US maims Japanese installation and air elements at Rabaul. The squeeze on the Japanese here increases in intensity; surrounding the Imperial troops is replaced by direct attack.

*October 18*

US attacks Japanese air base at Buin on Bougainville.

*November 1*

US forces invade Bougainville

*November 2*

Naval engagements begin near Rabaul, New Britain Island.

*November 9*

Japanese reinforcements cause heavy fighting on Bougainville.

*November 13*

US begins bombing of Tarawa in the Gilbert Islands.

*November 20*

US troops land on Makin and Tarawa in the Gilberts, which shrinks Japan's defense perimeter of the Home Islands. The later invasion of Wake Island also helped.

*November 23*

Submarine Lipscomb Bay sunk in the Solomons. Fierce Tarawa battle won by US.

*November 26*

US forces land on Cape Gloucester in New Britain Island. MacArthur's landing on New Britain Island and Halsey's pressure on Bougainville, a strategy called "Operation Cartwheel," complete the isolation of Rabaul.

*December 4*

US and Japanese Naval battles near Kwajalein in the Marshall Islands.

*December*

US forces occupy the airfield at Cape Gloucester in New Britain.1


*Janary 9 1944*

British and Indian troops secure Maungdaw, Burma.

*Janary 23*

US forces invade Parry in the Eniwetok Atoll, bomb Saipan, Tinian, and Rota in the Marianas. Invasions here and those in the Marshalls and Carolinas advance the Allies across the Pacific. Occupying the Marinas enables air strikes for US B29s against Japan.

*Janary 25*

Chinese begin counteroffensive against Japan in Burma.

*Janary 29*

US forces occupy Admiralty Islands.

*Janary 31*

US landings on Marshall Islands.

*February 7*

US forces take Kwajalein in Marshall Islands; the Japanese are pushed from a northern direction now.

*February 18*

US naval air force strikes Truk Island in the Carolines, which, with Rabaul, constituted the two major Japanese air centers.

*March 8*

In Burma, British and Indian divisions advance from the Irrawaddy enroute Mandalay.

*March 15*

The 17th Indian Division, with US air support, holds Meiktila.

*March 16*

US forces capture airfield on Manus in the Admiralties. The Japanese defense perimeters are pushed farther back every day. Soon the Home Islands would be all that remained of the Empire of Japan.

*March 24*

Admiral Mineichi Koga, Yamamoto's successor, meets the same fate – death in the air. US forces encircle a 100,000 troop Japanese holdouts on Rabaul, New Britain Island, isolating them. MacArthur's "Operation Cartwheel" is a brilliant success.

*April 22*

US forces land in Hollandia, New Guinea, and surprise the Japanese, as they expected a landing elsewhere.

*April 23*

US forces capture Hollandia, New Guinea.

*May 7*

Fortieth Division of US Sixth Army secures Hoskins Airdome in New Britain.

*May 22*

US bombards Wake Island.

*May 27*

US forces land on Biak Island, New Guinea.

*June 5*

Debut of B-29 Superfortress. 29 of them bomb railways in Bangkok, Thailand.

*June 15*

US bombs Tokyo. General Curtis LeMay has developed a low-flying incendiary strategy known as "scorched earth," where planes fly on a 24-hour per day basis. US troops land on Saipan in the Mariana Islands. By time the air battle ends, 220 Japanese and 20 US planes are downed. Battle is named "The Great Marianas Turkey Shoot."

*June 19*

Battle of the Philippine Sea. US win. Japan suffers heavy losses including 300 aircraft and the carriers, Taiho and Shokaku. A pilot dives onto a torpedo to save his ship, becoming the founder of the kamikazi missions. This was the largest carrier battle of the war. FDR signs the GI Bill, providing financial and educational benefits to returning veterans.

*June 22*

Japan retreats in India.

*July 9*

In a raging battle, US forces land on Saipan Island in the Marianas east of Luzon.

*July 19*

Tojo resigns as Japan's Prime Minister.

*July 21*

US forces land on Tinian; napalm used for the first time in the Pacific Theater.

*July 24*

US invades Guam in the Mariana Islands to retake the first American holding captured by the Japanese. The Lexington's Admiral Raymond Spruance does not allow the enemy to lure him away from his designated assignment, and his superior radar enables him to calculate Japanese direction, speed, etc.

*July 27*

FDR meets with MacArthur, Nimitz, and other COs in Hawaii to plan strategy.

*July 28*

US wins battle of Biak. The US objective becomes denying the home islands the resources of SE Asia and providing a staging area for the final assault in November, 1945, on Kiyushu. Okinawa is needed, as the Japanese fleet remains a formidable factor to be reckoned with.

FDR is standing for a fourth term, and US political as well as military leaders like General Marshall convince Admirals King and Halsey that the Philippine liberation needed to be the objective. At the time, it was not clear whether the Japanese had pulled their inner defensive perimeter prior to Leyte or during the campaign.

The conclusion of the New Guinea campaign secures all objectives, covering 1,000 miles in fourteen months. Now, planning for the Philippine campaign takes place on New Guinea at Lake Santini above Hollandia. The Leyte invasion is scheduled for October 20, Mindinao for December 15, and Luzon for January 9. Forces are convened in Hollandia from all over the Pacific, as far in the rear as Noumeia 800 miles in the rear (it was not wrested from the Japanese). Hollandia, the major staging area, is 2100 miles from Leyte.

*August 10*

US secures Guam, to complete the conquest of the Marianas.

*August 24*

Japan continues to withdraw from India. Japanese transport ship, Ukishiima Maru, carrying POWs and comfort women, sunk by US submarine.

*September 6*

The Pacific Task Force 38 attacks Palau in the Carolines, a pre-bombardment before the landing.

*September 15*

US forces capture Morotai in the Halmeheras, which brings the Philippines in range of bombers and fighter planes. Some consider this the first strike in the Philippine campaign.

*September 23*

US forces land on Ulithi, northeast of the Palu Islands, and announce the Palus are secure a week later, which pushes the Japanese back and neutralizes some of their Philippine invasion forces.

*October 20*

Admiral Kincaid's US Seventh Fleet escorts the Sixth Army's first landing parties on Leyte. 130,000 US troops come ashore, including MacArthur, who announces, "I have returned."

*October 24*

US 1st Cavalry Division units cross from Leyte to Samar. 64,000-ton Japanese battleship Musashi, four carriers, three other battleships sunk in Leyte Gulf.

*October 25*

Admiral "Bull" Halsey tricked by the Japanese into abandoning his post in the San Bernardino Strait. However, we sink the battleship Yamashiro in the last action fought between battleships. The first kamikaze missions sink four US escort carriers.

*October 26*

US Navy wins Battle of Leyte Gulf. The momentous Battle of the Philippine Sea – actually four different engagements – plays a fundamental role in the capture of Leyte. 216 US ships are involved and 64 Japanese. Owing to errors in judgment on both sides, the outcome remains in doubt throughout the engagement, but the US wins. Now our navy has no major opposition in the Pacific, as Japan's navy sustains calamitous losses.

*November 7*

US forces repel Japanese airborne Leyte operation and capture Bloody Ridge on Leyte. Around Ormoc and the San Ysidro Peninsula, 35,000 Imperial troops oppose 183,000 Sixth Army troops. Losses at that point are 2200 US dead and 24,000 Japanese. During the next months, another 1500 US troops die on Leyte, out of a peak strength of 260,000. Japanese dead are between 50,000 and 80,000, depending on the source.

*November 23*

US sinks four enemy destroyers and a cruiser.

*November 17*

Aircraft carrier Junyo sunk by US submarine in the China Sea.

*November 29*

Japanese carrier Shinano sunk by US submarine Archerfish. The "unsinkable" carrier's life lasted only 17 hours. .

*December 3*

Japanese retreat in Burma.

*December 13*

Heavy cruiser Nashville damaged by kamikaze enroute to Mindinao.

*December 15*

US forces land on San Augustin, Mindoro. The island is secured after a three-month campaign from December, 1944, until February, 1945, waged primarily by the Sixth Army. Kamikazes and naval assaults against US PT boats slow the conquest

*December 18*

Typhoon hits US Task Force 38 in Philippine Sea. Three destroyers sink, others damaged.


*Janary 2 1945*

US landing force for the Philippines leaves Leyte: six battleships, sixteen escort carriers, ten cruisers, and dozens of destroyers, landing ships, and support vessels carrying over 200,000 troops. Kamikazes attack. Japanese bomb Saipan in the Marianas.

*Janary 6*

US fleet begins preliminary bombardment of Luzon in preparation for landing. A minesweeper is sunk and twelve other vessels damaged.

*Janary 9*

S-Day, or Strike Day: 30,000 US troops from the Sixth Army, including the 40th Division, land on Luzon to face 250,000 Japanese troops commanded by the "Tiger of Malaya," General Tomoyuki Yamashita. The US troops are the vanguard; they will be joined by 170,000 others later. They establish a large beachhead in Lingayen Gulf. B-29 Bombers attack targets on Formosa and Okinawa.

### Janary 13

MacArthur goes ashore.

### Janary 15

US forces move out from the Lingayen beachheads, heading north, south, and east under withering fire from the enemy. The Japanese are well entrenched and supplied, and they far outnumber US troops. US forces close on Rosario.

### Janary 16

Linguayen airstrip becomes functional, so air coverage repels kamikaze assaults. On the nights of the 16 and 17th, part of the Fortieth Division wipes out a Japanese banzai charge. The Fortieth Division drives ahead, expanding beachhead to a depth and front of 30 miles in each direction. Captures Yamashita's headquarters. The taking of Rosario seals him into a defensive position in the Iocos Mountains of NE Luzon with 150,000 troops.

### Janary 20

As a result of these US military successes, Japan's leaders set forth a new outline of army and navy operations, with the "final defensive battle" to be waged on Japan proper. The outer defensive perimeter will be Formosa, the Bobins, part of the China coast, and So. Korea.

### Janary 21

US Fortieth Division takes Tarlac on Luzon.

### Janary 23

US Fortieth division forces a bridgehead at Bambam and encounters the main Japanese lines in the Bambam Mountains.

### Janary 25

US forces take Calapam and secure Mindoro. MacArthur urges the Sixth Army to dash to Manila. Krueger demurs because of logistic problems: inexperienced support troops and engineers unused to supporting large troop movements and the requisite railroad and pipeline construction required supplies available to create the infrastructure.

### Janary 27

Krueger's Sixth Army, reinforced by two divisions, works on securing Clark Field and simultaneously rolls south on highway 3 toward Manila.

US XI Corps lands at San Antonio on Luzon in an amphibian operation to open up the neck of the Bataan Peninsula. US Army Fortieth Division Artillery Rangers liberate POWs at Cabantuan. Another shore-to-shore amphibian operation from Subic Bay puts troops of the Eleventh Airborne ashore south of Manila. After heavy fighting, they find themselves on the ridge between Laguona De Bay SE of Manila and Manila Bay.

*February 1*

Elements of the 40th Division reach Clark Field in Luzon. Encountering stiff resistance, Allies still struggle to open neck of the Bataan Peninsula. The First Cavalry Division and Tank Battalion with MC air coverage heads south and passes over the Bulacan River at Novalicks Bridge, which is saved from demolition within two days.

*February 3*

US Eleventh Airborne Division lands on Luzon. 3,700 POWs, survivors of the Bataan Death March, are freed from Santo Tomas prison. The troops rush on and secure another specialized objective: the City of Aacona Palace Prison across the Pasig river.

*February 4*

The Thirty-seventh enters Manila on February 4 and releases 1024 POWs from Bilbad and reaches the Posig River.

*February 5*

US forces reach Manila, defended by 20,000 Japanese. General Eichelberger lands paratroopers from his Eighth Army in southern quadrant of the city, which prompts MacArthur to prematurely announce, "Manila is secure."

*February 12*

US bombers hit Corregidor and landing sites around Manila Bay.

*February 14*

The Kenbu Group of 30,000 troops continue to threaten Clark Field from formidable defensive mountain activity. Sacobia ridge behind the airfield renders it vulnerable. Artillery installation on Sacobia Ridge spotted during fatal reconnaissance flight. Locating site enables the securing of Clark Field. Lt. Col. Wallace takes over command of the 143rd battalion.

## February 16

Corregidor is recaptured and Manila bay secured. Harbor facilities rapidly expanded. By August 24,111 ships could be berthed at once.

Yamashita evacuates Manila and fights in the mountains around Baguio east of the city. He leaves behind a small force, which then comes under the command of the imperial navy, commanded by Admiral Iwabachi. He dedicates himself and his troops to a fight to the death, along with Yamashita's remnants, 3700 men. US forces seal off Manila. The subsequent vicious house-to-house combat decimates the city, due to artillery fire. The fighting above Manila and Nicholas Field on the isthmus overlooking the city becomes especially violent, prompting a senior officer to signal that Halsey can stop looking for the Japanese fleet. It's dying on Nichols Field.

US seaborne and airborne landings on Corregidor. Task Force 58 carrier aircraft attack Tokyo. Another column from the north crosses the Quezon Bridge over the Pasig River, and after fierce fighting liberates 3767 Allied internees. MacArthur convenes a provisional military government and declares the Philippine Commonwealth reestablished.

## February 23

Combined artillery and infantry assault by the Fortieth Division. Subsequent offensive action renders this remnant of the enemy army to small forays and ultimate annihilation by disease and Filipino guerillas.

## February 19

30,000 Marines land on Iwo Jima to battle 20,000 Imperial Forces. As with Luzon, landing is unopposed; then the enemy opens fire. Joe Rogers remembers, "One of the Marine Corps greatest heroes, Sgt. John Basilone, led the charge, but when we hit the beach, a Japanese pillbox had us cold. Basilone stood up to get the others moving, but a mortar got him. A Medal of Honor winner, he was only 29 years old and had been on Iwo Jima an hour and a half."

## February 21

Japanese fire puts US carrier Saratoga out of commission for three months. Carrier Bismark Sea is sunk by kamikazes, who have been inflicting heavy damage on US Navy support ships around Iwo Jima. The

Bismark Sea burns and explodes for three hours before it sinks. By time Skipper J. L. Pratt commands, "Abandon ship," twenty percent of the crew has died. Three destroyers with their escorts spend two days and a night picking up survivors.

*February 23*

Sacobia Ridge behind Clark Field on Luzon captured and renamed Ribbel Ridge.

*February 25*

US forces secure Mt. Suribachi in Iwo Jima, and hoist the flag. The photograph of the moment becomes the most famous image of World War II. The marines had endured six weeks of horrific casualties, which prompted the famous saying, "Uncommon valor was a common virtue."

*February 26*

US troops secure Corregidor.

*February 28*

At MacArthur's insistence, we move to capture the southern Philippine Islands by attacking Palawan.

*March 3*

US forces capture Manila.

*March 4*

Manila, though cleared of Japanese, is as desolate as Cologne or Hamburg. The enemy forces of South Luzon are annihilated by the Legapsi amphibious operation by the Sixth Army on April 6, 1945, so the San Berdini Straits are secure. The passage to Manila Bay and Leyte will be shorter now.

Yamashita's remaining troops have dwindles to well under 100,000. Some of his men fight to control the dams, the city's water supply. On VJ Day, only 6,200 surrender. The remaining 50,000 eventually surrender after lingering in the mountains of No. Luzon as long as possible.

*March 5*

In Burma, British General Wingate begins operations behind enemy lines.

*March 9*

US firebombs Tokyo, ultimately killing 80,000.

*March 15*

US Fleet enters Manila Bay and docks. The harbor handles 50,000 tons of shipping per week; in April, 70,000 tons, and in May, 90,000 tons.

*March 18*

US carrier-based planes from Task Force 58 bomb Japanese Home Islands.

*March 21*

Japan uses Mitsubishi bombers to launch first Ohka piloted bombs. Allies capture Mandalay, Burma.

*March 26*

14,000 more US troops land on Luzon. US forces secure Iwo Jima.

*March 29*

US 165th Regiment troops land on Philippine island of Negros.

*April 1*

US forces land at Legaspi, Luzon. Invasion of Okinawa begins.

*April 5*

Prime Minister Suzuki wishes to consider any possible peace offers. Emperor Hirohito refuses.

*April 8*

More US troops land on Negros in the Philippines. On Okinawa, US 111 Corps crosses Motobu Peninsula.

*April 10*

Mauban on Luzon captured.

*April 12*

President Roosevelt dies. Vice-President Truman succeeds the Presidency. The revisionists start complaining. Before Pearl Harbor, Americans were isolationists; only 2.5 percent favored fighting Nazi Germany, and 37.5 percent wanted to sell to both sides on a "cash and carry" basis. The notion took hold that FDR deliberately let the Japanese attack Pearl Harbor to jolt us into the war; proponents cited Agnes Meyer Driscoll's code-breaking skill as proof. Maj. Richard Bradshaw later tells me, "We were all on highest alert, and we did break the code. Hawaii command received a telegram, but since it was Sunday, it arrived delivered too late. The bicycle messenger had overslept. The day before Pearl Harbor, FDR sent the emperor a coexistence proposal, calling himself a 'son of man' who just sent a message to 'the Son of God.'"

*April 16*

US forces land on Ie Shima near Okinawa.

*April 17*

Japan attacks US air bases in East China.

*April 20*

US forces secure Northern Okinawa. On Luzon, we encounter heavy resistance around Baguio.

*April 25*

Delegates meet in San Francisco to form the United Nations.

*April 27*

US forces capture Baguio, former Yamashita headquarters.

*May 3*

Rangoon liberated.

*May 10*

More US troops land at Macalajar Bay in the Philippines. Around Okinawa, the kamikazes hit the destroyer Hadley, but the skipper, Commander B. J. Mullaney, survives.

*May 17*

US carrier Ticonderoga attacks Taroa and Maleolap in the Marshalls.

*May 23*

US bombs Japanese homeland. 750,000 phosphorous bombs dropped by 500 bombers; a similar number will bomb Tokyo the next day in a "scorched earth" policy.

*June 10*

Australian forces invade Borneo.

*June 11*

US secures Okinawa. During the Okinawa engagement, the Japanese air force and what remains of the naval fleet is virtually destroyed. However, victory is costly, as US casualties are also high.

*June 12*

Mass Japanese suicides in Oruku, Okinawa.

*June 18*

US General Buckner killed by enemy fire on a visit to Okinawa.

*June 28*

Fifty countries sign the UN Charter in San Francisco.

*June 30*

After more than six months of bitter fighting, the Philippines are re-captured. The Luzon campaign has lasted 173 days, from January 9 through June 30. Our casualties were 8297 dead and 29,557 wounded on the ground, plus 2000 navy men, mostly from kamikaze attacks. By mid-February most of the naval transports are freed for the upcoming actions if the Central Pacific. Japanese naval and ground losses are now incalculable, and the Imperial Navy has ceased to be an offensive weapon.

*July 2*

Another B-29 bombing raid on Dai Nippon. Mass exodus from cities.

*July 14*

Last of Japanese shipping sunk in Tsugaru Strait.

*July 16*

Atomic bomb tested in New Mexico, USA.

*July 20*

US test flight from Marianas simulates delivery of A-Bomb.

*July 26*

Potsdam Declaration: Allies demand unconditional surrender from Japan. Yamamoto's onetime flagship Yamato is sunk off Okinawa. Japanese radio no longer broadcasts messages like, "Come out, MacArthur, then we will send you tumbling to hell."

*July 28*

Japanese Prime Minister Suzuki makes ambiguous but hostile response to Potsdam Declaration.

*August 2*

Heaviest US air raid against Japan yet.

*August 6*

Col. Paul Tibbetts delivers first atomic bomb at 8:15 a.m. The uranium 235 fission weapon is dropped from the aircraft named the "Enola Gay," after his mother. Explosion equals 20,000 tons of TNT. A horrible choice, but less costly in human life than an invasion. Fewer civilian lives were lost than in the Allied bombing of Hamburg. General Walter Krueger agrees, saying at least 1.6 million Imperial troops were garrisoned on Japan's home islands to defend them.

*August 7*

A reticent Japanese broadcast refers to "new type of bomb" used on Hiroshima.

*August 8*

Japanese broadcast describes US as "having surpassed Genghis Khan in hideous cruelty." US mines Korean and Japanese harbors to create blockades. USSR declares war on Japan.

*August 9*

US drops second A-Bomb on Nagasaki. Soviets deploy 1,500,000 troops to fight Dai Nippon in Manchuria.

*August 10*

Japan broadcasts acceptance of Potsdam Declaration provided the Emperor remains on the throne.

*August 15*

Emperor Hirohito broadcast, telling his people to "endure the unendurable" and surrender. Prince Higashi-Kuni, a Yamato, will head new government.

*September 2, 1945*

Surrender treaty ratified on US battleship Missouri. Americans celebrate AVJ (Victory over Japan) Day.

# EPILOGUE

On October 25, 1945: UN Charter signed. MacArthur orders all military statues in Japan destroyed, so naval officers cut Yamamoto's in half and throw it into a lake. However, they make a chart of where it sinks, and later men dredge up the head and shoulders.

Liberated American POWs are forced to sign confidentiality documents drawn up by the Army stating they will not tell what happened in the Japanese biological warfare and slave labor prisons. If they do, they face Court Martial.

At the War Crimes trials, MacArthur finds some Japanese guilty, exonerates others. Mitsuo Fuchida of Pearl Harbor fame, for example, survives, prospers, and writes his memoirs. The men who hang go to the gallows shouting, "Banzai!" The day of the executions, Crown Prince Akihito cancels the birthday party he'd planned for himself. Still, he manages to get in his usual round of golf.

On February 23, 1946, General Yamashita is executed at Los Banos, the Philippines, after a brief military trial. In 1989, the Japanese government offers the Philippine government $250 million to return General Yamashita's bones for a proper Shinto burial. The Philippine government refuses. In 1989, Hirohito dies after the longest reign of any 20th century monarch. On August 1, 2001, Prime Minister Ichiro Koizumi makes an official visit to the Yasukuni Shrine, where the bodies of the war criminals hung by the allies are interred. In protest, China and Korea threaten to sever relations with Japan.

Sixteen million American men and women served in uniform during the war, two-thirds in the army and army air force, one-third in the navy and marines. Merchant marines supplied the troops. The approximate death toll: 50,000,000. The US, at least 300,000; Britain, 500,000; Germany, over 4,500,000; Japan, around 2,000,000; France, 500,000; Russia, 20,000,000; Holland, 200,000; China, 30,000,000; India, 1,500,000; Yugoslavia, 1,000,000; Hungary, Poland, Rumania, and Bulgaria, 500,000; Italy, 1,500,000.

Estimated costs of the war in millions of US dollars, 1946 value:

Allies: Australia, $10,036; Belgium, $6,324; Canada, $20,104; China, $49,072; France, $111,272; India, $4,804; Netherlands, $9,624; New Zealand, $2,560; Norway, $992; South Africa, $2,152; United Kingdom, $103,150; United States, $288,000; USSR, $93,012;

Axis: Germany, $212,336; Italy, $21,072; Japan, $41,272.

Governmental expenditures during World War Two for war materials and armaments added up to $1,154 billion (1946 value). Britain, $120 billion; the United States, $317 billion; the Soviet Union, $192 billion; Italy, $4 billion; Germany, $272 billion.

Official government expenditures did include allowance for damage to civilian property. Approximate losses due to damage, 1946 values:

Soviet Union, $128 billion; Britain, $5 billion; Germany, $75 billion; and other European countries, approximately $230 billion total. If these costs seem high, adjust for inflation; i.e., multiply by twelve for cost in 2009 currency.

# PRIMARY SOURCES

Diaries and letters of Maj. Frank E. Ribbel, jr., Mary-Helen Ribbel Gwynn, Ruth Ribbel Peyton, Arthur Ribbel, and Myra Austin Ribbel.

Interviews with men in the Fortieth Division, especially Stanley Dollar and General Rapp Brush.

Interviews with Admiral Julian Wheeler.

The US Army Archives of Maj. Frank E. Ribbel, jr.

Letters and conversations: General Harcourt Hervey

Letters and conversations: General Rapp Brush

# SECONDARY SOURCES

After years of reading I concluded, varying opinions existed on every aspect of the Pacific War, from whether FDR knew about Pearl Harbor in advance to the exact casualties in various battles. The sources listed below appear to represent the most widely held views and have the most thorough research, especially from primary sources.

"Hirohito, Behind the Myth" by Edward Behr (Willard Books, 1989)

"Hirohito and the Making of Modern Japan" by Herbert P. Bix (Harper Collins, 2000)

"War Letters" by Andrew Carroll" (Scribner, 2001)

"The Japanese Art of War" by Thomas Cleary (Shambadha, Boston and London, 1992)

"The Battle for Manila" by Connoughton, Pimlott, Anderson (Presidio, 2002)

"MacArthur and Defeat in the Philippines" by Richard Connoughton (Overlook 2001)

"The Pacific War" by John Costello (Atlantic Communications, 1981)

"The Fall of Japan" by William Craig (Dial Press, 1967)

"The Oxford Companion to World War II" by I.C.B. Dear (Oxford

University Press, 2000)

"Chronology of World War II" by Edward Davidson and Dale Manning (Cassell, 1999)

"The West Point Atlas of American Wars" - Chief editor, Maj. General Vincent J. Esposito (Praeger, 1959)

"War in the Pacific" by Harry A. Gailey (Presidio Press, 1995)

"Prisoners of the Japanese" by Gavin Daws (Morrow, 1994)

"No Ordinary Time" by Doris Kearns Goodwin, (Simon & Schuster, 1994)

"History of the 40th Infantry Division" (California National Guard Archives, 2000)

"Factories of Death" by Sheldon H. Harris (Routlege 1995)

"Comfort Woman" by Maria Rosa Henson (Routledge, 2000)

"The Years of MacArthur," Volumes I, II & III, by Clayton D. James (London, 1970)

"Freedom from Fear" by David M. Kennedy (Oxford, 1999)

"From Down Under to Dai Nippon" by General Walter Krueger (Combat Forces Press 1953)

"The Atlantic Monthly"

"Life" and "Time" magazines, 1941 - 1945

"A Diary of the Japanese Occupation" by Juan Labrador, O.P. (Santo Tomas University Press, 1989

"A History of Far Eastern Art" by Sherman Lee (Prentice Hall, 1965)

"Los Angeles Times" - Col. Wallace Nickel Lt. interview

"Ghosts of the Skies" by Philip MakAnna (Chronicle Books, 1998)

"American Caesar" by William Manchester (Little Brown, 1970)

"Goodbye, Darkness" by William Manchester (Little Brown, 1979)

"The Rising Sun in the Pacific" by Samuel Eliot Morrison (1948. Castle Books, 2001)

"Leyte" by Samuel Eliot Morrison (Castle Books, 2001)

"The Liberation of the Philippines" by Samuel Eliot Morrison, (1948. Castle Books, 2001)

"The Struggle for Guadalcanal" by Samuel Eliot Morrison (Illinois 2001)

"Tears in the Darkness" by Michael Norman and Elizabeth M. Norman (Farrar Straus Giroux, 2009)

"At Dawn We Slept" by Gordon W. Prange (McGraw-Hill, 1981)

San Francisco Chronicle (1944-1945)

The San Francisco Call Bulletin 1945

"Yamamoto, the Man Who Menaced America," John Deane Potter (Viking, 1965)

"Samurai Sketches," Romulus Hillsborough (Ridgeback, San Francisco, 2001).

"The Yamato Dynasty," Sterling Seagrave and Peggy Seagrave (Broadway Books, 1995)

"World War II," Eric Sevareid and the editors of Time-Life Books (Prentice Hall,1957)

"The Rise and Fall of the Third Reich," William L. Shirer (Simon and Schuster, 1959)

"The Pacific War Atlas," David Smurthwaite (Facts on File, 1999)

"At War At Sea," Ronald H. Spector (Viking, 2001)

"Eagle Against the Sun," Ronald Spector (Vintage, 1989)

"Day of Deceit," Robert Stinnet (Free Press, 2000)

"Hidden Horrors," Yuki Tanaka (Westview Press, 1998)

"A Pictorial History of the Second World War," William Wise, (Wm. H. Wise, 1944)

LaVergne, TN USA
06 December 2009
166168LV00002B/51/P